What Research Has to Say About
Fluency Instruction

S. Jay Samuels
Alan E. Farstrup
Editors

INTERNATIONAL
Reading Association
800 BARKSDALE ROAD, PO BOX 8139
NEWARK, DE 19714-8139, USA
www.reading.org

IRA BOARD OF DIRECTORS

Dick Allington, University of Tennessee, Knoxville, Tennessee, President • Timothy Shanahan, University of Illinois at Chicago, Chicago, Illinois, President-elect • Linda B. Gambrell, Clemson University, Clemson, South Carolina, Vice President • Charline J. Barnes, Andrews University, Berrien Springs, Michigan • Rita M. Bean, University of Pittsburgh, Pittsburgh, Pennsylvania • Carrice L. Cummins, Louisiana Tech University, Ruston, Louisiana • David Hernandez III, Glendale Elementary School District, Glendale, Arizona • Susan Davis Lenski, Portland State University, Portland, Oregon • Jill Lewis, New Jersey City University, Jersey City, New Jersey • Diane Barone, University of Nevada, Reno, Nevada • Maureen McLaughlin, East Stroudsburg University of Pennsylvania, East Stroudsburg, Pennsylvania • Karen K. Wixson, The University of Michigan, Ann Arbor, Michigan • Alan E. Farstrup, Executive Director

The International Reading Association attempts, through its publications, to provide a forum for a wide spectrum of opinions on reading. This policy permits divergent viewpoints without implying the endorsement of the Association.

Director of Publications   Dan Mangan
Editorial Director, Books and Special Projects   Teresa Curto
Managing Editor, Books   Shannon T. Fortner
Acquisitions and Developmental Editor   Corinne M. Mooney
Associate Editor   Charlene M. Nichols
Associate Editor   Elizabeth C. Hunt
Production Editor   Amy Messick
Books and Inventory Assistant   Rebecca A. Fetterolf
Permissions Editor   Janet S. Parrack
Assistant Permissions Editor   Tyanna L. Collins
Production Department Manager   Iona Muscella
Supervisor, Electronic Publishing   Anette Schütz
Senior Electronic Publishing Specialist   R. Lynn Harrison
Electronic Publishing Specialist   Lisa M. Kochel
Proofreader   Stacey Lynn Sharp

Project Editors   Shannon T. Fortner and Elizabeth C. Hunt

Cover   Design, Linda Steere; Photo, © 2006 JupiterImages Corporation

Copyright 2006 by the International Reading Association, Inc.

All rights reserved. No part of this publication may be reproduced or transmitted in any form or by any means, electronic or mechanical, including photocopy, or any information storage and retrieval system, without permission from the publisher.

Web addresses in this book were correct as of the publication date but may have become inactive or otherwise modified since that time. If you notice a deactivated or changed Web address, please e-mail books@reading.org with the words "Website Update" in the subject line. In your message, specify the Web link, the book title, and the page number on which the link appears.

Library of Congress Cataloging-in-Publication Data
What research has to say about fluency instruction / S. Jay Samuels, Alan E. Farstrup, editors.
     p. cm.
  Includes bibliographical references and index.
  ISBN 0-87207-587-7
  1. Reading. 2. Fluency (Language learning) 3. Language and languages--Study and teaching. I. Farstrup, Alan E. II. Samuels, S. Jay.
  LB1050.W4347 2006
  428.4--dc22
                                                                              2006003125

Contents

Note From the Editors

Long before the federal government mandated that educational decisions should be evidence based, we went to leading U.S. reading researchers and asked them to explain the research base that supported their recommendations for effective reading instruction. This was the origin of the highly successful book *What Research Has to Say About Reading Instruction*, now in its third edition. Each new edition brought forth the latest research and evidence for developing sound instructional practices. In this tradition, the International Reading Association presents the newest book in this series, *What Research Has to Say About Fluency Instruction*.

Presently, reading fluency is both a popular and important topic, and reading conferences usually offer several presentations with the term *fluency* in the title. As editors, we had several purposes in mind in offering this book to you. First, fluent reading represents a very high level of skill development, meaning that fluency is not a dichotomous variable where one is either fluent or not. It is a developmental variable, meaning that with continued instruction and the growth in skill that comes from years of independent reading, the student can become fluent at reading more and more difficult texts. We are well aware that teachers are open to promising new approaches that may help their students acquire advanced reading skills. However, if these approaches do not work after giving them a fair trial, teachers will abandon the tried-but-failed methods. Some methods fail not because the methods are ineffective but because the methods were not applied appropriately. One of our purposes is to bring together within the covers of this book leading experts in the field to provide teachers with the best information on how to promote and develop fluency through good instruction and assessment.

Second, we believe that teachers deserve more than a "cookbook" of successful fluency recipes. As much as teachers want to know what works in the development of reading fluency, they also want to know why something works, why certain assessments are recommended, and why caution is advised in other instances. To achieve this goal, we solicited the help of our scholars and asked them to explain the reasons, the research, and the theories that underlie their recommendations.

Within the pages of this book, you will find the thoughts of powerful thinkers who have something worthwhile to say; however, they may not all agree with one another. As editors of this volume, we expected diverse and vigorous viewpoints. Unanimity of expert opinion does not exist in education any more than it does in disciplines such as medicine or law. We wanted to provide you with learned opinions, and we wanted you to decide the issues for yourself.

As you read through the chapters, look for the definitions of fluency used by the authors. In the case of fluency, definitions are not an ivory tower concern that are of no importance, but just the opposite. The definitions of fluency that are either explicitly stated or implied may help to explain the recommendations contained in the chapters. Is fluency simply reading speed, or ease of decoding, or ability to read orally with expression, or is it something more? We believe that how one defines fluency is critical to the future of fluency. The definitions of fluency that teachers and researchers finally settle on will influence the future of fluency instruction—whether it will continue to be a hot topic or not.

The chapters in this volume embrace a variety of topics, such as the history of fluency, curriculum-based measurement, text difficulty, English-language learners, students with reading handicaps, development of fluency, measurement of fluency, reading rate, and oral-language skills. As in our editions of *What Research Has to Say About Reading Instruction*, we thought of our audience primarily as teachers or students who were training to be teachers. We wanted our teachers to have the best information available on fluent reading. Now with the U.S. No Child Left Behind legislation and its goal of every child at the proficient level in reading by the year 2014, the ability to help our students become fluent readers has taken on new importance. Fluent readers are proficient readers.

As with our earlier edited volume, *What Research Has to Say About Reading Instruction*, Third Edition, we have included questions for discussion at the end of each chapter in this book. Most of the questions were not designed to have a right or wrong answer, but to provoke thoughtful reflection and higher order critical thinking and discussions. We found that schools were using our book for staff development and in college courses, and the questions helped guide the discussions on the chapters. Furthermore, for individuals who read the book by themselves, the questions allow reflection and a sense of ownership of the ideas presented.

In closing, we hope that readers of this book will increase their understanding of practices that promote fluency, as well their knowledge of the research and theory that underlie reading fluency.

SJS, AEF

About the Editors

S. Jay Samuels

S. Jay Samuels started teaching elementary school shortly after the end of World War II. At that time, the schools were crowded and teachers were in short supply. Los Angeles needed teachers, so recruiters came to the New York area. Jay took a job offered by a recruiter because he knew that Muscle Beach, the Mecca for bodybuilding, would be conveniently located to where he would be teaching. He entered the University of California, Los Angeles, doctoral program, where he received a doctorate in educational psychology.

Jay later joined the Educational Psychology Department at the University of Minnesota and has been there for the last 40 years. Through Psychology Professor David LaBerge, Jay developed an interest in reading fluency. At the university, Jay received a Distinguished Teaching Award for his large teacher training lecture class on learning, cognition, and assessment. The National Reading Conference and the International Reading Association also have recognized Jay with research awards for reading. Jay was inducted into the Reading Hall of Fame in 1990.

Jay is also a member of the National Reading Panel. He points out that fluency is enjoying the attention it is presently receiving from researchers and teachers because of the panel's work on the subject.

Jay met Alan Farstrup when Alan was a doctoral student at the University of Minnesota. Over the years Alan and Jay have worked together to produce books that they trust will provide teachers with the latest in research and pedagogy from the leaders in the reading field.

Alan E. Farstrup

 Alan E. Farstrup is Executive Director of the International Reading Association (IRA) in Newark, Delaware. He completed his Bachelor of Arts degree at the University of Iowa in 1965, earned his teaching credential from the University of California at Berkeley in 1967, and received his PhD in Reading Curriculum and Instruction from the University of Minnesota in 1977.

Alan has been a junior high reading and English teacher and a member of reading education faculties of the University of Texas at San Antonio and the University of Rhode Island. He has served as a reading specialist and consultant. He directed the Institute of Human Science and Services at Rhode Island. He was also a U.S. Peace Corps volunteer in Afghanistan in 1965 and 1966.

Alan was IRA's director of research before assuming the post of Executive Director in 1992. His responsibilities include administrative leadership, supporting the IRA Board of Directors, and representing the Association on issues of reading research, policy, and classroom practice. He is a member of the United Nations Educational, Scientific and Cultural Organization's International Literacy Prize Jury; has extensive experience in the development of educational standards and assessments; and is IRA liaison to numerous organizations and agencies worldwide.

Alan is coeditor with S. Jay Samuels of *What Research Has to Say About Reading Instruction* (Second and Third Editions). He finds the work of IRA to be challenging, interesting, and important. Alan's wife, Susan, is a former teacher. They enjoy traveling and staying in touch with family and with their extensive network of friends and colleagues.

Contributors

Richard L. Allington
Professor of Education
University of Tennessee
Knoxville, Tennessee, USA

Stanley L. Deno
Professor of Educational
    Psychology
University of Minnesota
Minneapolis, Minnesota, USA

Alan E. Farstrup
Executive Director
International Reading Association
Newark, Delaware, USA

Lauren Fingeret
Doctoral Student
Michigan State University
East Lansing, Michigan, USA

Irene W. Gaskins
Founder and Director
Benchmark School
Media, Pennsylvania, USA

Elfrieda H. Hiebert
Adjunct Professor of Education
University of California, Berkeley
Berkeley, California, USA

Roxanne F. Hudson
Assistant Professor of Reading
    Education
Florida Center for Reading
    Research
Florida State University
Tallahassee, Florida, USA

Douglas Marston
Administrator for Research
    and Evaluation in Special
    Education
Minneapolis Public Schools
Minneapolis, Minnesota, USA

Theresa J. Palumbo
Instructor of Learning
    and Cognition
University of Minnesota Twin
    Cities
Minneapolis, Minnesota, USA

John J. Pikulski
Author, Houghton Mifflin
    Company
Professor Emeritus, University
    of Delaware
Newark, Delaware, USA

Michael Pressley
University Distinguished
    Professor
Michigan State University
East Lansing, Michigan, USA

Timothy V. Rasinski
Professor of Education
Kent State University
Kent, Ohio, USA

S. Jay Samuels
Professor of Educational
    Psychology
University of Minnesota Twin
    Cities
Minneapolis, Minnesota, USA

Keith J. Topping
Professor of Educational
and Social Research
University of Dundee
Dundee, Scotland, United
Kingdom

Joseph K. Torgesen
W. Russell and Eugenia Morcom
Chair of Psychology,
Department of Psychology
Director, Florida Center
for Reading Research
Florida State University
Tallahassee, Florida, USA

Jennifer R. Willcutt
Instructor of Learning
and Cognition
University of Minnesota Twin
Cities
Minneapolis, Minnesota, USA

Reading Fluency Instruction: Will It Be a Passing Fad or Permanent Fixture?

S. Jay Samuels and Alan E. Farstrup

O ut of the minds of humans came one of the greatest inventions of all time, the alphabet. If the alphabet can be considered one of humanity's greatest accomplishments, then the human brain's ability to learn to read alphabetic writing with fluency can be considered to be one of its greatest achievements. This book is all about fluency—its definition, development, and assessment.

Reading fluency is a hot topic. In *Reading Today*, Cassidy and Cassidy (2005/2006) reported the results of a study in which they asked reading experts, "What's hot and what's not?" in reading. The experts agreed that fluency was a very hot topic and deserved to be. Similarly, the highly influential *Report of the National Reading Panel* (National Institute of Child Health and Human Development, 2000) devoted an entire chapter to fluency. But interest in fluency is not new. Interest in this topic is traceable back for more than a century (see Timothy Rasinski's chapter in this book on the history of fluency). Interest in fluency, however, has not been constant, and there have been times when it was not a popular topic. Several factors seem responsible for rekindling interest in this topic. One is the No Child Left Behind legislation (NCLB, 2002), which has established a U.S. national goal that heretofore has been unobtainable. The legislation stipulates that all students, regardless of their learning abilities, will meet annual standards of achievement and that by the year 2014 all students will be proficient readers. Educators are very much aware of how difficult it will be to achieve this goal, and they are also aware that if all students can become fluent readers, it would contribute significantly to meeting this federal goal.

Another factor that brings fluency to the forefront is that we now have a far stronger evidence-supported knowledge base on how to

What Research Has to Say About Fluency Instruction, edited by S. Jay Samuels and Alan E. Farstrup. © 2006 by the International Reading Association.

develop reading fluency than we ever had before. The time is indeed ripe for us to more effectively help our students become fluent readers. In addition to possessing the knowledge of how to develop fluency, we also have access to the instructional tools that can assist in making this goal a reality. For example, to help a student achieve fluency, we know how important it is to have a close match between the student's reading ability level and the readability level of the books he or she uses for instructional and independent reading purposes. We are fortunate in having tools such as informal reading inventories and computerized interactive instruments that can quickly establish a student's reading level. We also have computerized tools that help us establish the readability level of texts the students will use. Although these helpful resources are available for developing fluency, mere availability is not enough. Teachers must not only know about research but be able to access available teaching resources so that they can better help students become fluent readers.

With the newborn importance of reading fluency has come two important problems: how one defines fluency and how one assesses it. The two problems are intertwined because how one defines fluency influences how it will be measured. Measurement is an important issue because of the controversy and concern about the validity of some of the methods that are widely used to measure fluency. As you read the chapters in this book that address some of these problems, you will have to decide for yourself which definitions and which approaches to assessing fluency make sense and which ones do not.

Although fluency is presently a hot topic, its fate will be similar to every other popular topic in the history of reading—its prominence may fade. What works will be retained, and what fails to work will be abandoned. You, the teacher, the knowledge you take from this book, and how you use it will influence in important ways what happens to the future of fluency instruction. Fluency is indeed a vital aspect of literacy. It deserves our serious attention. The chapters in this volume have been selected to support that attention and to expand our instructional horizons.

REFERENCES

Cassidy, J., & Cassidy, D. (2005/2006). What's hot, what's not for 2006. *Reading Today, 23*(3), 1, 8.
National Institute of Child Health and Human Development. (2000). *Report of the National Reading Panel. Teaching children to read: An evidence-based assessment of the*

scientific research literature on reading and its implications for reading instruction (NIH Publication No. 00-4769). Washington, DC: U.S. Government Printing Office.

No Child Left Behind Act of 2001, Pub. L. No. 107-110, 115 Stat. 1425 (2002).

SUGGESTED READINGS

Kuhn, M., & Stahl, S. (2000). *Fluency: A review of developmental and remedial strategies* (CIERA Rep. No. 2-008). Ann Arbor, MI: Center for the Improvement of Early Reading Achievement. Retrieved January 13, 2006, from http://www.ciera.org/library/reports/inquiry-2/2-008/2-008.html

Wolf, M., & Katzir-Cohen, T. (2001). Reading fluency and its intervention. *Scientific Studies of Reading, 5*(3), 211–238.

Chapter 1

A Brief History of Reading Fluency

Timothy V. Rasinski

The publication of the *Report of the National Reading Panel* (National Institute of Child Health and Human Development [NICHD], 2000) brought new visibility to reading fluency, an instructional concept in reading that had previously been relegated to a secondary or tertiary position. This panel of experts, who were given the charge of assessing "the status of research-based knowledge, including the effectiveness of various approaches to teaching children to read" (NICHD, 2000, p. 1-1), identified the most important research-based factors associated with high achievement in teaching and learning to read in the elementary grades. It identified reading fluency as one of four key areas for which instruction would most likely produce the desired results—proficient readers:

> It appears that oral reading practice and feedback or guidance is most likely to influence measures that assess word knowledge, reading speed, and oral accuracy. Nevertheless, the impact of these procedures on comprehension (and on total reading scores) is not inconsiderable, and in several comparisons it was actually quite high. (NICHD, 2000, p. 3-18)
>
> These (instructional) procedures help improve students' reading ability, at least through grade 5, and they help improve the reading of students with learning problems much later than this. (NICHD, 2000, p. 3-20)

This finding, that certain forms of guided oral reading and practice (i.e., instruction aimed at developing reading fluency) promote reading growth through most of the elementary grades, has been helpful in at least two ways. First, it has affirmed some of the instructional practices using oral reading that many teachers have been using successfully in their own classrooms. Second, it has been useful in guiding teachers to consider fundamental changes in the use of oral-reading instruction in their classrooms.

For some reading professionals, this finding was surprising. Reading fluency had not been on their instructional agendas. Indeed, a survey of

What Research Has to Say About Fluency Instruction, edited by S. Jay Samuels and Alan E. Farstrup. © 2006 by the International Reading Association.

reading methods textbooks and reading instructional materials from as little as 10 years ago is likely to find minimal attention, if any, given to the concept of reading fluency (Rasinski & Zutell, 1996). The subject was hardly mentioned in undergraduate- and graduate-level course work for teachers of reading. Yet today, professionals and practitioners are recognizing that the concept is key to success in reading.

Despite its relative obscurity, reading fluency has been part of the history of scholarly inquiry in reading. In this chapter, I present a brief overview to the concept of fluency from a historical point of view. My intention is not necessarily to provide a comprehensive historical treatment of the concept of reading fluency, but rather to make the case that reading fluency is an issue that has been considered by reading scholars through the history of reading instruction in the United States and that has enjoyed, from time to time, some degree of primacy in professional and scholarly circles.

One of the problems with reading fluency lies in its definition. To some, reading fluency is considered primarily an act of oral reading—specifically, the oral interpretation and expressiveness (prosody) associated with the oral production of a written text. To others, reading fluency has to do with accuracy and speed (automaticity) in word decoding. And to yet others, reading fluency has largely to do with the understanding, or comprehension, that comes as a result of reading with appropriate expressiveness or decoding speed and accuracy. Because the emphasis on what constitutes reading fluency has changed over time, and to this day the exact nature of reading fluency has yet to be resolved, a broad conception of reading fluency will be considered in this historical presentation.

Early Conceptions of Oral-Reading Fluency

Oral reading has been part and parcel of reading instruction in America since colonial times. In early schooling, oral reading was not viewed so much as a means to an end (i.e., fluent silent reading) as it was a legitimate goal or outcome for instruction. This goal for proficiency in oral reading was tied directly to the social context for literacy uses of the period. According to reading historians (e.g., Hyatt, 1943; Smith, 2002), in many early American homes there were few books, and only one person in the household may have been able to read. Thus, when reading occurred, someone had to read aloud so that the others could enjoy a book or other text. Expressive oral reading was considered a goal for classroom instruction because of its prominence in people's daily lives for entertainment and sharing information (Hyatt, 1943).

This development of "eloquent oral reading" became the focus of reading instruction in this period and was represented in most of the published reading programs of the time. Writing in 1835, Lyman Cobb expressed the goal of reading instruction to promote oral-reading skills in the following way:

> A just delivery consists in a distinct articulation of words pronounced in proper tones, suitably varied to the sense, and the emotions of the mind; with due attention to accent, to emphasis, in its several gradations; to rests or pauses of the voice, in proper places...and the whole accompanied with expressive looks, and significant gestures. (cited in Smith, 2002, pp. 40–41)

Schools in the 19th century began to use a form of oral recitation that focused on elocution as the preferred method and goal of reading instruction (Hoffman, 1987; Hoffman & Segel, 1983). The recitation lesson usually involved the teacher orally reading a text followed by the students orally practicing the passage on their own. Often the teacher would provide personal assistance and formative evaluation of the oral quality of individual students' reading. Then, after a sufficient period of practice, the students orally read or recited the passage for the teacher and fellow students. The students' reading was judged by the teacher on the quality of their oral reading and their recall of what they had read. According to Hoffman (1987), this approach to reading instruction became formalized at the beginning of the 20th century into what was termed the *story method* of instruction, the focal unit of instruction being an entire text, or story. Toward the end of the 19th century, oral reading had become such an ingrained and perceived necessary part of American education that philosopher William James (1892) indicated that "the teacher's success or failure in teaching reading is based, so far as the public estimate is concerned, upon the oral reading method" (p. 422).

Oral Reading in Decline

Near the end of the 19th and beginning of the 20th centuries, the dominant role of oral reading as the primary mode of instruction in reading was challenged. Education scholars studying in Europe and in the United States began to question the role of oral reading in American classrooms (Hyatt, 1943). They argued that the oral-reading instruction gave priority to elocutionary matters such as "pronunciation, emphasis, inflection, and force" (Hyatt, 1943, p. 27) over reading for understanding. In noting that reading instruction of the time had become more an "action of the organs of speech" rather than an "exercise of the mind in thinking and feeling," Horace Mann (1891) claimed that "more than eleven-twelfths of all the children in reading classes do not understand the meaning for the words they read" (cited in Hoffman & Segel, 1983, p. 4). Mann led the attack on reading instruction that he felt was too focused on the mechanical and oral aspects of reading.

Moreover, as reading material became more easily accessible and as common schools promoted literacy across a broader spectrum of American society, the need for oral reading for imparting information declined. Individual silent reading became a more common feature of family and community life. Francis Parker, most often associated with the Language Experience Approach to reading instruction, began to question the use of oral reading for instructional purposes while studying the educational theories of Froebel in Germany (Hyatt, 1943). He argued that oral reading in schools placed inappropriate emphasis on elocution over understanding:

> Many of the grossest errors in teaching reading spring from confounding the two processes of attention and expression. Reading itself is not expression.... Reading is a mental process.... Oral reading is expression, and comes under the heading of speech.... The custom of making oral reading the principal and almost the only means of teaching reading has led to many errors prevalent today. (Parker, 1894, cited in Smith, 2002, p. 150)

Science and scientific inquiry began to have an impact on reading education around the turn of the century. Some researchers, such as Edmund Huey (1908/1968), noted that oral reading had become an activity that was found only in schools. In everyday life, silent reading predominated:

> Reading as a school exercise has almost always been thought of as reading aloud, in spite of the obvious fact that reading in actual life is to be mainly silent reading.... The consequent attention to reading as an exercise in speaking, and it has usually been a rather bad exercise in speaking at that, has been heavily at the expense of reading as the art of thought-getting and thought manipulating.... By silent reading meanings from the first day of reading, and by practice in getting meanings

from the page...the rate of reading and of thinking will grow with the pupil's growth and with his power to assimilate what is read. (cited in Hyatt, 1943, p. 16)

To be fair, Huey did describe methods for reading instruction that focused on oral recitation of texts, but his instructional preference was on silent reading. Similarly, Huey discussed ways for improving reading rate in students, but he did not make a compelling connection between rate of reading and overall reading proficiency.

The focus on abstracting meaning from text over oral production of text began to take hold. Spurred by the work of Thorndike (1917), comprehension of text became a more important focal point of instruction than the oral interpretation of text. Silent reading was seen as the more logical path to good comprehension and therefore a more worthy goal for reading instruction than oral-reading proficiency.

Others noted that in the early 20th century the number of books, magazines, newspapers, and other materials available for adults and children began to expand at an increasingly rapid pace (Hyatt, 1943). In order for students and teachers to take advantage of and cover this growing body of print, silent reading, which was inherently more efficient than oral reading, needed to be emphasized. In their 1923 series of instructional reading books, Buswell and Wheeler noted that schools that employed oral reading used very few readers or other reading material:

In contrast with this, in the modern school, which emphasizes silent reading, a great many books are read in each grade.... It [silent reading] is the complex process of getting thought from printed page and involves an entirely new pedagogy. Silent-reading objectives will never be attained by oral-reading methods. (cited in Hyatt, 1943, pp. 39–40)

During this period, then, silent reading with a focus on comprehension began to replace oral reading with a focus on elocution not only as a goal for reading but also as the preferred mode of reading for instruction. Scholars felt that silent reading was a more authentic form of reading—for most readers in the real world, silent reading predominated over oral reading. Silent reading focused readers' attention on the apprehension of meaning—the goal of reading—while instruction in oral reading tended to focus attention on word-perfect, accurate, and expressive recitation of the text. Silent reading also was felt to maximize student engagement in reading and text coverage. Silent-reading instruction aimed at student understanding of the text with the first and only reading, thus increasing the opportunity to read many texts; oral-reading instruction aimed at expressiveness in reading and was obtained through intensive practice of a limited number of texts (Hoffman & Segel, 1983). Moreover, in oral-recitation reading activities, only one student read at a time, and the remaining students served as an audience for the reader. Reading volume was necessarily limited. Conversely, several students could simultaneously engage in silent reading. Thus, the Indianapolis Public Schools' "Course of Study" for 1902 advocated silent reading as the preferred mode of instruction:

> Reading...fundamentally is not oral expression. Children should do as much silent reading and be called upon to state the salient features of such reading in order to know how far they have grasped the thought. Silent reading is too much neglected in schools.... Pupils should be taught how to read silently with the greatest economy of time and with the least conscious effort. (cited in Hyatt, 1943, p. 21)

By the 1920s, the swell of support for silent reading reached out broadly into American educational circles. The following item from the 1923 "Course of Study" from the Ohio Department of Education reflects this fundamental change:

> During the past few years investigations have been in progress along several lines in reading, one of the most important having to do with the significant factors in silent reading and the emphasis due this type. It would be amiss not to suggest here some of the values of training in silent reading:
> 1. It is the most economical form of reading.
> 2. Silent reading bears a close relationship to the other school subjects in that attainment in other subjects depends largely upon ability to read.
> 3. Training in silent reading constitutes a real preparation for life reading.
> 4. Silent reading develops interest because thought plays a prominent part. (cited in Hyatt, 1943, p. 39)

According to Smith (2002), schools seemed to become obsessed with the notion of silent reading for improving comprehension. Silent reading became such a dominant focus of instruction that a program that emphasized silent reading exclusively was adopted in some of the Chicago schools in the late 1930s through the early 1940s. The approach, known as the "McDade non-oral" method of reading instruction, taught students to gain meaning directly from printed symbols, involving only the eyes and the central nervous system, without any inner speech (McDade, 1937, 1944; Rohrer, 1943). Beginning readers were taught to associate meaning directly from the printed words, without making an oral representation of the words. Even silent reading that involved internal sounding of words was discouraged. Although severely criticized (Rohrer, 1943) and eventually abandoned, the emergence of the "non-oral" method demonstrates the extent to which oral reading was viewed as unnecessary and, in some cases, detrimental to success in learning to read.

The standardized testing movement, which began in the early 20th century, also supported the shift away from oral reading and toward silent reading. Group-administered reading achievement tests in a silent reading format were being used to evaluate individual students as well as school progress. William S. Gray, a highly influential scholar in reading, used these tests in a series of school evaluation studies in the early 1900s, and the results of his studies showed that students who practiced reading silently performed best on the assessments (Hoffman, 1991). Fuchs, Fuchs, Hosp, and Jenkins (2001) have noted the ongoing decline of reading tests that incorporated a fluency component, both oral and silent, from the 1920s through the 1990s.

Similarly, Rasinski and Zutell (Rasinski, 1989; Rasinski & Zutell, 1996; Zutell & Rasinski, 1991) reported that by the later part of the 20th century, textbooks for training teachers in reading instruction provided little, if any, in-depth focus on defining, teaching, or assessing reading fluency. This historical trend in reading instruction and assessment in the United States demonstrates a gradual but sustained movement away from oral-reading fluency. Early in the country's history, oral reading for elocution (i.e., reading fluency) was a focal point of instruction. However, by the later part of the 20th century, oral-reading fluency was relegated, at best, to secondary status in reading instruction.

Round-Robin Reading

The demise of oral reading as a goal for reading instruction in the 20th century and the arguments for an emphasis on comprehension and silent reading as the best tools to lead students to high levels of success, however, did not lead to the disappearance of oral reading as an instructional practice. Research into classroom instructional practices (e.g., Austin & Morrison, 1963) revealed that oral reading continued as a mainstay of reading instruction. Despite criticisms, round-robin reading (unrehearsed sight reading, with turn-taking) persisted throughout the latter half of the 20th century as the dominant format for practice. Oral reading was used primarily as a method of checking students' word recognition after silent reading (Eldredge, Reutzel, & Hollingsworth, 1996). This change in the use of oral reading from reading for fluent expression to reading for checking word recognition became the genesis of round-robin reading. Integrated into the basal reading programs that assumed the preeminent position in elementary reading instruction from the early 1950s to the present (Hoffman, 1987; Hoffman & Segel, 1983), round-robin reading has become one of the most ubiquitous forms of reading in American reading instruction.

In the original form of round-robin reading, students read orally for a teacher who, rather than coaching students on their individual oral-reading performances, made note of any errors that were made during the reading. In some ways, it was analogous to the oral-reading portion of today's informal reading inventories or reading running records. Students were given additional instruction in the words missed or on any patterns of words that presented difficulty. Despite its pervasive use (Hoffman, 1987; Howlett & Weintraub, 1979), round-robin reading has never been widely advocated nor endorsed by scholars of reading (Beach, 1993).

More Recent Developments in Fluency

Despite its clear limitations, round-robin oral reading has continued for decades (and continues) to play a significant role in reading instruction and is considered by some practitioners a primary mode for developing reading fluency in students. Nevertheless, in the past three decades significant advances in our understandings of reading have caused reading scholars to look more closely at reading fluency. In their seminal volume on reading, Gibson and Levin (1975) made mention of oral reading, expressive reading, and reading rate, but failed to elucidate a strong connection between these aspects of reading and overall proficiency in reading. Indeed, they stated that, "Reading aloud in the early grades probably has little justification other than to give the teacher some insight into the child's progress" (p. 105).

One of the more important milestones in contemporary conceptions of reading fluency came with the publication of LaBerge and Samuels's (1974) theory of automatic information processing in reading. This was perhaps the first modern theoretical conception of reading fluency. LaBerge and Samuels argued that the surface-level processing of words in reading (visual perception, sounding, phrasing words together, etc.) should ideally be done at an automatic level, a level that required minimal attentional or cognitive capacity. In doing so, readers could reserve their finite cognitive resources for the more important task in reading—comprehension. LaBerge and Samuels hypothesized that for many readers poor comprehension could be explained by too much investment of their cognitive resources in the surface-level aspects of reading—slow, laborious, conscious-filled decoding of words. This investment of resources into the surface-level component of reading depleted or exhausted what could be invested in making sense of what they read.

Stanovich (1980) later refined this theory into what he termed the "interactive compensatory explanation" of reading fluency. Stanovich reasoned that a major difference between good and poor readers was in the way they processed text while reading. Poor readers were less able than good readers to employ automatic, attention-free, bottom-up processes in decoding reading. Rather, they compensated for their difficulty in using the more efficient automatic word-decoding processes by employing more context-bound strategies that required significant amounts of cognitive resources for word decoding. In doing so, they had fewer cognitive resources available for comprehension—a task in reading that requires top-down, contextually dependent, and conscious processing of the surface elements of text. These readers are characterized by slow, laborious, monotone, and unenthusiastic oral readings. Good readers, on the other hand, are quite able to use automatic, attention-free, bottom-up processes for word decoding and thus reserve their limited top-down, contextually dependent processes for comprehending what they read. These readers are characterized by accurate and nearly effortless word reading with appropriate phrasing and expression.

In a 1979 article in *The Reading Teacher*, Jay Samuels put the theory of automatic information processing in reading to a test. At the time he was a long-distance runner, and while on his runs he would think about possible analogies and applications to automaticity theory (Samuels, personal communication, October 30, 2004). While on one such run, he hypothesized that automaticity finds its way into many human activities—perhaps most notably athletics and music. Athletes and musicians are well known to have developed certain skills within their repertoire to a level where they can be performed seemingly without effort—automatically. They developed these skills to this level by first working with a teacher or coach who helped them develop the skills to a level of conscious mastery. Then, they practiced those skills until they became automatic in their execution. Practice seemed to be the key to the development of fluency.

Samuels then asked, How do teachers normally teach reading? He reasoned that for many students, especially those with severe difficulty in learning to read, the teacher tended to cover the reading curriculum at a pace that was too fast for them to develop conscious mastery (accuracy) or automaticity in critical reading skills. Thus, Samuels tested his ideas with a group of mentally retarded students from Minneapolis, Minnesota, USA. He asked students to read short passages of approximately 250 words in length repeatedly until they achieved a reading speed of 95 words per minute. Samuels explained to the students that like basketball players who need to practice plays over and over to develop their ability to execute the plays, readers need to practice reading a passage until they can read it well, or with fluency. As students practiced their passages, they traced their progress on graphs. Samuels found that this method of repeated readings lead to improvements in passage reading across a variety of dimensions, including accuracy, reading speed, and expression. Moreover, he found that when students moved on to other texts, their initial readings of the new passages were better than their initial readings of the earlier passages, and the number of repeated readings required to reach the criterion reading rate fell over time. Samuels explained his findings in terms of automatic information processing in reading. He argued that through their practiced or repeated readings of texts, readers were developing automaticity in word decoding and word processing. This automaticity was generalized to new passages that the students had not previously read. An important finding of Samuels's study was that fluency improvement was not limited to what the students were practicing but extended to new, never-before-read passages.

At about the same time that Samuels was testing his method of repeated reading for improving reading fluency, Carol Chomsky (1976) was testing a method for improving reading—a method that involved repeated reading but also included an approach first developed by Heckelman (1969), called the Neurological Impress Method (Hollingsworth, 1978; Hoskisson, 1975a, 1975b). Today this approach is referred to as assisted reading or reading while listening. Chomsky asked struggling readers to repeatedly read texts while simultaneously listening to audiotaped versions of the same text read fluently to them until they thought they could read the text fluently. Like Samuels, Chomsky reported remarkably positive results for students on text practices, on new texts never before read, and in attitude toward and confidence in their reading.

In 1980 Peter Schreiber (1980, 1991; Schreiber & Read, 1980) offered an alternative explanation for Samuels's positive results from repeated readings. Schreiber argued that through practice students were developing a greater awareness of the prosodic features of oral reading and speech. That is, they were learning to embed in their reading the expressive and intonational features of oral speech that help to mark phrase boundaries within and between sentences and convey meaning. Dysfluent readers tend to read in a slow, word-by-word manner that does not lend itself well to prosodic and syntactically appropriate phrased reading that carries meaning. Through repeated readings, even dysfluent readers are more able to capture the prosodic and syntactic essence of the text, thus improving the surface-level processing of the passage as well as text comprehension.

Both conceptualizations of reading fluency, automatic processing of the surface-level features of text and the ability to attend to the prosodic and syntactic features of text while reading, seem compelling. Indeed, both are considered central elements of current conceptions of reading fluency (Kuhn & Stahl, 2000) and instruction aimed at improving reading fluency.

Richard Allington presented his concept of reading fluency to the reading practitioner community in his 1983 article in *The Reading Teacher* titled "Fluency: The Neglected Reading Goal." Relying on the previous work in reading fluency mentioned in this section, Allington argued that reading fluency appears to be an important aspect of the reading process that holds great promise for improving the reading performance of many struggling readers. Equally important, Allington also noted that the reading community has largely ignored fluency. So, although the potential was strong for improving reading, teachers and developers of instructional material reading were not aware of its importance and did not include it as a central element of instructional methods, materials, and programs.

Allington's article began a slow but increasing awareness of the contribution of reading fluency to proficient reading. Subsequent research has pointed to an association between oral-reading fluency and reading achievement. A large-scale study of reading fluency (Pinnell et al., 1995) identified a significant relationship between the quality of fourth graders' oral reading and reading comprehension, and confirmed reading fluency as an important variable in the scholarship of reading. In this study, over 1,000 fourth-grade students who had previously taken the reading achievement assessment for the National Assessment of Educational Progress (NAEP) were asked to orally read a brief passage that was then analyzed qualitatively for expressiveness, phrasing, and accuracy of the reading. The relationship between oral-reading fluency and general reading achievement (NAEP reading assessment) was the focus of the study. Students who read orally with greatest fluency tended to score highest in overall reading achievement, and those who read with least fluency tended to manifest the lowest levels of reading achievement.

In a study of struggling elementary-grade readers, Rasinski and Padak (1998) found that students referred for supplementary instruction in reading were more likely to manifest significant difficulties in reading fluency than in word decoding or passage comprehension. Similarly, Fuchs, Fuchs, and Maxwell (1988) found a remarkably strong relationship (correlation coefficient = .91) between measures of reading fluency and students' performance on a standardized test of silent-reading comprehension.

These studies and others have begun to demonstrate a powerful and compelling relationship between reading fluency and more general measures of reading achievement and proficiency, including comprehension. Scholars were coming to the realization that oral, expressive, and automatic readings of texts were a significant contributor to overall proficiency in reading. Expressive reading was no longer important for the sake of expressive reading only; it was important because it appeared to lead to gains in reading achievement. Thus, the next step in this line of inquiry was to determine, through empirical study, if instruction in fluency would actually lead to generalized improvements in reading.

Subsequent articles have attempted to define and describe specific instructional activities for improving fluency in readers (e.g., Rasinski, 1989). These activities have included modeling fluent reading, practiced or repeated reading, assisted reading or reading while listening to a fluent rendering of the passage, and a focus on phrasing while reading.

A number of studies have examined the role of Samuels's repeated-reading method. In reviews of research related to repeated readings, Dowhower (1989, 1994) reported that studies of the repeated-reading method have demonstrated improvements in students' reading rates and word-recognition accuracy, better comprehension of both literal and higher level information, and its use as an effective study strategy. Moreover, Dowhower reported that improvements extend to unpracticed passages for students in primary through the middle grades and that repeated reading appears to be an effective intervention for students experiencing difficulty in learning to read.

Other studies have expanded on Chomsky's (1976) work and have examined various forms of assisted reading. These include students reading while listening to a more fluent partner read with them (paired or duolog reading; Eldredge, 1990; Eldredge & Quinn, 1988; Topping, 1987, 1989) and reading while listening to an audiotaped fluent reading of the text (Carbo, 1978, 1981; Pluck, 1995). These studies have generally demonstrated positive results for students (Kuhn & Stahl, 2000; Rasinski & Hoffman, 2003).

Although current research on the role of phrasing does not seem to be currently in vogue, Rasinski (1990) performed a review of research conducted over several decades related to instruction focused on text phrasing. The results of the review suggested that a focus on phrasing has substantial potential for delivering positive outcomes across a number of areas related to reading proficiency.

Instructional Programs in Reading Fluency

The research cited in the previous section demonstrates the promise of specific oral-reading practices for promoting improvements in fluency and general reading achievement. Some scholars have developed elaborated instructional routines aimed specifically at improving students' fluency. Holdaway's (1979, 1981) shared-book experience (SBE), or shared reading, has become one of the most widely used forms of fluency-directed instruction. In SBE the teacher introduces a book, reads the book to a class or group of students, and discusses it. Later, the students read and reread the text with the teacher, in small groups, with partners, and eventually on their own. In addition to the Eldredge et al. (1996) study of SBE described earlier in this chapter, Smith and Elley (1997) summarized a number of studies that demonstrate positive results from the use of the shared-book experience.

Hoffman (1987; Hoffman & Crone, 1985) described the Oral Recitation Lesson (ORL) as a substitute for a traditional basal reading lesson. The teacher initiates the lesson by expressively reading the assigned passage to the students, followed by a discussion that leads to the construction of a story map and a summary of the story. Students then read and reread a section of the story with the teacher. Following this step, students select, practice, and perform a segment of the story. In addition, students spend a brief period of time practicing stories covered in previous lessons and performing them for the teacher, who checks students' for accuracy and fluency. Studies of the ORL or an adaptation of the lesson reported positive results (Hoffman, 1987; Morris & Nelson, 1992; Reutzel & Hollingsworth, 1993).

Stahl and Heubach's (2005) Fluency-Oriented Reading Instruction (FORI) is a modified version of the ORL. Like the ORL, FORI is employed with basal reading passages and begins with the teacher reading the story aloud to the class. Following the reading are a discussion of the story, vocabulary and comprehension activities related to the story, and other instructional activities from the story, including rereading the story independently or with the teacher. Later, students reread the story at home with their parents or other adult (this particular step could occur over a number of days). On the following day(s), students reread the story with a partner—alternating pages while the partner listens to and monitors the reading. After some further extension activities, the class moves onto the next story.

In an implementation of FORI in 10 second-grade classrooms over two years, Stahl and Heubach reported a mean gain of nearly two years in reading achievement. Of the 105 students in the study, only 2 were reading below grade level at the end of second grade.

Rasinski, Padak, Linek, and Sturtevant (1994) developed a Fluency Development Lesson (FDL) that was a supplement to the normal basal reading lesson. In the 15-minute lesson, students read and reread a brief passage, usually an age-appropriate poem. The lesson begins with the teacher reading the poem to the students and briefly discussing its meaning. Next the children chorally read the text with the teacher several times. Then the students pair up and practice the text three times each with their partner (Koskinen & Blum, 1984, 1986). Finally, students perform the text for the class or another audience. Additionally, the students are assigned to read the text at home to their parents or other willing listeners.

In their implementation of the FDL in a second-grade classroom, Rasinski et al. (1994) found significant positive effects for reading rate in favor of the FDL group over a control group doing more traditional reading activities during the assigned time. Although a trend toward overall improved reading for the FDL group was apparent, it was not statistically significant.

Taken as a whole, these and other studies (e.g., Hasbrouck, Ihnot, & Rogers, 1999) suggest that dedicated oral-reading lessons that employ repeated and assisted readings have the potential to significantly and positively impact reading achievement among elementary-grade students.

Conclusions

The history of reading fluency in the United States is interesting and checkered. Fluency has gone from a primary focus in reading instruction to secondary status and has returned to an area of primacy in reading instruction. What has brought about such changes? I think fluency has been misunderstood, and it has been this misunderstanding that has led to these shifts in status.

Fluency essentially deals with the surface-level and easily observable aspects and characteristics of reading—it deals largely with oral reading, it deals with reading words accurately and with appropriate speed, and it deals with embedding in one's voice elements of expression and phrasing while reading. These aspects and characteristics are easy to observe, measure, and monitor. Thus, reading fluency was inviting for early reading scholars and practitioners to focus their efforts on these aspects of reading because they were open to observation and analysis. However, reading, at its heart, involves comprehension. Although comprehension is not easy to observe, scholars recognized that proficient reading had to be measured by the extent to which readers understood what they read. The link between the observable aspects of fluency in reading and the unobservable and hidden aspects of comprehension was not apparent to scholars in the early and mid-20th century. Thus, reading fluency lost favor and became a rather forgotten stepchild of reading. Finally, in the late 20th century, scholars and practitioners theorized a link between fluency and overall proficiency in reading and have provided empirical evidence of the link between the two. Comprehension requires the fluent mastery of the surface-level aspects of reading.

The link between fluency and overall reading proficiency is now well established. Several reviews of research related to reading fluency have come to this conclusion (Chard, Vaughn, & Tyler, 2002; Dowhower, 1994; Kuhn & Stahl, 2000; NICHD, 2000; Rasinski & Hoffman, 2003; Strecker, Roser, & Martinez, 1998). Nevertheless, our understanding of reading fluency and its place in the reading process and reading curriculum is far from complete. Many questions for the future exist. The following are just a few:

- What is the full complement of characteristics that define fluency? Is it more than decoding and prosodic reading?
- What is the full complement of outcomes of fluency instruction? Are there other outcomes besides improved accuracy and automaticity in decoding, gains in prosodic reading, better comprehension, and greater confidence in and attitudes toward reading?
- What is the role of the teacher in fluency instruction? While students practice passages and listen to fluently read passages while reading, what is the appropriate role for the teacher?
- What is the appropriate level of text difficulty for teaching fluency? Should texts that are practiced be relatively easy or challenging for students? Similarly, what genres of texts are best suited for fluency instruction?
- What are the appropriate grade levels for teaching fluency? Is it something best taught in the primary grades, or should fluency be taught and nurtured in the intermediate-, middle-, and secondary-grade levels?
- What are the best ways to assess reading fluency? Is a focus on reading speed best? What about a focus on prosodic reading? And, of course, how do we help teachers (and parents) understand that speed and prosodic reading are important insofar as they reflect the extent to which readers are able to focus their attention on comprehension—the meanings they construct as they read?

Fluency is an important part of the reading process, and it should be part of any effective reading curriculum. The potential for better understanding reading fluency and, in so doing, improving students' achievement in reading is strong. Let us hope that reading fluency remains a significant variable for theory building, research, and instruction in reading.

Questions for Discussion

1. Given the two conceptualizations of reading fluency (automatic and prosodic reading) presented in this chapter, describe a typical fluent and dysfluent reader. Which of the two conceptualizations captures the essence of reading fluency? What sort of instructional implications arise from each conceptualization?

2. Repeated readings have been shown to be an effective way to improve students' fluency. However, asking students to read a text more than once can be a somewhat artificial task. What are some authentic ways that you could motivate students to read a passage more than once beyond having them practice the text until they can read it at some level of proficiency in word accuracy, reading speed, or comprehension?

3. Reading fluency generally is developed through oral reading. Are there some texts that lend themselves better to oral-reading performance than others?

4. Round-robin oral reading is generally not a recommended instructional practice at any grade level. What are some oral-reading alternatives to round-robin reading?

5. Fluency has been described as a bridge between phonics and comprehension. Discuss how it might be such a bridge.

REFERENCES

Allington, R.L. (1983). Fluency: The neglected reading goal. *The Reading Teacher, 36,* 556–561.

Austin, M., & Morrison, C. (1963). *The first R: The Harvard report on reading in elementary schools.* New York: Macmillan.

Beach, S.A. (1993). Oral reading instruction: Retiring the bird in the round. *Reading Psychology, 14,* 333–338.

Carbo, M. (1978). Teaching reading with talking books. *The Reading Teacher, 32,* 267–273.

Carbo, M. (1981). Making books talk to children. *The Reading Teacher, 35,* 186–189.

Chard, D.J., Vaughn, S., & Tyler, B. (2002). A synthesis of research on effective interventions for building fluency with elementary students with learning disabilities. *Journal of Learning Disabilities, 35,* 386–406.

Chomsky, C. (1976). After decoding: What? *Language Arts, 53,* 288–296.

Dowhower, S.L. (1989). Repeated reading: Research into practice. *The Reading Teacher, 42,* 502–507.

Dowhower, S.L. (1994). Repeated reading revisited: Research into practice. *Reading & Writing Quarterly, 10,* 343–358.

Eldredge, J.L. (1990). Increasing reading performance of poor readers in the third grade by using a group assisted strategy. *Journal of Educational Research, 84,* 69–77.

Eldredge, J.L., & Quinn, W. (1988). Increasing reading performance of low-achieving second graders by using dyad reading groups. *Journal of Educational Research, 82,* 40–46.

Eldredge, J.L., Reutzel, D.R., & Hollingsworth, P.M. (1996). Comparing the effectiveness of two oral reading practices: Round-robin reading and the shared book experience. *Journal of Literacy Research, 28,* 201–225.

Fuchs, L.S., Fuchs, D., Hosp, M., & Jenkins, J.R. (2001). Oral reading fluency as an in-dicator of reading competence: A theoretical, empirical, and historical analysis. *Scientific Studies of Reading, 5*, 239–256.

Fuchs, L.S., Fuchs, D., & Maxwell, L. (1988). The validity of informal measures of read-ing comprehension. *Remedial and Special Education, 9*, 20–28.

Gibson, E.J., & Levin, H. (1975). *The Psychology of Reading.* Cambridge, MA: MIT Press.

Hasbrouck, J.E., Ihnot, C., & Rogers, G. (1999). Read naturally: A strategy to increase oral reading fluency. *Reading Research and Instruction, 39*, 27–37.

Heckelman, R.G. (1969). A neurological impress method of reading instruction. *Academic Therapy, 4*, 277–282.

Hoffman, J.V. (1987). Rethinking the role of oral reading in basal instruction. *The Elementary School Journal, 87*, 367–373.

Hoffman, J.V. (1991). Teacher and school effects in learning to read. In R. Barr, M. Kamil, P. Mosenthal, & P.D. Pearson (Eds.), *Handbook of reading research* (Vol. 2, pp. 911–950). White Plains, NY: Longman.

Hoffman, J.V., & Crone, S. (1985). The oral recitation lesson: A research-derived strat-egy for reading in basal texts. In J.A. Niles & R.V. Lalik (Eds.), *Issues in literacy: A re-search perspective* (34th yearbook of the National Reading Conference, pp. 76–83). Rockfort, NY: National Reading Conference.

Hoffman, J.V., & Segel, K. (1983). *Oral reading instruction: A century of controversy (1880–1980).* Paper presented at the annual meeting of the International Reading Association, Anaheim, CA. (ERIC Document Reproduction Service No. ED239237)

Holdaway, D. (1979). *The foundations of literacy.* Sydney, NSW, Australia: Ashton Scholastic.

Holdaway, D. (1981). Shared book experience: Teaching reading using favorite books. *Theory Into Practice, 21*, 293–300.

Hollingsworth, P.M. (1978). An experimental approach to the impress method of teach-ing reading. *The Reading Teacher, 31*, 624–626.

Hoskisson, K. (1975a). The many facets of assisted reading. *Elementary English, 52*, 312–315.

Hoskisson, K. (1975b). Sucessive approximation and beginning reading. *The Elementary School Journal, 75*, 442–451.

Howlett, N., & Weintraub, S. (1979). Instructional procedures. In R.C. Calfee & P. Drum (Eds.), *Teaching reading in compensatory classes* (pp. 87–103). Newark, DE: International Reading Association.

Huey, E.B. (1968). *The psychology and pedagogy of reading.* Boston: MIT Press. (Original work published 1908)

Hyatt, A.V. (1943). *The place of oral reading in the school program: Its history and devel-opment from 1880–1941.* New York: Teachers College Press.

James, W. (1892). *Psychology.* New York: Holt.

Koskinen, P.S., & Blum, I.H. (1984). Repeated oral reading and acquisition of fluency. In J.A. Niles & L.A. Harris (Eds.), *Changing perspectives on research in reading/language processing and instruction* (33rd yearbook of the National Reading Conference, pp. 183–187). Rochester, NY: National Reading Conference.

Koskinen, P.S., & Blum, I.H. (1986). Paired repeated reading: A classroom strategy for developing fluent reading. *The Reading Teacher, 40*, 70–75.

Kuhn, M.R., & Stahl, S.A. (2000). *Fluency: A review of developmental and remedial practices.* Ann Arbor, MI: Center for the Improvement of Early Reading Achievement.

LaBerge, D., & Samuels, S.J. (1974). Toward a theory of automatic information processing in reading. *Cognitive Psychology, 6,* 293–323.

McDade, J.E. (1937). A hypothesis for non-oral reading: Argument, experiment, and results. *Journal of Educational Research, 30,* 489–503.

McDade, J.E. (1944). Examination of a recent criticism of non-oral beginning reading. *The Elementary School Journal, 44,* 343–351.

Morris, D., & Nelson, L. (1992). Supported oral reading with low achieving second graders. *Reading Research and Instruction, 32,* 49–63.

National Institute of Child Health and Human Development (NICHD). (2000). *Report of the National Reading Panel. Teaching children to read: Reports of the subgroups* (NIH Publication No. 00-4754). Washington, DC: U.S. Government Printing Office.

Pinnell, G.S., Pikulski, J.J., Wixson, K.K., Campbell, J.R., Gough, P.B., & Beatty, A.S. (1995). *Listening to children read aloud.* Washington, DC: Office of Educational Research and Improvement, U.S. Department of Education.

Pluck, M. (1995). Rainbow Reading programme: Using taped stories. *Reading Forum, 1,* 25–29.

Rasinski, T.V. (1989). Fluency for everyone: Incorporating fluency instruction in the classroom. *The Reading Teacher, 43,* 690–693.

Rasinski, T.V. (1990). The effects of cued phrase boundaries in texts. Bloomington, IN: ERIC Clearinghouse on Reading and Communication Skills. (ERIC Document Reproduction Service No. ED 313689)

Rasinski, T.V., & Hoffman, T.V. (2003). Theory and research into practice: Oral reading in the school literacy curriculum. *Reading Research Quarterly, 38,* 510–522.

Rasinski, T.V., & Padak, N.D. (1998). How elementary students referred for compensatory reading instruction perform on school-based measures of word recognition, fluency, and comprehension. *Reading Psychology: An International Quarterly, 19,* 185–216.

Rasinski, T.V., Padak, N.D., Linek, W., & Sturtevant, E. (1994). The effects of fluency development instruction on urban second grade readers. *Journal of Educational Research, 87,* 158–164.

Rasinski, T.V., & Zutell, J.B. (1996). Is fluency yet a goal of the reading curriculum? In E.G. Sturtevant and W.M. Linek (Eds.), *Growing literacy* (18th yearbook of the College Reading Association, pp. 237–246). Harrisonburg, VA: College Reading Association.

Reutzel, D.R., & Hollingsworth, P.M. (1993). Effects of fluency training on second graders' reading comprehension. *Journal of Educational Research, 86,* 325–331.

Rohrer, J.H. (1943). An analysis and evaluation of the "non-oral" method of reading instruction. *The Elementary School Journal, 43,* 415–421.

Samuels, S.J. (1979). The method of repeated reading. *The Reading Teacher, 32,* 403–408.

Schreiber, P.A. (1980). On the acquisition of reading fluency. *Journal of Reading Behavior, 12,* 177–186.

Schreiber, P.A. (1991). Understanding prosody's role in reading acquisition. *Theory Into Practice, 30,* 158–164.

Schreiber, P.A., & Read, C. (1980). Children's use of phonetic cues in spelling, parsing, and—maybe—reading. *Bulletin of the Orton Society, 30*, 209–224.

Smith, J., & Elley, W. (1997). *How children learn to read.* Katonah, NY: Richard C. Owen.

Smith, N.B. (2002). *American reading instruction* (Special ed.). Newark, DE: International Reading Association.

Stahl, S.A., & Heubach, K.M. (2005). Fluency-oriented reading instruction. *Journal of Literacy Research, 37*, 25–60.

Stanovich, K.E. (1980). Toward an interactive-compensatory model of individual differences in the development of reading fluency. *Reading Research Quarterly, 16*, 32–71.

Strecker, S., Roser, N., & Martinez, M. (1998). Toward an understanding of oral reading fluency. In T. Shanahan & F. Rodriguez-Brown (Eds.), *47th yearbook of the National Reading Conference* (pp. 295–310). Chicago: National Reading Conference.

Thorndike, E.L. (1917). Reading and reasoning. A study of mistakes in paragraph reading. *Journal of Educational Psychology, 8*, 323–332.

Topping, K. (1987). Paired reading: A powerful technique for parent use. *The Reading Teacher, 40*, 604–614.

Topping, K. (1989). Peer tutoring and paired reading. Combining two powerful techniques. *The Reading Teacher, 42*, 488–494.

Zutell, J., & Rasinski, T.V. (1991). Training teachers to attend to their students' oral reading fluency. *Theory Into Practice, 30*, 211–217.

Chapter 2

Toward a Model of Reading Fluency

S. Jay Samuels

While from an intellectual perspective teachers have always recognized the importance of reading fluency, their instruction has infrequently promoted this high-level reading skill. Two decades ago, Allington (1983) recognized this problem and stated that fluency instruction was a neglected reading goal. Only recently have researchers and teachers shown a collective interest in this topic (Cassidy & Cassidy, 2003/2004). Along with this renewed interest in fluency, however, we have encountered some serious problems that relate to questions about what fluency is, how we can measure fluency, and whether independent reading is a useful practice. In this chapter, I will define fluency and suggest what teachers can do to assess students to determine if they are fluent. In addition, I will provide a historical backdrop for understanding fluency and will respond to the National Reading Panel report (National Institute of Child Health and Human Development [NICHD], 2000), which states that the panel could find no experimental evidence either for or against the value of independent reading.

Trends in Fluency Research

Historical Backdrop

Some of the earliest experimental work on what today would be thought of as research on fluency was done by psychologist James McKeen Cattell (1886). Using a tachistoscope, a device he developed that would expose a letter or a word for a set period of time, Cattell worked with highly skilled readers to find out which was easier to recognize, a letter or a word. He found that skilled readers could recognize a word as easily as a letter, and he concluded that the unit of recognition was the word. In addition, he found that recognition was facilitated if context preceded the target word.

A decade after Cattell's research investigated how skilled readers recognized words, Bryan and Harter (1897, 1899) studied the development

What Research Has to Say About Fluency Instruction, edited by S. Jay Samuels and Alan E. Farstrup. © 2006 by the International Reading Association.

of word recognition from the beginning to skilled stages using Morse code and found that beginning Morse code operators had experiences similar to children learning how to read. At first, the operators had difficulty identifying letters. After much effort, they could identify letters, but they had trouble with word identification. The word-identification process was so slow and required so much of their attention that the effort interfered with understanding the message. With extensive practice, however, the word-recognition process became easier, and they improved enough to be able to decode the message and understand it at the same time. What Bryan and Harter learned about the development of fluency in understanding Morse code provided additional insight into how beginning students learned to read printed texts.

In 1905, Edmond Huey (1905/1968) published his famous book, *The Psychology and Pedagogy of Reading*. In this book, he described with unusually keen insight how reading fluency developed. He observed that the first time a beginning reader encounters a new word, he or she has to pay close attention to it. However, Huey observed that as the same word is encountered repeatedly, each "repetition progressively frees the mind from attention to details, makes facile the total act, shortens the time, and reduces the extent to which consciousness must concern itself with the process" (p. 104). Thus, at about the same time that the Wright brothers were first learning how to fly with their heavier-than-air machine on the sands of Kitty Hawk, North Carolina, USA, Bryan and Harter and Huey were providing important psychological insights into how fluency developed.

In addition, Donald Olding Hebb (1949) introduced an important concept, unitization, for understanding what happens developmentally when students advance from beginning to fluent reader. For example, look at the letters *b*, *d*, *p*, and *q*. These letters are often the most difficult ones for students to learn. As a skilled reader, you see them as holistic units; that is, you have unitized them. Students who are learning the alphabet, however, do not perceive each letter as a single, holistic unit. In order to discriminate among these four letters, which share similar, confusing features, students must learn their distinctive features, that is, what combination of features makes each letter different from all the others. In order to learn the distinctive features, the student must decompose the letters into parts. Thus, in order to discover the features of the letter set *b*, *d*, *p*, and *q*, the student sees a vertical line with a ball that is either at the top or the bottom and to the left side or the right side of the vertical line. This supposedly simple task involves stages of learning. First, the student has to learn the features (i.e., vertical line with a ball at the top or bottom, and to the left or right of the line). Having learned the distinctive features, the student enters the accuracy stage. While the student's responses are accurate, they are slow and require considerable cognitive effort. With additional practice, all the components of the letters become unitized, and the student recognizes the letters automatically. When automatic, the responses are fast, accurate, and performed with little cognitive effort. Only with practice will the student advance to the stage in which the letters are unitized and seen as holistic units. A somewhat similar process occurs with word learning as students advance from beginning to fluent readers. That is, as students encounter the same high-frequency words repeatedly in the books they read—words like *mother, jumping, chair*, and *blue*—they go through the unitization process. When beginning readers encounter new words in the books they read, their unit of recognition is the letter, and they sequentially work through words letter by letter. In contrast, when skilled readers are required to recognize the same words, their unit of recognition is the word (Samuels, Bremer, & LaBerge, 1978). Fluent readers have unitized high-frequency words and recognize them as holistic units.

Despite this early interest and emphasis on fluency, reading fluency fell on hard times. Several factors account for this lack of interest. During the very early 1900s, behaviorism became the dominant paradigm governing education, and it maintained control until the late 1950s. Under the iron fist of behaviorism, researchers were prevented from studying inside-the-head components of reading like comprehension and fluency. Also, by the 1970s the whole language philosophy of Frank Smith and Ken Goodman began making significant inroads into the reading field, and fighting the "reading wars" took up the energy of many in the reading community (Pearson, 1996). Compared to fighting the reading wars, work on fluency was of lesser importance.

So what turned the tide and led the field of reading back to an interest in fluency? By the end of the 1950s, cognitive psychology had become the dominant paradigm, and researchers began studying comprehension and fluency. For example, at the University of Minnesota, David LaBerge and I entered into a yearlong series of discussions culminating in the publication of a theoretical article on automatic information processing in reading (LaBerge & Samuels, 1974). This article was important because it provided the scientific rationale for understanding how fluency occurs through automatic word recognition. However, the theoretical model did not address practical issues of instruction.

Repeated Reading

Because I had a strong belief that a good theory should lead to practical outcomes, I developed repeated reading, a method that promotes fluency. To test the method, I worked with mentally challenged beginning readers. I asked the students how to become good at sports, and they all said that it required practice. I then explained that getting to be a good reader was a lot like getting to be good at a sport and that we were going to practice getting good at reading stories.

Before meeting with the children, I took a children's story and broke it into 150 word segments. I then gave each student the same 150-word passage, and, as the students held the copy of the story and looked at the words, I read the short passage to them. In essence, I modeled good oral reading by reading it with proper expression. Then the students practiced alone at their desks; when a student thought that he or she was ready, the student read the short passage orally to the teacher, who recorded the word-per-minute reading rate for each student as well as the number of word-recognition errors. The student reread the 150-word passage a number of times until each one reached a criterion rate of 85 words per minute. After reaching the criterion reading rate, the student was given the next passage in the story to practice. All students progressed at their own pace, and their progress, in terms of numbers of errors and reading speed each time they read the story to the teacher, was charted. Thus, by looking at the chart, the students were able to note their progress.

With each rereading of a passage, the students could see that they made fewer errors and that their reading rates got faster. Before long, the students realized that as they orally reread the same passage a number of times, they began to sound like good readers. Sounding good was an exciting realization for students who had a history of failure. I described the method of repeated reading in an article for *The Reading Teacher,* and it was reissued as a classic study in reading (Samuels, 1979/1997). Unknown to me, at the same time that I was developing repeated reading, Carol Chomsky was developing a similar method at Harvard's School of Education for helping struggling readers. Chomsky tape-recorded a children's story and had the students listen to the tape several times while they looked at the words in their story. I later invited her to write a chapter for the first edition of *What Research Has to Say About Reading Instruction* (Chomsky, 1978).

The repeated-reading methods described above have become the basis for newer approaches to fluency instruction. (See Table 2.1 for a summary of the many forms that repeated reading has taken.) One problem with the old repeated-reading method was that it required the computation of reading rate to determine when a student reached the goal of 85 words per minute. However, O'Shea, Sindelar, and O'Shea (1985) found that students would get the fluency benefits from a passage in no more than four rereadings, thus eliminating the need for having the teacher compute the word-per-minute rate. After the teacher has modeled the oral reading of a passage for students during repeated reading, the students only need to practice reading the story four times, and then they can move on to the next passage or story.

At Webster Elementary School in St. Paul, Minnesota, USA, using the shortcut method suggested by O'Shea and colleagues (1985), we used repeated reading with a second-grade classroom in which the students only read the story four times. In this study, the students in the experimental classroom were paired up. First, the teacher read the selected passage orally to the children. Then each paired team took turns with one another, one person playing the role of teacher, who listened and asked a comprehension question, while the other played the role of student and read the story out loud. A typical prompt following oral reading was "Tell me what you can remember about the story you read." After the first oral reading, the paired students reversed roles. In all, the story was read a total of four times, two times by each student. The study lasted only three weeks, but we found that "compared to the control group, students in the Paired-Repeated Reading Group made statistically significant gains in reading rate, accuracy, and word recognition" (Semonick, Lewis, & Samuels, 2001, p. xi).

Rather than establishing a repeated-reading program on their own, teachers and schools now can obtain a computer repeated-reading program that manages all the repeated-reading fluency instruction, with the exception of deciding when to advance the student to a more difficult text readability level. The program helps each student achieve fluency by selecting an appropriate starting level of text difficulty to practice repeated reading, and it provides a wide variety of reading materials for repeated-reading practice at numerous levels of difficulty. In addition, it helps the student select a reading-rate goal, lets the student know when

Table 2.1. Oral reading methods for developing fluency

Method	Description
Oral repeated readings	
Individually based: Classic version	
Repeated readings	Students reread a short, meaningful passage of text typically four times. Alternatively, a criterion is set for speed, accuracy, and comprehension and perhaps expression. After four readings or when the criterion is met, they may proceed to the next section or to a new short passage.* (See Samuels, 1979/1997.)
Individually based: Technology centered	
Audiotapes: Commercially made Teacher made or student made	As described above, except that while rereading aloud, the student is following along with an audio-recorded version. Teachers are cautioned that commercially available tapes may be read too quickly for some students, and they may choose to make their own. Teachers may need to make certain the student is actually reading. Older students in need of fluency development may have their needs met by recording their best oral reading of a text to be used by younger students.*
Computer	
Stories on CD-ROM	As above, except stories are computer based. CD-ROMs (see Project LITT, 1998) can be programmed to read aloud word by word, sentence by sentence, or other combinations. (See above cautions.)
Systematic programs	Commercially available programs such as Fluent Reader (Renaissance Learning, 2004) provide a complete computer-based system. (See FCRR, 2003, for lists of other programs.)
Reading in pairs	
Partner reading	Each child must read the passage aloud to his or her partner a number of times. Students may be given simple feedback forms for their partner. Other variations (integration of other activities) exist. Comprehension activities may follow.*

(continued)

Table 2.1. Oral-reading methods for developing fluency *(continued)*

Method	Description
Guided pairs	The more skilled reader (teacher, parent, older peer) reads the passage once and then the pair reads it aloud in unison a number of times. In some variations, the more skilled reader instructs the less skilled reader to signal when the learner wishes to "try it solo." Comprehension activities may follow.*
Group contexts Readers Theatre	Involves repeated readings alone or in groups to reach acceptable reading for an ensemble performance; gives the student a "real-life" reason to do repeated readings. Performance criteria are similar to those given in "Repeating Readings" (above). Readers Theatre typically consists of plays or poems but may be material directly from textbooks.
Radio reading	Radio reading may be "news" (as from children's news magazines) or material directly from textbooks, read as a "news announcer" would read it.* (See Carrick, 2001.)
Choral reading	Teachers and class read material aloud in unison. May read entire selection, refrains (as in predictable texts), split the selection by group to read alternating lines, etc. This simple technique is often used to provide students with more reading time.*
Integrated fluency lessons	Combines a number of techniques; includes teacher model; discussion; repeated readings in the form of choral, partner, and individual readings; performance; activities relating to the text, oral and/or silent-reading assignments to do as homework and review.*

*This table was developed by University of Minnesota graduate student Terri Fautsch-Patridge.

the goal is reached, and charts the student's rate of progress with each rereading (Renaissance Learning, 2004). With all the instructional modifications that were being made to help students achieve fluency, it was inevitable that the National Reading Panel would examine these practices to evaluate their effectiveness.

National Reading Panel Report

The publication of the *Report of the National Reading Panel* (NICHD, 2000) was another factor that boosted the prominence of fluency instruction. The task of the panel was to search the research literature on reading in order to identify effective instructional methods that met the litmus test of being published in peer-reviewed journals, and the research used either an experimental or quasi-experimental design so that cause-and-effect relationships could be determined. Once the panel identified such studies on fluency that met the criteria, a meta-analysis was done on repeated reading. A meta-analysis is a method that allows a researcher to summarize numerous studies of a particular method, such as repeated reading, in order to determine the method's overall effectiveness. The statistic used in the meta-analysis as the indicator of the effectiveness was the effect size. Effect size represents how much better the treatment group is than the control group, and this statistic is expressed in standard deviation units. For example, an effect size of 1.00 means that the achievement level of the repeated-reading group was one standard deviation better than the level of the control group. Effect sizes were computed for reading accuracy, fluency, and comprehension, and the combined effect sizes over the outcomes averaged out to .5. The panel report states that repeated-reading "procedures led to the conclusion that such procedures had a consistent, and positive impact on word recognition, fluency, and comprehension, as measured by a variety of test instruments and at a range of grade levels" (NICHD, 2000, p. 3-3).

While the report identified repeated reading as a viable approach to fluency instruction, it also put forth a disclaimer about the effect of independent reading on reading achievement that upset many U.S. teachers. The disclaimer states, "Despite widespread acceptance of the idea that schools should encourage students to read more and that these increases in reading practice will be translated into better fluency and higher reading achievement, there is not adequate evidence to sustain this claim" (NICHD, 2000, p. 3-28). However, the Executive Summary of the report (p. 12) states, "Given the extensive use of these techniques, it is important that such research be conducted." Subsequent to the panel report, I conducted such a study.

Developing Reading Fluency Through Independent Reading

The number of routes to fluency are few. One route appears to be through reading a lot. Keith Stanovich's (1986) Matthew effect in reading takes a wise saying from the Bible, namely that the rich get richer and the poor get poorer, and applies it to reading and developing fluency. In essence, the Matthew effect refers to the observation that students who read a lot improve and those who do not read a lot show little improvement. There is an abundance of correlational evidence in support of this observation that students who read a lot are good readers and those who do not read a lot tend to be poor readers. However, correlation is not the same as causation. It is possible that the amount of reading that good readers engage in did not cause them to improve in reading. For example, naturally good readers may read a lot because reading is easy and enjoyable for them.

Until 2003, experimental studies were lacking that showed that the amount of reading, as well as ease of reading early on, caused reading skill to develop. Because it was so apparent to teachers and to researchers that if a student practiced reading, there would be improvement, no one bothered to test the obvious. However, the National Reading Panel report (NICHD, 2000) states that because the panel could not find experimental studies in the literature showing that independent reading led to gains in achievement, the panel could neither support nor condemn this practice. The failure of the National Reading Panel to support independent reading was one of the most controversial aspects in the report and led me to conduct an experimental study to determine how differences in time spent in independent reading might affect reading outcomes (Samuels & Wu, 2003).

Our study was conducted over six months in 2 third-grade and 2 fifth-grade classrooms at a St. Paul inner-city school, where the teachers assigned students to classrooms so as to balance their reading abilities. Of the 4 classrooms, we randomly assigned 2 as the experimental and 2 as the controls. The experimental variable was the amount of time the students would spend in independent reading. In the experimental treatment, the students read independently for 40 minutes each day, while in the control treatment, the students read independently for only 15 minutes each day. To ensure that the students' time in the control condition equaled the time spent by the experimental students, teachers read children's literature to control students and discussed the stories with them for 25 minutes each day in addition to the 15 minutes of independent reading. All the teachers in the study were highly experienced. Independent reading for the control and the experimental classes occurred in class so that we could maintain control over how much time was actually spent reading. The independent reading was done in addition to a regular balanced reading instructional plan that all the students received. All students selected books for independent reading that were taken from the school library; color coding indicated to the students which books matched their level of reading ability. As soon as students in the control and experimental treatments finished reading a book, they took a computer-administered comprehension quiz on the book. Students were encouraged to read their books carefully so they could achieve an overall average of 85% to 92% across all quizzes attempted.

We compared the gain between pre- and posttest scores of the experimental and control groups. Students were given a variety of tests such as the curriculum-based measurement (CBM) speed of reading test; the Star Test, which measured comprehension; the Woodcock–Johnson Word Recognition Test; and the Vocabulary section of the Metropolitan Achievement Test. The outcomes from this six-month study were not exactly as anticipated. For example, contrary to a general impression that more time spent in independent reading should lead to greater gains for all students regardless of ability, we found instead that for the lower ability students in this study, more time did not necessarily lead to greater gains. However, for the higher ability students, those who spent 40 minutes on independent reading had significantly greater gains in comprehension, vocabulary, and word recognition than the higher ability students who received only 15 minutes of independent reading. For the lower ability students, those who spent only 15 minutes on independent reading had significantly greater gains in reading speed and vocabulary than the higher ability students who only spent 15 minutes on independent reading.

How should one interpret these results in terms of the National Reading Panel disclaimer that there was no evidence one way or another on the effects of independent reading? In general, the extra independent reading does have positive effects, but the amount of time spent in independent reading should match the student's reading ability. For higher ability readers, 40 minutes of independent reading proved to be effective. However, for the lower ability readers, 15 minutes of independent reading proved effective. This finding makes sense if one views it in terms of the student's ability to maintain motivation to stay on task and to attend to the task. Soli and Devine (1976), for example, found that students who have lower achievement scores cannot maintain attention for as long as their peers who have higher achievement. When the results from this experimental study on the effects of independent reading on outcomes such as reading speed, comprehension, word recognition, and vocabulary are added to the findings from correlational studies, I can state with confidence that when the amount of time spent in independent reading is matched to the student's ability to maintain attention, there are positive reading outcomes. Matthew effects do operate in reading. Those who read more get better.

Automaticity Theory

Unfortunately, the human brain has only limited capacity to process information. Because of this processing limitation, not only are beginning and fluent readers using different strategies when they read, but also the strategy used by beginning readers places a heavier burden on their short-term memory than the strategy used by fluent readers. To understand this difference in strategy use, I will briefly discuss four essential components of the reading processes:

1. **Decoding**. Decoding simply means the ability to generate a phonological—or sound—representation of each printed word on the page. Some may think of decoding as subvocalizing, or saying the word silently to oneself while reading. For example, when a beginning reader sees the word *house*, he or she may subvocalize and silently say /house/. However, reading theorists such as Gough (1972) believe that in high-speed fluent reading, subvocalizing does not actually happen because the speed of silent reading is faster than what would occur if readers said each word silently to themselves as they read. The silent reading speed for 12th graders when reading for meaning is 250 words per minute, whereas the speed for oral reading is only 150 words per minute (Carver, 1990). However, in beginning reading, when the word-recognition process is far slower than in skilled fluent reading, subvocalization—or saying the word silently in one's head—may be taking place because the reading speed is so much slower.

2. **Comprehension.** Years ago comprehension was thought of as getting meaning from the printed page, but modern conceptualizations of the process lead us to believe that the reader actually takes

the information that is on the page and combines that information with prior knowledge and, in so doing, constructs a meaningful understanding of the text. In order to understand the sentence "The executive ate his steak in the corporate dining room," the reader may form a mental image of a scenario that goes beyond the text information. For example, the reader may form the image of a well-dressed man who is wearing a business suit and holding a fork with his left hand and a knife in his right hand while cutting the steak on a plate that sits atop a white tablecloth. The added information that was used to construct meaning came from prior knowledge of how one eats in a formal setting and went well beyond the information contained in the text.

It is important to emphasize that comprehension is not a unitary skill. In fact, it is multifaceted and can be separated into simpler and more complex components such as literal comprehension, inferential comprehension, critical reasoning, and so on. In the discussion that follows, I will refer to comprehension as if it were a unitary construct for the sake of simplicity; however, when fluent readers simultaneously decode and comprehend, it may only be for the lower level aspects of this multifaceted comprehension process.

3. **Metacognition**. Metacognition refers to the active monitoring and regulation of one's reading. It involves self-awareness of whether or not one understands the material in the text, and it involves knowledge of fix-up strategies to use during a comprehension breakdown. These metacognitive self-monitoring skills improve with practice and differentiate unskilled and skilled readers (Collins, Dickson, Simmons, & Kame'enui, 2002; Garner, 1987). Furthermore, some of these self-monitoring skills can become automatic, thus contributing to fluency.

4. **Attention**. Kahneman (1973) defines attention as the cognitive energy or effort used to process information. For example, when I read an important article I am struggling to understand, I use my attentional resources for reading each of the words in the text and for constructing meaning. In addition, I keep attention focused on my work and do not allow my attention to drift to other matters that are unrelated to my task at hand.

Reading tasks such as decoding, comprehension, and metacognition require attention for their processing, but herein is the crux of a potential problem. If these tasks require more attention than is available, *the tasks cannot all be completed at the same time.* To explain how readers use attention in order to decode, comprehend, and monitor their comprehension, I will describe the processes used by beginning and by fluent readers.

Beginning Readers

Figure 2.1 shows how beginning readers use attention to decode, comprehend, and monitor comprehension. Figure 2.1A illustrates how attention is directed first at decoding. The solid black arrow from attention to decoding indicates that the decoding task is completed but requires so much of the reader's attention that the other reading tasks, such as comprehension and monitoring comprehension, cannot be done simultaneously. Next, Figure 2.1B shows how the student switches attention to comprehension, and the solid black arrow indicates that this task gets accomplished but uses so much attention that other tasks, such as comprehension monitoring, cannot be done at the same time. Figure 2.1C shows how, after the comprehension task is done, the student switches attention to self-monitoring comprehension (metacognition) in order to decide if the level of comprehension is satisfactory. However, again, this task uses up so much attention that other tasks cannot be performed. By switching attention back and forth from decoding to comprehension to self-monitoring, the beginning reader manages to work through the text, but the process is slow and places a heavy load on short-term memory.

In addition, research using a variety of techniques consistently found that the size of the visual unit used in word recognition by beginning readers is smaller than the entire word (Samuels et al., 1978). Thus, what the beginning reader puts into short-term memory is a unit that has no meaning. To make a difficult situation even more difficult, the student must figure out the meaning of the entire word quickly, in less than 18 seconds, or what was placed in short-term memory will be lost (Peterson & Peterson, 1959). Observing the oral reading of beginning readers often shows how, as they slowly work their way word by word through a sentence, they regress and start sounding out a word at the beginning of the sentence again. This repetitive behavior is driven by the fact that they took too long trying to solve the puzzle of what is the word on the page, and by taking too long they lost the word fragment that was stored in memory. Thus, they have to start over again. Adams (1994) states, "If it takes a child too long to identify successive words, the beginning of the sentence will fade from memory before the end has been registered" (p. 857). With perseverance, however,

Figure 2.1. Comprehension of beginning readers

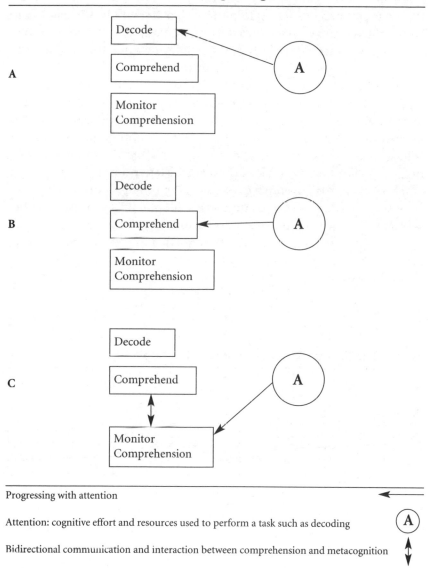

Progressing with attention   ←

Attention: cognitive effort and resources used to perform a task such as decoding   (A)

Bidirectional communication and interaction between comprehension and metacognition   ↕

going word by word, the student works through the sentence, switching attention from decoding to comprehension until the meaning of the sentence is completed. No wonder the learning-to-read process is so difficult, and some children would rather watch television than read a book.

Fluent Readers

With repeated practice a most important transformation takes place as to how printed words are recognized. For common, high-frequency words that are encountered regularly in day-to-day reading, the unit of word recognition enlarges to become the entire word, which leads to fluent reading (Samuels et al., 1978), and these words are usually meaningful for students who have grown up in English-speaking homes. Another important change also occurs: Now, during the decoding process, the printed words on the page are recognized with automatic decoding, or with so little attention that another process can take place simultaneously. In fact, at this point the bulk of the available attention may be used for other processes such as comprehension and metacognition.

Just as decoding becomes automatic with practice, so, too, can many skills used in metacognition become automatic with practice. In each case, the tasks will require so little attention that the bulk of the cognitive resources can be focused on the task of constructing meaning. Figure 2.2 shows how decoding and metacognitive comprehension monitoring

Figure 2.2. Comprehension of fluent readers

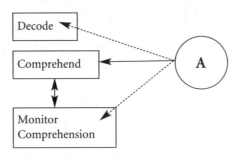

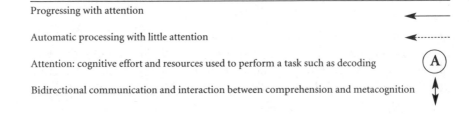

are done automatically while at the same time comprehension processing takes place. In the many years that researchers have worked on skill building in reading, they have come to the realization that with practice almost every component of the reading process has elements that can become automatic, including aspects of comprehension (Thurlow & van den Broek, 1997) and metacognition (Samuels, Ediger, Willcutt, & Palumbo, 2006). In general, however, even though aspects of comprehension, such as making inferences, can become automatic, considerable attention will always be required in order to construct a meaningful and coherent representation of a text.

A Definition of Fluency

As stated earlier in this chapter, there are two controversial aspects of fluency. The first relates to its definition and the second to its measurement. Definitions are not trivial, ivory tower concerns that are of no importance—how we define a construct such as fluency determines and influences to a large degree how we will measure it. Using automaticity theory as the basis for the definition, reading fluency is defined as the ability to decode and comprehend at the same time. However, fluency is situational. This means that fluency is like happiness, in that we are not happy all the time, nor are we fluent all the time. One of the major factors influencing fluency is the readability level of the text (see Hiebert, this volume). For example, a student may be fluent on a text with a second-grade readability level but not be fluent on a text written at the sixth-grade readability level. Another factor is the text topic. If the reader is familiar with the topic, he or she not only understands its concepts but also is probably familiar with its vocabulary and its written words. Other behaviors such as oral reading with speed, accuracy, and expression are simply indicators of fluency. These indicators are like temperature readings on a thermometer. A high temperature is an indicator of a possible disease, but it is not the disease itself. In fact, the high temperature may be misleading and contribute to a false diagnosis.

The ability to decode and comprehend at the same time is profoundly important to understanding how to determine if a student is fluent. Cognitive psychologists define automaticity as the ability to perform two difficult skills at the same time as the result of extended practice, whereas prior to practice only one task could be performed at a time. If two complex tasks can be performed simultaneously, then at least one of them is automatic. For example, at the beginning stage of reading, only one skill could be done at a time; first decoding, followed by comprehension. However, at the skilled stage, both decoding and comprehension can be performed together. Thus, the critical test of fluency is the ability to decode a text and to understand it *simultaneously*.

Fluency Measurement Controversies Over DIBELS

One problem with fluency measurement is the Dynamic Indicators of Basic Early Literacy Skills (DIBELS; Good & Kaminski, 2002). Presently, DIBELS is being used widely by school districts all across the United States as a way to measure student achievement in reading. The DIBELS's many tests include ISF (initial sounds fluency), PSF (phoneme segmentation fluency), NWF (nonsense word fluency), ORF (oral reading fluency), and RF (retell fluency). Note that the term *fluency* is attached to all of the tests although, in fact, they are simply one-minute tests of speed. For example, in the ORF test, the student is given one minute to read orally from a passage while the examiner counts the number of words read correctly within the minute. During the RF test, the student reads orally for one minute and then the student is asked to retell what he or she can recall from the passage. While the student is retelling the story, the tester counts the number of words uttered by the student.

My concern with DIBELS extends well beyond the labeling issue of calling all the tests fluency measures when they are simply measuring speed of performance. For example, when the ORF test is used with certain student populations for whom English is their second language, the test may give false impressions of the students' reading ability. Because the United States has a large ESL population of students, teachers should be cautious about making diagnostic decisions based on the use of the DIBELS test of oral-reading fluency. There are English as a second language (ESL) students who can read rapidly but have little comprehension of what they have read. For example, at Hayden Heights Elementary School in St. Paul, there is a very large Hmong population. Many Hmong students who attend school there speak Hmong at home and to one another. For these students, however, English is the language of the classroom and television, but Hmong is the language they use for personal communication. I have personally gone to the school and worked one on one with approximately 60 Hmong students in grades 4–6 to find out if it was common to find students whose reading speed was adequate but who had trouble understanding what they had read. I gave Hmong students passages to read that were appropriate for their reading ability and said, "Read this story to me out loud, and when you are done I want you to tell me what you remember about the story." About 20% of the ESL students at this school could read orally with accuracy and speed, but had poor recall of the passage. Even when I probed them with literal comprehension questions about the passage, they could not answer them. In essence, the one-minute ORF DIBELS test gave a false sense of fluency for these ESL students. Later, when I talked to Hayden Heights teachers about the problem of assessing students' reading using only reading speed as the measure, they were aware that many of their Asian students had adequate decoding skills but had trouble understanding what they had read. The teachers thought the comprehension difficulty their ESL students were having was linked to inadequate vocabulary knowledge, as well as a mismatch between the grammar of the Hmong language and the grammar used in English reading passages.

In another example, in the Minneapolis School System the eighth graders were given a CBM test, which establishes students' reading rate. Comprehension is not a concern on this test. The same students also took the Minnesota Basic Skills Test that has a reading comprehension component. When Hmong students with a 100-word-per-minute reading rate took the Minnesota Basic Skills Test, only 45% of them could pass the Basic Skills Test. However, when the entire student body with a reading rate exactly that of the Hmong (100 words per minute) took the Basic Skills Test, 70% passed. The results can be explained by the difference between the two groups in familiarity with English grammar and vocabulary.

A second concern that I have relates to the way studies were conducted to show that the ORF is a valid instrument. These studies were conducted in the following way: Students were given a one-minute oral-reading test and scored on their correct words per minute. At a later time, these same students were given a second test that measured their comprehension, or their performance on a state reading test. Correlations were computed between the two scores, and the correlations were high enough that the researchers concluded the one-minute speed-reading sample was a good predictor of comprehension (Elliott, Lee, & Tollefson, 2001; Good & Jefferson, 1998). However, it is important to note that on these validation tests where reading speed was measured, the students were not required to decode and comprehend at the same time. This is not a trivial point. Beginning readers first decode and later they comprehend. Thus, it appears that the method used to validate the one-minute reading-speed score reflects what nonfluent readers do, not what fluent readers do. For example, students may be given a test of reading speed and then given a test of comprehension at a later time. This is precisely what beginning readers do when they read. First, they decode what they are reading, and later they try to understand the text. By separating the times of the tests of decoding speed from tests of comprehension, the very essence of what is meant by fluency has been ignored. The proper way to determine if a student is fluent is to require simultaneous decoding and comprehension, and this requirement was not observed.

During investigations that require simultaneous decoding and comprehension, the outcomes may be different from what the DIBELS organization uses to justify its measurement tools. Cramer (2005) instructed students to read orally for comprehension. Two sets of correlations were computed, one between students' oral-reading speed and accuracy of word recognition, and the other correlation between oral-reading speed and comprehension. She found there was a significant correlation between reading speed and accuracy of word recognition, but the correlation between oral-reading speed and comprehension was not significant. Using her study as an example, it appears there might be different results in the predictive validity of one-minute samples of reading speed depending on the reading task demands imposed on the students. The findings from testing in which the student is required to decode and comprehend at the same time may be very different from testing in which the student is only asked to decode and the information of interest is the number of correct words read per minute.

There is nothing we do so well that we cannot do better. It is time to take another look at validating how reading speed correlates with comprehension, but it should be done in such a way that the task demands for the reader require simultaneous decoding and comprehension. For example, it is possible to set up a situation where the task demands require that two things—decoding and comprehension—be done at the same time. Researchers could instruct a student to read orally a short but complete text of about 200 words and, when finished, answer comprehension questions. The researcher could then use the word-per-minute reading score and correlate it with the comprehension score as measured by the score on the comprehension test. This procedure would have construct validity because the task demands that the students perform two reading tasks at the same time, which is what fluent readers do when they read.

A third concern is directed at the DIBELS test of RF, retell fluency. This test requires the student to decode and comprehend material at the same time. The student is told that he or she will be required to read the material orally and then will be asked to recall as much of what he or she read as possible. At the end of one minute, the student is stopped and asked to recall what has been read. The problem with this test is the scoring procedure, during which the examiner is asked to do an accurate count of the number of words uttered by the student in the retelling. Often the stream of student speech is faster than the examiner can count accurately. By the time the examiner makes a decision about the number of previously uttered words, the student will have uttered new words that will be missed.

Some of my concerns about the DIBELS test are reflected in a recent research study by Pressley, Hilden, and Shankland (2005). They investigated the adequacy of the DIBELS oral-reading fluency test and the oral retell test. In testing the student retells, the examiner tape recorded the retell and at the same time also counted words as the student uttered them. Later, the examiner went back to the recording to check on the accuracy of word counting as the words were uttered. The data show statistically significant errors in counting words as the student uttered them in comparison to counting words taken off the tape recorder. In other words, the method recommended by DIBELS for counting words as spoken is unreliable, which calls into question the validity of the oral-reading retell test. Furthermore, the research conducted by Pressley and colleagues showed low correlations between speed of oral reading and retelling when measured in idea units. This lack of significant correlation between speed of oral reading and idea-unit recall is not surprising. After all, there is not much of a story narrative that can be covered in only one minute of reading. Given their findings, this research team stated,

> Based on available data, the fairest conclusion is that DIBELS mispredicts reading performance on other assessments much of the time, and at best is a measure of who reads quickly without regard to whether the reader comprehends what is read. (p. 2)

Consequently, they strongly suggested that the whole issue of validating DIBELS should be reopened. When taking into consideration that the DIBELS tests are so widely used to evaluate students, and that serious misgivings about their reliability and the validity have been expressed, I believe it would be prudent for an independent group to reexamine the validity of these tests.

Conclusions

How does one summarize this journey into the history and current status of the field of fluency? Fluency as an important aspect of skilled reading is enjoying a rebirth, but it is labored. The history of reading is filled with hot topics that were replaced with new hot topics and methods. Fluency will only remain prominent if teachers are convinced that the methods used to develop fluency work and the methods used to measure fluency are reliable and valid. The time is ripe for our field to reexamine these issues.

Questions for Discussion

1. What is your definition of fluency? Is your definition of fluency an indicator of fluency or does it embrace the critical attributes of fluency as described in this chapter? What were your reasons for deciding on the definition that you chose?

2. What methods are available to teachers to help students become fluent readers? What methods are available to parents to help their children become fluent readers?

3. Not everyone becomes a fluent reader. What factors might account for the fact that not everyone becomes fluent in reading? What solutions can you think of that can overcome each of the factors that might impede development of fluency? Some students who were diagnosed as being dyslexic overcame this handicap, and they became good readers. How do you think they overcame this handicap?

REFERENCES

Adams, M.J. (1994). Modeling the connections between word recognition and reading. In R.B. Ruddell, M.R. Ruddell, & H. Singer (Eds.), *Theoretical models and processes of reading* (4th ed., pp. 838–863). Newark, DE: International Reading Association.

Allington, R.L. (1983). Fluency: The neglected reading goal. *The Reading Teacher, 36,* 556–561.

Bryan, W.L., & Harter, N. (1897). Studies in the physiology and psychology of the telegraphic language. *Psychological Review, 4,* 27–53.

Bryan, W.L., & Harter, N. (1899). Studies on the telegraphic language. *Psychological Review, 6*, 345–375.

Carrick, L. (2001). Internet resources for conducting Reader's Theatre. *Reading Online, 5*(1). Retrieved December 9, 2004, from http://www.readingonline.org/electronic/elec_index.asp?HREF=carrick/index.html

Carver, R.P. (1990). *Reading rate: A review of research and theory.* New York: Academic Press.

Cassidy, J., & Cassidy, D. (2003/2004). What's hot, what's not for 2004. *Reading Today, 22*(3), 1.

Cattell, J.M. (1886). The time it takes to see and name objects. *Mind, 11*(41), 63–85.

Chomsky, C. (1978). When you still can't read in third grade: After decoding, what? In S.J. Samuels (Ed.), *What research has to say about reading instruction* (pp. 13–30). Newark, DE: International Reading Association.

Collins, V., Dickson, S., Simmons, D., & Kame'enui, E. (2002). *Metacognition and its relation to reading comprehension: A synthesis of the research.* Eugene: National Center to Improve the Tools of Educators, University of Oregon.

Cramer, K. (2005). *Effect of degree of challenge on reading performance.* Unpublished manuscript.

Elliott, J., Lee, S.W., & Tollefson, N. (2001). A reliability and validity study of Dynamic Indicators of Basic Early Literacy Skills-Modified. *School Psychology Review, 30*, 33–49.

Florida Center for Reading Research (FCCR). (2003). *Summary table for FCRR reports.* Tallahassee: Author. Retrieved January 25, 2005, from http://www.fcrr.org/FCRR Reports/table.asp

Garner, R. (1987). *Metacognition and reading comprehension.* Norwood, NJ: Ablex.

Good, R.H., & Jefferson, G. (1998). Contemporary perspectives on curriculum-based measurement validity. In M.R. Shinn (Ed.), *Advanced applications of curriculum based measurement* (pp. 61–88). New York: Guilford Press.

Good, R.H., & Kaminski, R.A. (2002). *Dynamic Indicators of Basic Early Literacy Skills* (6th ed.). Eugene, OR: Institute for the Development of Educational Achievement. Retrieved October 7, 2005, from http://dibels.uoregon.edu

Gough, P. (1972). One second of reading. In J. Kavanagh & I. Mattingly (Eds.), *Language by ear and by eye* (pp. 331–358). Cambridge, MA: MIT Press.

Hebb, D.O. (1949). *The organization of behavior.* New York: Wiley.

Huey, E.B. (1968). *The psychology and pedagogy of reading.* Cambridge, MA: MIT Press. (Original work published 1905)

Kahneman, D. (1973). *Attention and effort.* Englewood Cliffs, NJ: Prentice Hall.

LaBerge, D., & Samuels, S.J. (1974). Toward a theory of automatic information processing in reading. *Cognitive Psychology, 6*, 293–323.

National Institute of Child Health and Human Development (NICHD). (2000). *Report of the National Reading Panel. Teaching children to read: An evidence-based assessment of the scientific research literature on reading and its implications for reading instruction* (NIH Publication No. 00-4769). Washington, DC: U.S. Government Printing Office.

O'Shea, L.J., Sindelar, P.T., & O'Shea, D.J. (1985). The effects of repeated readings and attentional cues on reading fluency and comprehension. *Journal of Reading Behavior, 17*, 19–142.

Pearson, P.D. (1996). Reclaiming the center. In M. Graves, P. van den Broek, & B.M. Taylor (Eds.), *The first R: Every child's right to read* (pp. 259–274). New York: Teachers College Press; Newark, DE: International Reading Association.

Peterson, L.R., & Peterson, M.J. (1959). Short-term retention of individual verbal items. *Journal of Experimental Psychology, 58,* 193–198.

Pressley, M., Hilden, K., & Shankland, R. (2005). *An evaluation of end grade-3 of Dynamic Indicators of Basic Early Literacy Skills (DIBELS): Speed reading without comprehension, predicting little.* Unpublished manuscript, Michigan State University, Literacy Achievement Research Center.

Project LITT. (1998). *Software lists.* Retrieved January 25, 2005, from http://edtechfm.sdsu.edu/SPED/ProjectLITT/lists.html

Renaissance Learning. (2004). Fluent reader [Computer software and materials]. Wisconsin Rapids, WI: Author.

Samuels, S.J. (1997). The method of repeated readings. *The Reading Teacher, 32,* 403–408. (Original work published 1979)

Samuels, S.J., Bremer, C., & LaBerge, D. (1978). Units of word recognition: Evidence for developmental changes. *Journal of Verbal Learning and Verbal Behavior, 17,* 715–720.

Samuels, S.J., Ediger, K., Willcutt, J., & Palumbo, T. (2006). Role of automaticity in metacognition. In C. Block & S. Israel (Eds.), *Metacognition and literacy learning* (pp. 41–59). Thousand Oaks, CA: Corwin Press.

Samuels, S.J., & Wu, Y.C. (March 21, 2003). Effect of increased individual reading time on reading achievement. Retrieved February 22, 2006, from http://www.tc.umn.edu/~samue001

Semonick, M.A., Lewis, M., & Samuels, S.J. (2001). The effects of paired-repeated reading on second graders' oral reading and on-task behavior. Unpublished doctoral dissertation, University of Minnesota.

Soli, S.D., & Devine, V.T. (1976). Behavioral correlates of achievement: A look at high and low achievers. *Journal of Educational Psychology, 68,* 335–341.

Stanovich, K.E. (1986). Matthew effects in reading: Some consequences of individual differences in the acquisition of literacy. *Reading Research Quarterly, 21,* 360–406.

Thurlow, R., & van den Broek, P. (1997). Automaticity and inference generation during reading comprehension. *Reading & Writing Quarterly, 13*(2), 165–185.

Chapter 3

Instruction and Development of Reading Fluency in Struggling Readers

Michael Pressley, Irene W. Gaskins, and Lauren Fingeret

What do we as educators want for young readers? Yes, like other authors in this volume, we want readers to read words fast and accurately and with expression (i.e., read prosodically), but we want more. We want readers also to read with high comprehension, and for that to happen, we are convinced that they must be constructively responsive as they read (Pressley & Afflerbach, 1995), which includes the following: Excellent comprehenders overview text and scan it. They relate their prior knowledge to ideas in the text. They notice when they are confused or need to reread and do so. They construct images in their mind's eye reflecting the content of the text. Good readers summarize, and they interpret, often with intense feeling, rejecting or embracing the ideas of an author. Such reflective reading, actually, can be pretty slow. Speed in reading and accurate word reading are not the goals. Understanding, appreciating, and thinking about the ideas in text are. Yes, fluency at the word level, as operationalized as reading accurately and quickly, is necessary so that the reader can choose to slow down and employ the comprehension strategies previously described. When word-level reading is fluent, enough cognitive capacity is available (LaBerge & Samuels, 1974) to permit the decision to execute the comprehension strategies and profit from them. Thus, fluent readers can and do think hard about what they are reading.

Constructively responsive fluent readers do not become fluent in an instant; there is no magical moment when fluency is achieved once and for all. Moreover, even a presumably fluent, proficient adult reader might falter if presented with a very difficult and unfamiliar text. Thus, there are probably stages of fluency, with word-level fluency a precursor to fluent, constructively responsive reading, which varies in adequacy depending on the difficulty of the text for the reader.

What Research Has to Say About Fluency Instruction, edited by S. Jay Samuels and Alan E. Farstrup. © 2006 by the International Reading Association.

Our reading of the literature is that no one knows with certainty how to produce fluent reading in all readers, let alone fluent reading in the constructively responsive sense. Enough is known, however, to provide some guidelines about methods to try to promote reading in initially struggling, dysfluent readers with high comprehension.

We wish to emphasize that the methods of instruction discussed in the following sections are methods for teachers to try—and, as a teacher tries a method with a struggling reader, the teacher should also monitor whether the method is having an impact. We feel especially strongly about this "try and monitor" approach, as we near completion of a study documenting the instruction at Benchmark School, Media, Pennsylvania, USA (Pressley, Gaskins, Solic, & Collins, 2005), which, in the first author's opinion, is one of the premier, evidence-based schools in the country targeting struggling readers in grades 1–8 (Gaskins, 2005). A centerpiece of Benchmark School's instruction is that the teachers are always monitoring whether what they are trying is working with students, and, if it is not, they try something else.

Such an approach seems imperative to us because the range of struggling readers, those who are at risk for long-term dysfluency, is great. Some children struggle in kindergarten and first and second grade because there is very little instruction occurring in their mainstream classroom, or, at least, instruction is not as explicit, systematic, and complete in word learning as they need to "get it." If there were systematic teaching of the code, most of these children would get it. Other struggling readers are receiving instruction, perhaps very systematic decoding instruction, but somehow it does not click with them, whereas another form of systematic decoding instruction might. Still others can sound out words but do so very, very slowly, with the result that all of their conscious capacity is used up, and they call out words but have no idea what the message is in the text they just read (Cromer, 1970; LaBerge & Samuels, 1974). Then, there are those children for whom blending and synthesizing individual sounds is their very problem, and systematic, synthetic phonics instruction just does not help them. They just cannot blend individual sounds into recognizable words. In some cases, such children can work with larger word chunks just fine and are able to blend onsets and rhymes (e.g., able to blend *fl* and *at* to read *flat*) or syllables that they recognize as wholes (e.g., able to read *carpet* because they already have *car* and *pet* memorized). In other cases, the children seem to be able to learn whole words only—fortunately, sometimes multisyllabic words (i.e., they can memorize *carpet* but cannot sound it out on first encounter even though they know *car* and *pet* already). Finally, some children seem to have normal vision, except for their perceptions of letters and words. These are the children who read and write *b*s and *d*s reversed, among other errors. They seem not to have acquired the metacognitive knowledge that, although physical objects are the same whether viewed from left to right or right to left, this is not the case with letters and words. And bear in mind that we are limiting our discussion to children with at least normal intelligence. In addition, many children with less-than-normal intelligence experience difficulties learning to read. They will not be taken up here. Our focus in this chapter is on struggling readers who are at least of average intelligence or greater and are reading at beginning levels (like the students who enter Benchmark School).

For struggling readers, diversity in instruction is essential. One reason is that these children are not a homogenous population; they differ greatly in their needs and responses to reading instruction of various sorts. Some need and benefit from traditional phonics. Some need and benefit from a different form of word-recognition instruction. Some will only learn to read words through instruction emphasizing sight words. Unfortunately, we do not have at present a really good diagnostic test that permits identification of the various types of struggling readers in advance of trying to teach them. More positively, the perceptive teacher can discover much about the specific difficulties experienced by a reader by carefully monitoring the child's reaction to instruction.

Another reason that instruction must be diverse is that skilled reading involves diverse skills. Much must be taught to cover the waterfront of competencies that the skilled reader possesses. In this chapter, we detail our thinking about how such instruction might proceed and why we think the way we do about instruction by offering a series of suggestions about how and what to teach struggling readers who read at the beginning levels.

Try Systematic Decoding Instruction

The evidence is simply overwhelming that many struggling readers do, in fact, make great progress in learning to read if they are given systematic decoding instruction (National Institute of Child Health and Human Development [NICHD], 2000). Especially if it is not known whether a child received such instruction already (and often, it is not), it makes good sense to attempt teaching phonics and seeing how much progress the child makes. One possibility is that the child experienced exceptionally deficient instruction, that no one attempted systematic decoding instruction previously. If that is the case, there might be rapid progress in the child learning the code and being able to sound out words and eventually becoming fluent in sounding out words. Alternatively, it may be that the particular form of decoding instruction is not well matched to the child, but that another form would permit more certain progress. Finally, sometimes the child makes progress in learning to decode but does not become fluent in sounding out words. The child can only sound out words slowly. We reflect on each of these possibilities in the context of research findings that should be on the minds of anyone concerned with the development of fluency in struggling readers.

Word-Recognition Progress, Perhaps to the Point of Fluency (or Close)

Systematic phonics instruction may be powerful because it influences basic neurological processing, at least in some struggling readers. A little background information will set the stage for understanding this point. Brain-imaging techniques now exist that permit the detection of more and less active areas of the brain as people read (see Shaywitz & Shaywitz, 2004, for a review, which is the basis for this subsection; also, Goswami, 2004). One important finding is that normal, mature readers especially activate a set of three sites on the left side of the brain more reliably than readers with dyslexia (Shaywitz et al., 2002). One especially active area is in the parieto-temporal region, with its healthy functioning associated with the ability to analyze words phonologically (e.g., sound out words). This area is about three quarters of the way toward the back of the brain and two thirds of the way toward the top of the brain. A second very active region in normal functioning is in the occipito-temporal region, which is near the back of the brain and the bottom of the cortex. The healthy functioning of this region is important to recognizing words as wholes, that is, as sight words, rather than sounding out. The third region, Broca's area, is closer to the front of the brain and is implicated in analysis of spoken words. In good readers, these three areas work well in coordination, with the result that readers recognize familiar words automatically without sounding them out and can quickly and accurately sound out less familiar words.

Good readers probably are not born with these left side areas more active. For example, Turkelbaum, Gareau, Flowers, Zeffiro, and Eden

(2003) reported in a cross-sectional developmental study that activity in these areas increased with increasing age, that is, as children learned to read. Also interesting was that with development, the activation of areas on the right side of the brain decreased. Brain activation in response to words changes as people learn to read. Some areas of the brain turn on, while others turn off.

Shaywitz et al. (2004) reported an interesting initial study supportive of the possibility that systematic phonics instruction may, in fact, stimulate the development of the brain regions associated with skilled reading. That is, they explored whether brain activation in the left side areas associated with skilled reading was more likely in students receiving phonics instruction than in those not receiving such instruction. Participants in the study were children at the end of first or second grade who were performing below the 25th percentile on standardized tests of word-recognition and word-attack skills. Students receiving the phonologically based intervention received systematic phonics instruction for the school year, including reading of decodable books, complemented by reading of trade books as decoding skill increased. Other students who were below the 25th percentile on word-level skills experienced the regular school reading curriculum in grade 2 or 3, which varied from school to school but did not focus on phonological skills. After the year of intervention, the students who received the phonological intervention were reading better than those who did not receive the intervention; those who received the intervention had better word recognition, slightly faster reading, and very slightly better comprehension. In spite of their gains, however, the phonological students remained far behind same-age normal readers on standardized reading measures.

Brain images during reading were also recorded at the beginning and end of the year of the intervention. The most striking result was that after a year of intervention, the phonologically treated students had brain images resembling nonimpaired age-mates. In particular, the areas of the brain associated with sounding out words showed normal activation. The disabled readers receiving regular reading instruction had less pronounced brain activations in the areas associated with skilled reading. The researchers also collected brain-imaging data a year after intervention concluded for the students who received phonics instruction. The findings were very encouraging; they indicated more activity in the occipitotemporal region, the area that presumably mediates recognition of words as wholes. The hypothesis that phonologically based interventions may have effects beyond teaching students how to sound out words gathers momentum with the results of this study, although much additional study needs to occur, especially mapping out the long-term effects of phonologically based interventions in the primary grades, both on behavioral data (i.e., accurate reading of words, fluency, and comprehension) and brain functioning. The brain-imaging data are suggestive at this point, hardly definitive.

More positively, however, when students who are at risk for reading failure, but who have not yet evidenced any reading failure, are provided systematic phonics instruction in kindergarten and grade 1, these students' reading is almost as fluent (i.e., fast) in the later elementary grades as the general population of late elementary readers (Torgesen, 2004). For many at-risk readers, systematic phonics instruction is probably close to a cure for their beginning reading problems, at least at the word-recognition level.

Alternative Forms of Word-Recognition Instruction

Since Chall's (1967) book, synthetic phonics instruction has been favored over all other forms of phonics. Adams's (1990) review of the data, however, suggests that both synthetic and onset-rime phonics are viable alternatives for teaching beginning readers to break the code once phonemic awareness has been attained. Synthetic phonics instruction focuses on the individual sounds in words, with students taught to map the letters and letter combinations in words to their component sounds, and then blend the sounds together to pronounce the word. Many phonics programs in the marketplace are some form of synthetic phonics. Instruction in onset-rime (analogy) phonics teaches students to use the consonant(s) (onset) before the vowel plus the vowel and what follows (rime) to decode words (e.g., blending the onset *r* with the rime *ide* to decode *ride*).

Irene Gaskins and her colleagues at Benchmark School regularly receive students who experienced some form of synthetic phonics instruction and failed to make much progress in learning to read in their first year or two of school. Hence, they end up at Benchmark, frustrated. Based on their clinical experiences and understanding of the research literature on decoding, the Benchmark faculty recognized that there is more than one way to decode a word. Rather than decoding sound by sound, readers can decode by analogy to other words (Ehri & Robbins, 1992; Peterson & Haines, 1992), and some struggling readers do better decoding that way (Berninger, Yates, & Lester, 1991; Freebody & Byrne, 1988; Wise, 1992).

Thus, once a person knows basic letter–sound associations for consonants and the word *cat*, the reader can decode by analogy *hat, fat, hat, mat, Nat, pat, rat, sat*, and *vat*. At the heart of the Benchmark Word Identification program (Gaskins, Gaskins, Anderson, & Schommer, 1995; Gaskins, Gaskins, & Gaskins, 1991, 1992), a very systematic approach to word-recognition instruction, are 120 keywords that capture the most frequent spelling patterns (e.g., *-at*) associated with the six English-language vowels. In addition, the program includes keywords for the two sounds of *g* (e.g., *girl, giraffe*) and the two sounds of *c* (e.g., *can, city*). Some word parts that always sound the same (e.g., *-tion*) are taught as wholes.

For example, to decode the word *dispatcher*, a student using the Word Identification program would learn to identify a keyword for each syllable of the word. For the first syllable, *dis-*, the keyword *this* could be used, because the vowel *i* is followed by a consonant. For the second syllable, *-patch-*, the keyword could be *cat* or *catch*, because the *a* in *-patch-* is followed by a consonant. For the final syllable, *-er*, the keyword *her* would apply. Thus, the student, who is also learning the simple consonant–sound associations of English plus the digraphs and consonant blends, would know the sequence of vowel sounds and would then be able to sound out the word. Thus, rather than *this-cat-her* being pronounced, the student would sound out the word *dispatcher*.

Does the Word Identification program approach work? With severely reading-disabled readers, it works as well as synthetic phonics (Lovett et al., 2000). If it were the case that some children do better with synthetic phonics and some do better with the analogy approach of Word Identification, then you would expect that there would be greater performance in a situation where both are taught. Both Gaskins and her colleagues (Gaskins, Ehri, Cress, O'Hara, & Donnelly, 1996/1997) and Lovett et al. (2000) included such a condition in their work and found that greater performance was indeed the case. The lesson learned is that if synthetic phonics is not working, an alternative based on decoding by analogy is available, and, to the extent that it has been tested, it appears to be as powerful as synthetic phonics (NICHD, 2000). Nevertheless, the severe readers in Lovett et al.'s (2000) work were far from fluent at the word level after receiving 70 hours of any of the three types of instruction evaluated (synthetic phonics, analogy Word Identification, combined). However, a longitudinal study of students who entered Benchmark School as beginning readers revealed that after one year of a combined sound–letter and analogy approach, these struggling readers on average attained the 50th percentile for their grade level in word reading. Students who entered the school as beginning readers and who received only the analogy approach did not attain the 50th percentile until they had been instructed in the analogy program for three years. That finding is the critical point. A combined program appears to enable more students to acquire decoding skills that are typical of their grade level and to do so in a shorter time period.

Fluency Is Not a Byproduct of Phonics Instruction With Severely Struggling Beginning Readers

With many of the most-difficult-to-remediate struggling readers, fluency does not follow from systematic phonics alone (see Torgesen, 2004, for a review; also Torgesen, Rashotte, & Alexander, 2001). Such students read much more slowly in the later elementary grades than the general population of readers (e.g., Bowers & Swanson, 1991; Hogaboam & Perfetti, 1978; Lovett, 1984; Vukovic, Wilson, & Nash, 2004; Wolf & Bowers, 1999; Wolf, Bowers, & Biddle, 2000; Wolf, Pfeil, Lotz, & Biddle, 1994). A group at the University of Kansas is studying one possibility with respect to these children. Many struggling readers may process verbal material, in general, more slowly than other children. Their problem is not phonological processing per se but speed of verbal processing. To date, the Kansas group has found support for that possibility, with speed of processing of verbal material predictive of reading achievement over and above phonological processes in its analyses of second and fourth graders (Catts, Gillispie, Leonard, Kail, & Miller, 2002; see also Denckla, 1972; Denckla & Rudel, 1976; Levy, Bourassa, & Horn, 1999; McBride-Chang & Kail, 2002; Scarborough, 2001). Slow reading is a real problem, for those who read slowly comprehend slowly (Vukovic et al., 2004). Slow reading of words consumes the limited consciousness available for processing text, with the result that no consciousness is left over for understanding what is read (LaBerge & Samuels, 1974).

With the knowledge that decoding instruction is not a cure-all, it becomes clear that more is needed to deal with problems of fluency than phonics. Researchers have been working hard to identify other approaches that can increase fluency, with some having more support than others. Even so, there are a few ideas in the marketplace, taken up in the next section, that should be on the minds of all those who are teaching struggling readers.

Try Frequent Student Oral Reading With Teacher or Tutor Feedback

Reading fluency can be increased through repeated oral reading with feedback and guidance (NICHD, 2000). That is, accuracy in reading and speed of reading can be increased through such teacher-supported oral reading. However, the procedures for doing so are a real "mulligan stew," as described by Stahl (2004). They vary in how much repeated reading occurs in the intervention as well as whether an adult assists reading, an adult tutors the child, or the child reads along with audiotapes. Moreover, the National Reading Panel (NRP; NICHD, 2000) did not attempt to separate the various alternative procedures for increasing fluency with respect to their relative potency.

As we reflected on Stahl's (2004) mulligan stew, we realized that one reason that the analogy-plus-letter–sound students in Benchmark's longitudinal study made such rapid progress toward the mean word-reading score for their grade level (Ehri, Satlow, & Gaskins, 2006) may be that, during their initial year in the program, students practiced daily echo and choral reading of text saturated with decodable and high-frequency words, both at school and at home. In later years some of the analogy-plus-letter–sound students participated in Readers Theatre, but not with the consistency that is probably necessary to influence gains in fluency. Readers Theatre is an activity that most Benchmark students find motivating, and thus should probably be revisited on a consistent basis. This activity appears to be especially valuable for developing fluency and for pulling together major concepts in content areas (see Flynn, 2004/2005).

Kuhn and Stahl (2003) looked again at the studies included in the NRP report (NICHD, 2000) and broadened the criterion so that more than just experimental and quasi-experimental studies were included in their analyses, as well as more than studies that provided enough quantitative information to be included in a meta-analysis. Their analyses of the studies examined by NRP and the additional investigations highlighted some important points: (a) Kuhn and Stahl concluded that adult assistance was quite important with respect to increasing fluency, with simple repeated reading by the child much less certain to produce a positive outcome as repeated reading with adult assistance. (b) Kuhn and Stahl also noted no difference in fluency or other reading outcomes between repeated reading of same text and the same amount of time spent reading a variety of texts (Homan, Klesius, & Hite, 1993; Mathes & Fuchs, 1993; Rashotte & Torgesen, 1985; von Bon, Boksebeld, Font Freide, &

van den Hurk, 1991). (c) Assistance during repeated reading promoted both fluency and comprehension. (d) Evidence supported readers reading aloud slightly challenging texts rather than easy texts. (e) Although most of the research on fluency instruction has been carried out with one-to-one tutoring, promising whole-group approaches (Rasinski, Padak, Linek, & Sturtevant, 1994; Stahl, Heubach, & Cramond, 1997) deserve more evaluation. (f) Nevertheless, the fluency instruction evaluated to date certainly is not catching weak readers up to regularly achieving readers with respect to fluency! A need definitely exists for more than just teacher-supported oral reading, if struggling readers are to become very good readers (if that is possible at all). One aspect of fluency instruction that deserves further attention is the percentage of high-frequency words found in the texts used in reading instruction.

Try Developing Sight Words and Vocabulary Knowledge

Given the emphasis on reading at the word level in the most popular conceptions of fluent reading, it makes sense for all concerned with reading education to be thinking about what words students are learning to read. Readers must both decode words and access their meanings automatically (i.e., once the word is read, they know what it means). With millions of words in English—consider, for example, that the complete *Oxford English Dictionary* comprises 20 volumes—how could this happen? It can happen because readers do not need to know all of the words in English!

Dolch Words

Consider first a historically prominent reading fluency intervention. Edward W. Dolch (1939, 1941, 1945, 1951, 1960) believed that children should be taught the words most often encountered in text as sight words or words they should recognize automatically. Through his research, he identified 220 words that made up between 50% and 75% of texts children read, with these being mostly function words (e.g., *the, a*), conjunctions (e.g., *and*), pronouns, prepositions, and common verbs. He also identified 95 nouns that commonly occurred in texts read by children. Both of these lists were part of his larger list of the 1,000 most commonly encountered words.

Dolch had a view of reading and reading instruction that was far ahead of his time (see Pressley, 2005), but in this chapter we will cover only those elements most pertinent to our discussion on fluency. Although he believed that much learning of sight words could occur in a decontextualized fashion, he developed many literary stories filled with the common sight words so that students could have many encounters with the Dolch words in context. For struggling readers, in particular, Dolch felt that these stories should be orally read by students with substantial feedback from the teacher, including feedback about how to sound out words (i.e., the stories contained plenty of words that were not Dolch words that could be attacked with phonics skills, which Dolch believed in teaching explicitly). Dolch was emphatic that reading stories was not about reading words but about getting meaning from text, often very personalized meanings informed by students' prior knowledge.

The reading of interesting texts was just part of a larger pedagogy in Dolch's approach that emphasized motivation, filled with practices consistent with what is now known about how to motivate students based on substantial research (see Pintrich & Schunk, 2002): Dolch advocated asking students to read texts that were just a bit challenging, providing lots of praise, practicing reading skills in the context of games, and practicing reading in cooperative classrooms rather than ones emphasizing competition between students.

Dolch did not live in an era when experimental research was common or even much understood as a means of evaluating curriculum. Campbell and Stanley's (1966) classic monograph on designs for research appeared several years after the final edition of Dolch's best-known textbook. Thus, the Dolch ideas about instruction have never been subjected to a credible scientific test. What has been studied is whether intense, short-term teaching of sight words in a decontextualized fashion improves student reading of text containing those words. Although the data are mixed on whether such teaching improves reading (Fleisher, Jenkins, & Pany, 1979; Levy, Abello, & Lysynchuk, 1997), such an exclusive focus on short-term, intensive, decontextualized practice at recognizing words was not what Dolch proposed. What Dolch proposed was long-term teaching of sight words and reading of real stories containing the words occurring in a balanced reading instructional program that extends across the school day.

Dolch's idea of making certain that students know a core set of commonly encountered words makes even more sense today in light of some recent analyses. Much is now being learned about just what words K–12 students really need to know, the basic vocabulary of children and adolescents. Biemiller and Slonim (2001) provide the most recent chapter in this effort. They performed analyses to identify words understood by 80% of children at each grade level (i.e., the children know the meanings of these words). It is important to note that these researchers were focusing on root words. For example, *fish* is a root word for *fishing*, *fishy*, and *fished*. By the end of grade 2, children know about 5,000 root words. After that, through grade 12, students gain about 1,000 words a year to a total of about 15,000 words. In their study, Biemiller and Slonim identified the words that children at each grade level need to understand. Although their list has more words than the Dolch basic 1,000-word list, it is not an overwhelming number of words. Because many of these words are not especially high-frequency words in English or in texts children encounter, it should be possible to further list in order of priority those words that should be the targets for sight-word development and to make certain that students have fluent access to the meanings of the words (i.e., know these meanings automatically when they see the words).

Benchmark School Approach

The Benchmark School staff supports students in learning sight words by fully analyzing the words they are learning during Word Identification lessons (Gaskins et al., 1996/1997). In addition, teachers support students in acquiring sight words through contextual guessing, letter–sound decoding, and analogy (Gaskins, 2004). New words that students will encounter during reading group lessons are placed on index cards with the word in isolation on the front of the card and, on the reverse side, decoding strategies the child can apply independently for identifying unknown words. For example, if the new word were *then*, the teacher might write a context clue and the analogy strategy on the reverse side of the index card (e.g., "She will work and *then* she can play." "If I know ten, *then* I know *then*."). Word cards are punched with one hole and added to each student's word ring, which is checked each day by the teacher. When a child falters, the teacher asks the child what decoding strategy he or she knows that might work for decoding the word. If the child is still unable to decode the word, the teacher turns the card over and reminds the child of the strategies he or she might use to decode the word. Each time a child quickly and correctly identifies the word in isolation on the front of the card, a check mark is placed on the word card. When a child has five check marks indicating that he or she quickly and correctly identified the word on five different days, the card is removed from the word ring and filed.

In addition, a parent (or sometimes a sibling, grandparent, or other family member) enhances the sight vocabulary of the Benchmark's beginning reader by reading for 20 to 30 minutes each evening with the child. Children choose from several sources of materials to fulfill this nightly home-reading requirement. One source for this reading is Benchmark's Books in Bags program. Books published by the Rigby and Wright Group have been grouped in plastic zip-close bags according to the number of words in the text and the frequency count of those words. The books chosen for this program are books that feature the 100 most frequently used words in written English. The bags of books are sent home, and parents are asked to read each book to their child as the parent finger points and the child follows. Next, the parent and child echo read and choral read the book until the child feels ready to read the book to a parent on his or her own. The bags of books are returned twice a week so that children can have a checkout with the Books in Bags lady. If a child is able to read with 98% accuracy and adequately discuss the content of the book, a new bag of books is given to the child.

A second source of reading material for home reading is the books in bags that are part of the analogy Word Identification program. Each day during the Word Identification lesson, students practice reading these books. On some days, they echo read or choral read, or do both. On other days, they read with a partner as the teacher monitors the reading. These little books contain the word patterns that have been introduced to date in the Benchmark Word Detectives program. Copies of these books are placed in plastic bags and kept at home for children to practice reading them with their parents and anyone else they can find to listen. Students obtain "autographs" from those to whom the books are read. The bag of Word Identification books is returned each week for two new books that feature the word patterns being studied that week. In addition to reading these books, each evening students analyze the words in the books and dictate five "discoveries" to their parents about how our language works (e.g., "I noticed in the word *Nathan* that the *t* and *h* represent one sound, just like the *n* and *g* in *sing* represent one sound. The letters *a-u* in *caught* represent the same sound that *a-w* represent in *saw*.").

Beginning readers at Benchmark also take home a folder of stories written by the teacher that feature the high-frequency sight words that have been introduced in reading group as part of their basal reader program. In addition, once students have acquired a preprimer sight vocabulary, they go to the library each day to pick out books to take home from the preprimer section. In short, the school provides many opportunities for students to practice reading sight words.

Limits of Sight-Word Learning

Reading is not just about decoding words. Even the simplest view of reading (e.g., Gough & Tunmer, 1986) posits that reading involves decoding the words and then comprehending them, largely by listening to one's own reading of the words. Hence, reading comprehension is viewed as determined by a combination of word-recognition skills and listening-comprehension abilities.

In an important study, Catts, Hogan, Adlof, and Barth (2003) assessed the word-recognition, listening-comprehension, and reading-comprehension skills of a group of students who ranged in reading ability when they were in second, fourth, and eighth grades. Word recognition was much more predictive of reading comprehension at grade 2 than at grade 4, and more predictive at grade 4 than at grade 8, where it accounted for a negligible portion of the variance in reading comprehension. The researchers also examined the weakest readers at each of the grade levels. Word-recognition difficulties were more prominently associated with poor reading when students were younger than when they were older. With increasing age, listening-comprehension problems were more prominent in the reading problems of the older students. Based on these data, we see more reason to be concerned about word-recognition and sight-word learning with younger compared to older students, but for poor readers, word-recognition problems are still obvious in grade 8. At all grade levels, however, reading comprehension reflected a balancing of word-recognition and listening-comprehension skills. These analyses indicate the need for a balanced development of skills, consistent with a message in research of the last decade (Pressley, 2006) that a balancing of factors is essential in effective reading instruction.

Sight-Word Learning as Compensation

Finally, in making the point that teaching sight words and vocabulary to struggling readers makes sense, we point to another aspect of the brain-imaging data. Some adults who were dyslexic as children have, somehow, somewhat compensated for it as adults (Shaywitz et al., 2003). They recognize well-familiar words. We find it very interesting that these compensating readers have more pronounced activity in the occipito-temporal region than do adults with dyslexia who do not recognize familiar words (i.e., the compensating adults with dyslexia have more pronounced activity in the area of the brain responsible for recognizing words as wholes rather than by sounding the words out). Because these compensating readers also seem to have more connection between the functioning of the occipito-temporal region and regions of the brain responsible for short-term memory than other readers (including normal readers), it seems likely that they have somehow memorized the sight words. In contrast, normal readers have stronger connections between the parieto-temporal and occipito-temporal regions, suggesting that repeated sounding out of words rather than rote memorization brings about the fluent reading of familiar words in them. The normal reader first sounds out the word and over repeated encounters comes to recognize the word as a sight word, with some evidence in young readers of active functioning of the parieto-temporal region preceding the active functioning of the occipito-temporal region as beginning readers who are good at sounding out begin to develop sight vocabulary.

In addition, consider the childhood dyslexics who seem to compensate as adults. Their reading is still not fluent because they have trouble with unfamiliar words. They still cannot sound out words, with the brain-imagery data confirming that there is less than optimal functioning in their parieto-temporal regions (see Shaywitz et al., 2003, for the original data on this fascinating study that we consider potentially very important as thinking about reading education proceeds). Shaywitz et al.'s (2003) observation that fluent reading depends on automatic recognition of high-frequency words and skilled sounding out of lower frequency words is consistent with other recent analyses (Compton, Appleton, & Hosp, 2004). Even so, Shaywitz and others (2003) made a significant finding, a counterintuitive one, about comprehension by the compensating readers: The compensating readers did about as well as nonimpaired adults on a comprehension measure and better than the noncompensating adult dyslexics. This finding raises the possibility that even if the compensation from memorizing familiar words does not produce as fluent reading as occurs in normal adult readers, it can still improve comprehension. On the basis of one study, this finding should be considered a hypothesis; however, it is an important hypothesis, one that should be a priority for study in the immediate future, as should instruction aimed at promoting the comprehension skills of struggling readers. If that hypothesis holds up in other studies, then emphasizing sight-word instruction for struggling beginning readers will gain much additional impetus.

Try Teaching Comprehension Strategies

At the beginning of this chapter, we stated that fluency and comprehension are not so much linear processes but are interdependent in a "blurry" sort of way. In this section we assert that comprehension strategies should be taught to all readers from the beginning of reading instruction, even if they have not yet become fluent. This approach may be the best practical demonstration of the interrelatedness of fluency and comprehension we described earlier and, more important, the best intervention to address it. In effect, weak readers can become better readers through teaching of comprehension strategies. The work of Brown, Pressley, Van Meter, and Schuder (1996) and Anderson (1992) is especially powerful evidence of this. In the former study, weak second-grade readers were taught a small repertoire of comprehension strategies over the course of a school year of instruction, with huge gains in reading achievement at the end of the year. In the latter study, weak readers in grades 6 through 9 were provided similar instruction, with similar large gains in reading achievement. In both studies, researchers found positive effects across a variety of measures. Many of the children in both of these studies were far from being fluent readers at the word level, even at the conclusions of the interventions. However, using the comprehension strategies very much seemed to make up for the lack of fluency as demonstrated by several measures of comprehension.

In addition, learning to use comprehension strategies presents a bonus. Students get more out of reading, which, if they are reading quality material, increases their knowledge of the world, including their vocabulary, with such richer world knowledge empowering future comprehension of topically related texts (Anderson & Pearson, 1984). So by teaching comprehension strategies that permit students to read books with worthwhile content, teachers can do much for potential literacy development, even of students who are not as word fluent as their classmates.

When students are first learning comprehension strategies, the teacher must often cue their use, and the student only responds to such cuing with some effort. Use of the strategies is far from fluent. Over several years of instruction and practice, however, many students come to use the strategies on their own and seem to execute them more as habits of mind, doing so with much less effort than when they were first learning to employ the techniques (Pressley et al., 1992; Gaskins, 2005). Over the course of the four to seven years of Benchmark School, teachers make a substantial effort for students to practice these strategies from their first days in the school as 7-year-olds to their concluding lessons as middle schoolers. Just as the development of fluency at the word level takes years, becoming a fluent, constructively responsive reader takes years.

Try All of the Recommendations at Once— Try Balanced Instruction

Every day, every student at Benchmark School experiences some form of word-recognition instruction, oral reading with teacher support, development of sight-word knowledge, development of vocabulary, and comprehension strategies instruction. The components recommended in this chapter to improve student reading to the point of fluency are at the center of the Benchmark curriculum, which includes many other elements as well—the reading of fine literature, extensive reading of expository materials, and composing, as well as the full range of elementary and middle school content that is in any combined elementary–middle school. We emphasize *every day* because becoming an excellent reader, one who is fluent at the word level and constructively responsive, occurs over years, not over a few lessons, a few months, or even a year or two. Reading acquisition is a longitudinal development if ever there was one.

Not every Benchmark student becomes fluent at the word and comprehension levels, but all make progress toward fluency. In a middle school class, some students are fluent with respect to most words encountered and facile in using the comprehension strategies. Some are fluent at the word level but have not mastered independent and habitual use of the comprehension strategies. Other students depend more on the comprehension strategies because they know many sight words but still struggle with unfamiliar words.

And, finally, some students struggle reading words, period—the children who have a biological difference that impairs their ability to perceive words as quickly and accurately as others do. These children are the ones who have been ignored in the recent flurry of interest in reading disabilities. Yes, most children with reading disabilities suffer principally from verbal difficulties. A few, however, have speed-of-response and perceptual problems. Although treatment is not yet well understood, the teacher clinicians at Benchmark do work with these children so they can make as much sense as possible from text.

An important key to the success of the treatment of the struggling readers at Benchmark School is that the treatment is multidimensional (Gaskins, 1998, 1999, 2005). Realizing that children learn differently, teachers implement a variety of approaches; they are responsive to the aspects of the Benchmark program that work best for each student and make students aware of what appears to work for them. In addition, just as Kuhn (2004/2005) found, the Benchmark staff has learned that opportunities for students to spend a great deal of time during the school day and at home involved in wide reading (sometimes echo reading, sometimes choral reading, and much of the time silent or oral reading in texts in which at least 98% of the words are sight words) leads to improved fluency and comprehension. We believe that the number of words read each day is one of the most important ingredients of a program that develops fluent readers.

In addition, the Benchmark staff has found that the text in which children read does make a difference. The staff has noted that their students appear to acquire sight vocabulary more quickly and easily when students read in basal readers that were published in the heyday of controlled vocabulary. For example, some of the basal readers that have proved successful for Benchmark's struggling beginning readers are the preprimers, primers, and first readers published in the 1970s. In these texts the most frequent words in written English account for a large portion of the words, and the percentage of less common multisyllabic words is lower than is typical of the current literature readers. In the readers of the 1970s, word overlap (i.e., word families that end in the same sound) tends to be frequent, which seems to be helpful to struggling readers in gaining fluency. The best texts for aiding struggling readers to become fluent readers appear to be those that have a controlled vocabulary consisting of a high percentage of both high-frequency words (e.g., *the, dog*) and words with consistent and decodable patterns (e.g., *rug, sun*). This conclusion is based on experiences at Benchmark School and is consistent with more formal research-based conclusions produced by Hiebert (2003) and Hiebert and Fisher (2002).

Conclusions

Tremendous progress has been made in understanding how to promote better and more fluent reading in struggling beginning readers. We are far from having a cure for all such readers, although progress in alleviating their symptoms has been made. Every instructional direction discussed in this chapter requires additional study and should receive it as part of the quest for instruction that will work to permit all children to become fluent readers—readers who can process the words on the page and respond to the ideas reflectively and intelligently. The progress has been great, but so are the challenges to get beyond where we are right now.

Then, an even larger challenge exists: There is only one Benchmark School. More positively, because of the emphasis on evidence-based approaches to reading instruction, the instructional practices reviewed in this chapter are being tried in more and more schools. Nonetheless, it is not certain how well these components are being implemented or how completely. As we come to understand more fully how to develop better, more fluent readers, we must simultaneously work on making certain that the light from a lighthouse such as Benchmark finds its way as far and as wide as possible, wherever there are children who are struggling to learn how to read—and, by the way, they are everywhere.

Questions for Discussion

1. How can all the suggestions for encouraging fluent reading be incorporated in every "reading morning"?

2. Why is measuring the number of words a child can read per minute an inadequate measure of fluency based on the perspective of this chapter?

3. Why should the development of fluent reading be a focus of instruction throughout the elementary years?

REFERENCES

Adams, M.J. (1990). *Beginning to read.* Cambridge, MA: Harvard University Press.

Anderson, R.C., & Pearson, P.D. (1984). A schema-theoretic view of basic processes in reading. In P.D. Pearson, R. Barr, M.L. Kamil, & P.B. Mosenthal (Eds.), *Handbook of reading research* (pp. 255–291). New York: Longman.

Anderson, V. (1992). A teacher development project in transactional strategy instruction for teachers of severely reading-disabled adolescents. *Teaching & Teacher Education, 8,* 391–403.

Biemiller, A., & Slonim, N. (2001). Estimating root word vocabulary growth in normative and advantaged populations: Evidence for a common sequence of vocabulary acquisition. *Journal of Educational Psychology, 93,* 498–520.

Berninger, V.W., Yates, C., & Lester, K. (1991). Multiple orthographic codes in reading and writing acquisition. *Reading and Writing: An Interdisciplinary Journal, 3,* 115–149.

Bowers, P.G., & Swanson, L.B. (1991). Naming speed deficits in reading disability: Multiple measures of a single process. *Journal of Experimental Child Psychology, 51*, 195–219.

Brown, R., Pressley, M., Van Meter, P., & Schuder, T. (1996). A quasi-experimental validation of transactional strategies instruction with low-achieving second grade readers. *Journal of Educational Psychology, 88*, 18–37.

Campbell, D.T., & Stanley, J.C. (1966). *Experimental and quasi-experimental designs for research*. Chicago: Rand-McNally.

Catts, H.W., Gillispie, M., Leonard, L.B., Kail, R.V., & Miller, C.A. (2002). The role of speed of processing, rapid naming, and phonological awareness in reading achievement. *Learning Disabilities Quarterly, 35*, 510–525.

Catts, H.W., Hogan, T.P., Adlof, S.M., & Barth, A.E. (2003, June). *The simple view of reading: Changes over time*. Paper presented at the annual meeting of the Society for the Scientific Study of Reading, Boulder, CO.

Chall, J.S. (1967). *Learning to read: The great debate*. New York: McGraw-Hill.

Compton, D.L., Appleton, A.C., & Hosp, M.K. (2004). Exploring the relationship between text-leveling systems and reading accuracy and fluency in second-grade students who are average and poor decoders. *Learning Disabilities Research & Practice, 19*, 176–184.

Cromer, W. (1970). The difference model: A new explanation for some reading difficulties. *Journal of Educational Psychology, 61*, 471–483.

Denckla, M.B. (1972). Color naming deficits in dyslexic boys. *Cortex, 8*, 164–176.

Denckla, M.B., & Rudel, R.G. (1976). Rapid automatized naming (R.A.N.): Dyslexia differentiated from other learning disabilities. *Neuropsychologica, 14*, 471–476.

Dolch, E.W. (1939). *A manual for remedial reading*. Champaign, IL: Garrard.

Dolch, E.W. (1941). *Teaching primary reading*. Champaign, IL: Garrard.

Dolch, E.W. (1945). *A manual for remedial reading* (2nd ed.). Champaign, IL: Garrard.

Dolch, E.W. (1951). *Teaching primary reading* (2nd ed.). Champaign, IL: Garrard.

Dolch, E.W. (1960). *Teaching primary reading* (3rd ed.). Champaign, IL: Garrard.

Ehri, L.C., & Robbins, C. (1992). Beginners need some decoding skill to read words by analogy. *Reading Research Quarterly, 27*, 12–27.

Ehri, L.C., Satlow, E., & Gaskins, I.W. (2006). *Word reading instruction: Graphophonemic analysis strengthens the keyword analogy method for struggling readers*. Manuscript submitted for publication.

Fleisher, L.S., Jenkins, J.R., & Pany, D. (1979). Effects on poor readers' comprehension of training in rapid decoding. *Reading Research Quarterly, 15*, 30–48.

Flynn, R.M. (2004/2005). Curriculum-based Readers Theatre: Setting the stage for reading and retention. *The Reading Teacher, 58*, 360–365.

Freebody, P., & Byrne, B. (1988). Word-reading strategies in elementary school children: Relations to comprehension, reading time, and phonemic awareness. *Reading Research Quarterly, 23*, 441–453.

Gaskins, I.W. (1998). There's more to teaching at-risk and delayed readers than good reading instruction. *The Reading Teacher, 51*, 534–547.

Gaskins, I.W. (1999). A multidimensional reading program. *The Reading Teacher, 53*, 162–164.

Gaskins, I.W. (2004). Word detectives. *Educational Leadership, 81*(6), 70–73.

Gaskins, I.W. (2005). *Success with struggling readers: The Benchmark School approach.* New York: Guilford.

Gaskins, I.W., Ehri, L.C., Cress, C., O'Hara, C., & Donnelly, K. (1996/1997). Procedures for word learning: Making discoveries about words. *The Reading Teacher, 50,* 312–327.

Gaskins, R.W., Gaskins, I.W., Anderson, R.C., & Schommer, M. (1995). The reciprocal relationship between research and development: An example involving a decoding strand for poor readers. *Journal of Reading Behavior, 27,* 337–377.

Gaskins, R.W., Gaskins, J.C., & Gaskins, I.W. (1991). A decoding program for poor readers—and the rest of the class, too! *Language Arts, 68,* 213–225.

Gaskins, R.W., Gaskins, J.C., & Gaskins, I.W. (1992). Using what you know to figure out what you don't know: An analogy approach to decoding. *Reading & Writing Quarterly, 8,* 197–221.

Goswami, U. (2004). Neuroscience and education. *British Journal of Educational Psychology, 74,* 1–14.

Gough, P.B., & Tunmer, W.E. (1986). Decoding, reading, and reading disability. *Remedial & Special Education, 7,* 6–10.

Hiebert, E.H. (2003). *The role of text in developing fluency: A comparison of two interventions.* Ann Arbor, MI: Center for the Improvement of Early Reading Achievement.

Hiebert, E.H., & Fisher, C.W. (2002, April). *Text matters in developing reading fluency.* Paper presented at the annual convention of the International Reading Association, San Francisco.

Hogaboam, T.W., & Perfetti, C.A. (1978). Reading skill and the role of verbal experience in decoding. *Journal of Educational Psychology, 70,* 717–729.

Homan, S., Klesius, P., & Hite, S. (1993). Effects of repeated readings and nonrepetitive strategies on students' fluency and comprehension. *Journal of Educational Research, 87,* 94–99.

Kuhn, M.R. (2004/2005). Helping students become accurate, expressive readers: Fluency instruction for small groups. *The Reading Teacher, 58,* 338–344.

Kuhn, M.R., & Stahl, S.A. (2003). Fluency: A review of developmental and remedial practices. *Journal of Educational Psychology, 95,* 3–21.

LaBerge, D., & Samuels, S.J. (1974). Toward a theory of automatic information processing in reading. *Cognitive Psychology, 6,* 293–323.

Levy, B.A., Abello, B., & Lysynchuk, L. (1997). Transfer from word training to reading in context: Gains in reading fluency and comprehension. *Learning Disabilities Quarterly, 20,* 173–188.

Levy, B.A., Bourassa, D.C., & Horn, C. (1999). Fast and slow namers: Benefits of segmentation and whole word training. *Journal of Experimental Child Psychology, 73,* 115–138.

Lovett, M.W. (1984). A developmental perspective on reading dysfunction: Accuracy and rate criteria in the subtyping of dyslexic children. *Brain and Language, 22,* 67–91.

Lovett, M.W., Lacerenza, L., Borden, S.L., Frijters, J.C., Steinbach, K.A., & De Palma, M. (2000). Components of effective remediation for developmental reading disabilities: Combining phonological and strategy-based instruction to improve outcomes. *Journal of Educational Psychology, 92,* 263–283.

Mathes, P.G., & Fuchs, L.S. (1993). Peer-mediated reading instruction on special education resource rooms. *Learning Disabilities Research and Practice, 8,* 233–243.

McBride-Chang, C., & Kail, R.V. (2002). Cross-cultural similarities in the predictors of reading acquisition. *Child Development, 73,* 1392–1407.

National Institute of Child Health and Human Development (NICHD). (2000). *Report of the National Reading Panel. Teaching children to read: Reports of the subgroups* (NIH Publication No. 00-4754). Washington, DC: U.S. Government Printing Office.

Peterson, M.E., & Haines, L.P. (1992). Orthographic analogy training with kindergarten children: Effects of analogy use, phonemic segmentation, and letter–sound knowledge. *Journal of Reading Behavior, 24,* 109–127.

Pintrich, P.R., & Schunk, D.H. (2002). *Motivation in education: Theory, research, and applications* (2nd ed.). Englewood Cliffs, NJ: Prentice-Hall.

Pressley, M. (2005). *Dolch professional development guide.* Columbus, OH: Science Research Associates.

Pressley, M. (2006). *Reading instruction that works: The case for balanced teaching* (3rd ed.). New York: Guilford.

Pressley, M., & Afflerbach, P. (1995). *Verbal protocols of reading: The nature of constructively responsive reading.* Hillsdale, NJ: Erlbaum.

Pressley, M., El-Dinary, P.B., Gaskins, I.W., Schuder, T., Bergman, J.L., Almasi, J., et al. (1992). Beyond direct explanation: Transactional instruction of reading comprehension strategies. *The Elementary School Journal, 92,* 511–554.

Pressley, M., Gaskins, I.W., Solic, K., & Collins, S. (2005). *A portrait of Benchmark School: How a school produces high achievement in students who previously failed.* East Lansing: Michigan State University Literacy Achievement Research Center.

Rashotte, C.A., & Torgesen, J.K. (1985). Repeated reading and reading fluency in learning disabled children. *Reading Research Quarterly, 20,* 180–188.

Rasinski, T.V., Padak, N.D., Linek, W., & Sturtevant, B. (1994). Effects of fluency development on urban second-grade readers. *Journal of Educational Research, 87,* 158–165.

Scarborough, H.S. (2001). Connecting early language and literacy to later reading (dis)abilities: Evidence, theory, and practice. In S.B. Neuman & D.K. Dickinson (Eds.), *Handbook of early literacy research* (pp. 97–110). New York: Guilford.

Shaywitz, B.A., Shaywitz, S.E., Blachman, B.A., Pugh, K.R., Fulbright, R.K., Skudlarski, P., et al. (2004). Development of left occipito-temporal systems for skilled reading in children after a phonologically-based intervention. *Biological Psychiatry, 55,* 926–933.

Shaywitz, B.A., Shaywitz, S.E., Pugh, K.R., Mencl, W.E., Fulbright, R.K., Skudlarski, P., et al. (2002). Disruption of posterior brain systems for reading in children with developmental dyslexia. *Biological Psychiatry, 52,* 101–110.

Shaywitz, S.E., & Shaywitz, B.A. (2004). Neurobiologic basis for reading and reading disability. In P. McCardle & V. Chhabra (Eds.), *The voice of evidence in reading research* (pp. 417–442). Baltimore: Paul H. Brookes.

Shaywitz, S.E., Shaywitz, B.A., Fulbright, R.K., Skudlarski, P., Mencl, W.E., Constable, R.T., et al. (2003). Neural systems for compensation and persistence: Young adult outcome of childhood reading disability. *Biological Psychiatry, 54,* 25–33.

Stahl, S.A. (2004). What do we know about fluency? Findings of the National Reading Panel. In P. McCardle & V. Chhabra (Eds.), *The voice of evidence in reading research* (pp. 187–211). Baltimore: Paul H. Brookes.

Stahl, S.A., Heubach, K., & Cramond, B. (1997). *Fluency-oriented reading instruction.* Athens, GA: National Reading Research Center; Washington, DC: U.S. Department of Education, Office of Educational Research and Improvement, Educational Resources Information Center.

Torgesen, J.K. (2004). Lessons learned from research on interventions for students who have difficulties learning to read. In P. McCardle & V. Chhabra (Eds.), *The voice of evidence in reading research* (pp. 355–382). Baltimore: Paul H. Brookes.

Torgesen, J.K., Rashotte, C.A., & Alexander, A.W. (2001). Principles of fluency instruction in reading: Relationships with established empirical outcomes. In M. Wolf (Ed.), *Dyslexia, fluency, and the brain* (pp. 333–355). Timonium, MD: York.

Turkelbaum, P.E., Gareau, I., Flowers, D.L., Zeffiro, T.A., & Eden, G.F. (2003). Development of neural mechanisms in reading. *Nature Neuroscience, 6,* 767–773.

von Bon, W.H.J., Boksebeld, L.M., Font Freide, T.A.M., & van den Hurk, A.J.M. (1991). A comparison of three methods of reading-while-listening. *Journal of Learning Disabilities, 24,* 471–476.

Vukovic, R.K., Wilson, A.M., & Nash, K.K. (2004). Naming speed deficits in adults with reading disabilities: A test of the double-deficit hypothesis. *Journal of Learning Disabilities, 37,* 440–450.

Wise, B.W. (1992). Whole words and decoding for short-term learning: Comparisons on a "talking-computer" system. *Journal of Experimental Child Psychology, 54,* 147–167.

Wolf, M., & Bowers, P.G. (1999). The double-deficit hypothesis for the developmental dyslexias. *Journal of Educational Psychology, 91,* 415–438.

Wolf, M., Bowers, P.G., & Biddle, K. (2000). Naming-speed processes, timing, and reading: A conceptual review. *Journal of Learning Disabilities, 33,* 387–407.

Wolf, M., Pfeil, C., Lotz, R., & Biddle, K. (1994). Towards a more universal understanding of the developmental dyslexias: The contribution of orthographic factors. In V.W. Berninger (Ed.), *The varieties of orthographic knowledge: I. Theoretical and developmental issues* (pp. 137–171). London: Kluwer Academic.

Chapter 4

Fluency: A Developmental and Language Perspective

John J. Pikulski

Fluency, which has been referred to as a "neglected" aspect of reading (National Institute of Child Health and Human Development [NICHD], 2000), currently is receiving substantial attention from both researchers and practitioners. One likely reason for the recently heightened attention to fluency in the reading community is that the *Report of the National Reading Panel* (NICHD, 2000) identifies fluency as one of only five critical components needed for the acquisition and advancement of reading skills. That report has been particularly influential because it is seen as the blueprint for the No Child Left Behind (NCLB; 2002) and Reading First legislation and funding.

Perhaps from an overly optimistic perspective, I would also speculate that another possible reason for the heightened interest in fluency is that the divisive issues surrounding the topics of phonological and phonemic awareness, and even more so, phonics, may finally be coming to a state of resolution for many teachers and other educational practitioners. The consistency of conclusions about the need for early, direct, systematic phonics instruction in major research syntheses—dating back to the classic, pioneering work of Jeanne Chall (1965) through the *Report of the National Reading Panel*—makes further debate of this topic seem tedious; however, some in the field continue to question the conclusions of these reports. Nevertheless, with diminished preoccupation with the topics of phonological and phonemic awareness and phonics, both researchers and practitioners may become free to focus on what I would consider the far more challenging, higher order topics of fluency, vocabulary, and comprehension. This trend could be very encouraging and potentially highly productive.

Defining Reading Fluency

Clearly defining fluency is critical to any discussion of it. In the past fluency received little attention because it was often viewed essentially

What Research Has to Say About Fluency Instruction, edited by S. Jay Samuels and Alan E. Farstrup. © 2006 by the International Reading Association.

as an oral-reading phenomenon (Chard, Pikulski, & McDonagh, 2006; Pikulski & Chard, 2005). In defining fluency as "the ability to read text quickly, accurately, and with proper expression" (p. 3-5), the *Report of the National Reading Panel* (NICHD, 2000) appears to support such a view. However, the importance of oral reading pales dramatically in comparison to that of silent-reading comprehension. Most readers, particularly mature readers, spend a minuscule amount of time engaged in oral reading as compared to silent reading. Although oral reading is not nearly as widely used or as utilitarian as silent reading, oral reading is vitally important because it is an observable reflection of decoding and fluency, which are nothing less than *essential* for reading comprehension. Reading comprehension requires translating or transcoding written symbols into their meaning. However, comprehension, particularly comprehension of more complex texts, requires that those printed symbols be translated rapidly and automatically.

A major advancement in the understanding of fluency took place with the seminal 1974 article by LaBerge and Samuels. These researchers argue that, as human beings, we can attend to only one thing at a time. We are able to do more than one thing at a time if we alternate our attention between two or more activities or if one of the activities is so well learned that it can be performed automatically. Reading successfully is a complex interaction of language, sensory perception, memory, and motivation.

To understand and illustrate the role of fluency, it helps to characterize the multiple interacting processes involved in reading as including *at least* two major activities: (1) word identification, or decoding, and (2) comprehension, or the construction of the meaning of text. This simple view of reading (Gough, Hoover, & Peterson, 1996) as involving decoding and comprehension is a fundamental part of the conceptualization of fluency reflected in this chapter. For reading to proceed effectively, a reader cannot focus attention on both activities. Constructing meaning involves making inferences, responding critically, and so on, and it *always* requires attention. The nonfluent reader can alternate attention between the two processes; however, this makes reading a laborious, often punishing process. If decoding words drains attention, little or no capacity is available for the attention-demanding process of comprehending. Therefore, automaticity of decoding—a critical component of fluency—is essential for high levels of reading achievement. Thus, the definition contained in the *Report of the National Reading Panel* does address important aspects of fluency, but from the position taken in this chapter, is incomplete.

A definition of fluency needs to encompass more than oral reading. In *The Literacy Dictionary: The Vocabulary of Reading and Writing*, Harris and Hodges (1995) define fluency as "freedom from word identification problems that might hinder comprehension" (p. 85). This definition enlarges our understanding of reading fluency to include comprehension. Samuels (2002), a pioneer in research and theory in reading fluency, cites the adoption of an expanded definition of fluency as a major force in elevating its importance in the field of reading.

A large-scale data analysis from the National Assessment of Educational Progress in Reading (Pinnell et al., 1995) clearly established the correlation between fluency and comprehension. In that study, 44% of the subjects were not fluent when reading grade-level appropriate materials; the study also showed a significant, positive relationship between oral-reading fluency and reading comprehension. However, the relationship between fluency and comprehension is fairly complex. This complexity is summed up well by Stecker, Roser, and Martinez (1998) in their review of fluency research: "The issue of whether fluency is an outgrowth or a contributor to comprehension is unresolved. There is empirical evidence to support both positions" (p. 300). However, in the end they conclude, "Fluency has been shown to have a 'reciprocal relationship' with comprehension, with each fostering the other" (p. 306). In her classic review of the research on beginning reading, Adams (1990) draws similar conclusions, which are reflected in much more recent works, such as that by Stahl and Heubach (2005).

This chapter builds on the evidence that a reciprocal relationship between reading fluency and comprehension exists; this reciprocal, interactive relationship between decoding and comprehension is so central to fluency that it is included as part of the definition of fluency proposed in this chapter. This chapter, however, also takes the position that adopting a *developmental perspective* will enhance our understanding of fluency, as well as its instruction and assessment, and that the foundations for fluency need to be built earlier than the stage of reading development where it is typically expected and assessed. The position of this chapter is that the foundations of fluency need to be considered as early as the preschool level if skills are to be maximally developed. Indeed, the central theme of this chapter is that the better, safer, more effective approach to fluency is to consider its roots, even though much can be accomplished through intervention strategies for students who are reading in a slow, laborious, nonfluent fashion. Fluency is equally or, perhaps more importantly, simultaneously grounded in the systematic development of decoding skills and language and vocabulary skills.

A comprehensive definition, then, would relate the centrality of fluency to reading comprehension and address its developmental nature. The definition of fluency proposed for this chapter is a modification of that offered by Pikulski and Chard (2005) and also incorporates elements of the definitions cited earlier from the *Report of the National Reading Panel* and *The Literacy Dictionary*:

> Reading fluency is a developmental process that refers to efficient, effective decoding skills that permit a reader to comprehend text. There is a reciprocal relationship between decoding and comprehension. Fluency is manifested in accurate, rapid, expressive oral reading and is applied during, and makes possible, silent-reading comprehension.

In this chapter, I will try to build the case that an exclusive focus on the development of decoding skills will produce a shallow root system that will not support the growth that the fluent processing of challenging, advanced, and content area texts require. The nature of this development, based on research and theory, is laid out in the pages that follow.

Theoretical Foundations for a Developmental Approach to Fluency

A reasonable way to think about a developmental approach to fluency is to think about stages that a reader goes through to become fluent and what it takes to extend and refine the initial emergence of fluency. Stage theories of reading development have existed for some time. The theories of Chall (1983) and Ehri (1995, 1998) have received particularly wide attention in the area of reading. In a recent publication, Stahl and Heubach (2005) describe how the six stages of Chall's theory are helpful for understanding the way in which fluency develops over time, and they explore the implications of that theory for understanding fluency, thus supporting the conceptualizing of fluency as a developmental process. However, Stahl and Heubach acknowledge that Chall's theory is a "global" conceptualization that extends to very high levels of comprehension involving critical evaluations and responses to text materials that seem beyond the construct of fluency (see Samuels, this volume). Ehri's theory of stages of reading development focuses much more on the decoding aspects, recognizes and acknowledges the important role of language and construction of meaning, and seems more directly related to fluency and its development. Her theory offers a coherent view of much of the research on the developmental nature of fluency and a framework for instruction designed to promote and improve fluency. Much of the remainder of this chapter will be devoted to summarizing, in some detail, the stages of development that she has identified, because her theoretical formulations are the foundation for much of the content of this chapter. Understanding her developmental stages can serve as a valuable guide to understanding the behaviors of students as they approach the development of fluency and, consequently, for providing interventions that will facilitate that development.

Ehri distinguishes four stages of reading development: (1) pre-alphabetic, (2) partial alphabetic, (3) fully alphabetic, and (4) consolidated alphabetic. Readers at the **pre-alphabetic stage** have no appreciation of the alphabetic principle—the idea that in languages such as English a systematic relationship exists between the limited number of sounds of the language and the graphic forms (letters) of the language. At the pre-alphabetic stage, children attempt to translate the unfamiliar visual forms of print into familiar oral language through visual clues in the print. Children might remember the word *monkey* by associating the descending shape of the last letter with a monkey's tail. Obviously, this approach is not productive and quickly leads to confusion because *my*, *pony*, and many, many other words would also be read as *monkey*.

At the **partial alphabetic stage**, readers have learned that letters and sounds are related, developed an understanding of the alphabetic principle, and begun to use that insight. However, they are not able to deal with the full complexity of the sounds in words, and so they aren't able to make a complete use of the letter–sound relationships. Therefore, children focus on the most vibrant and salient parts of a word and consequently use initial and, later, final letters as the clues to a printed word's pronunciation. If readers at this stage learn that the letter sequence *g-e-t* is *get*, they may focus just on the *g* and the sound it represents to identify the word. However, using this strategy of focusing on the first letter, the letter sequences *game*, *gem*, *give*, *girl*, and *gorilla* might also be identified as *get*. While children at this stage of development will make errors in identifying words, they can make progress toward becoming fluent because they have developed the insight that the letters of a word are clues to the sounds of the word, and they have a tendency to increase the number of graphic features that they process as their familiarity and phonemic-awareness skills advance.

Thus, as children become more familiar with letters and sounds, they move into the **fully alphabetic stage**. Now, even though they may never have seen a word in print before, if they know the sounds commonly associated with the letters (e.g., *b-u-g*), they can think about the sounds for each of the letters and blend them together to arrive at the pronunciation of the word. As a result of encountering the printed word *bug* several times, as few as four according to a widely cited study (Reitsma, 1983), they come to accurately, instantly identify the word *bug* without attending to the individual letters, sounds, or letter–sound associations. Ehri (1998) describes this more mature, more skilled reading in the following way:

> Most of the words are known by sight. Sight-reading is a fast-acting process. The term *sight* indicates that sight of the word activates that word in memory including information about its spelling, pronunciation, typical role in sentences, and meaning. (pp. 11–12)

This instant, accurate, and automatic access to all these dimensions of a printed word is the needed fluency that will allow readers to focus their attention on comprehension rather than on decoding. According to Ehri (1995, 1998), careful processing of print in the fully alphabetic stage leads to this rapid, instant recognition. Partial alphabetic readers store incomplete representations of words and, therefore, confuse similar words such as *were, where, wire,* and *wore*. However, once the word form is fully processed, with repeated encounters of the word, it is recognized instantly and accurately.

Readers who recognize whole words instantly have reached the **consolidated alphabetic stage**. This stage represents the ability to recognize words rapidly and accurately, characteristics most closely associated with fluency. Readers who have reached this stage also develop another valuable, attention-saving, effective decoding skill. In addition to storing words as units, repeated encounters with words allow a reader to store letter patterns across different words. A multiletter sequence (e.g., *-ent*) will be stored as a unit as a result of reading the words *went, sent,* and *bent*. Upon encountering the word *dent* for the first time, a consolidated alphabetic reader would need to connect only two units—*d* and *-ent*—rather than the four units that the fully alphabetic reader would need to combine. Although this approach of using "chunks" in order to read a word is faster than blending the individual phonemes, it is not as fast and efficient as sight recognition of the word. Readers who have reached the consolidated stage of reading development are in a good position to progress toward increasingly efficient fluency; however, in addition to these advanced word-identification skills, they also need to increase their language vocabulary development in order to reach advanced levels of fluent reading. For example, the words *claustrophobia* and *onychophagia* are both very low-frequency words in their printed forms; *claustrophobia*, however, is much more common in oral language. In many demonstrations with teachers and other educators, I repeatedly find that though both of these words are low-frequency words in print, *claustrophobia* is consistently identified far more fluently than *onychophagia*. Although many readers have encountered *claustrophobia* very infrequently in print and *onychophagia* even less frequently, if ever, another major difference is that many adult readers have heard and know the meaning of *claustrophobia*. An interactive model of reading and Ehri's stage theory predicts that when the brain is processing the perceived visual image of a word, the recognition of that image will be greatly facilitated and speeded up if it connects with meaning for a word stored in the reader's mental lexicon.

This need to connect a word to a meaning for recognition to occur led Pikulski and Chard (2005) to suggest that thinking of fluency both as *basic* and *advanced* is helpful. In the early grades, perhaps through grades 3 and 4 for most readers, the preponderance of the words that children are meeting in their reading are words for which they know the meaning. As readers encounter more advanced texts, particularly more complex, informational texts, these authors suggested, a very critical dimension of fluency will be the extent of the readers' language and vocabulary skills.

According to this position, a heavy emphasis on phonological awareness, phonics, and related decoding skills may very well allow for the development of basic fluency skills; however, if there has not been a simultaneous emphasis on the development of vocabulary and language, children may falter in their reading progress after making initially good progress. The lack of such simultaneous emphases may very well be the reason behind the well-documented "fourth-grade slump" (Chall & Jacobs, 1983).

A consideration of Ehri's (1995) stage theory along with the recognition of the central role that vocabulary and language development play in achieving fluency have important implications for reading instruction at all grade levels. The next section of the chapter attempts to draw some of these implications and to offer suggestions for teaching and developing fluency.

Instructional Implications of a Developmental Approach to Fluency

Until fairly recently, many, though certainly not all, educators often appeared to take a rather simplistic approach to developing fluency that is summed up in the admonition: "Read, read, read." The expectation was that if students read more, they would achieve fluency. However, at least some students will need expert instruction and teacher guidance to progress efficiently through the stages of reading development. Readers need all the foundation skills necessary for passing from the pre-alphabetic into the partial and fully alphabetic stages of development. As children enter into the fully alphabetic stage, but not before, they are in a position to do wide reading, which, indeed, has been shown to contribute to fluency and reading achievement (Anderson, Hiebert, Scott, & Wilkerson, 1985; Stanovich, 1986). As suggested previously in this chapter, I think it is efficient and instructive to begin with a simple view of reading and to consider both the decoding and language skills needed to develop fluency.

Decoding Skills Needed for Fluency

Foundations for fluency. Ehri lists three prerequisite skill areas as foundations for fluency: (1) letter familiarity; (2) phonemic awareness—that is, becoming consciously aware of the sounds that make up oral language; and (3) phonics—that is, the knowledge of how graphemes, printed letters, or letter combinations typically represent phonemes, the sounds of the language, in words. These are the primary skills required to move students from the pre-alphabetic stage of development. From a developmental perspective, these skills will have the greatest influence on reading achievement, including fluency, at the earliest stages of learning to read. The graphophonic skills allow beginning readers to capitalize on the oral-language skills they have been developing to engage in beginning reading. The importance of these three prerequisite skill areas to fluency is fully documented in numerous research reports (e.g., Adams, 1990; NICHD, 2000).

To move from the pre-alphabetic stage to the partial and fully alphabetic stages, students need to grasp the alphabetic principle and to efficiently apply information about the relationship between the letters and sounds to recognize words. This clearly requires a high level of familiarity with letter forms as well as the ability to segment and blend phonemes. Strickland and Schickendanz (2004) offer practical, research-based approaches to developing graphophonic skills, including letter familiarity, in emergent readers. Instruction in the area of phonological awareness has been addressed widely. For example, Adams, Foorman, Lundberg, and Beeler (1998) offer a comprehensive approach to dealing with phonological awareness from kindergarten through first grade that presents many games and activities that begin with easier rhyming actives and build to blending, segmenting, and manipulating of phonemes. O'Connor, Notari-Syverson, and Vadasy (1998) offer a similar range of activities that are most developmentally appropriate for kindergarten but are easily adapted for use beyond that level for students who are experiencing difficulty.

High-frequency vocabulary. High-frequency words are those words that appear over and over again in our language, such as *the, of, and, at,* and *to.* A substantial number of these words (e.g., *the, of, to*) do not lend themselves to simply blending the most commonly associated sounds for each of the letters, as a fully alphabetic reader might try to do. Therefore, if developing readers cannot instantly identify these words, they are unlikely to become fluent because of the widespread presence of these words.

One approach to building fluent recognition of high-frequency vocabulary, exceedingly popular with primary-grade teachers, is the use of word walls where high-frequency vocabulary is posted and practiced (P.M. Cunningham, 2000). Cunningham also offers a variety of other approaches to bring high-frequency words to fluency, such as having students manipulate letter cards to form words and to make minimal changes to create new words, an activity she calls "making words." Bear, Invernizzi, Templeton, and Johnston (1996) also offer many useful, practical suggestions for reinforcing student familiarity with word forms, including many "word sort" activities that involve sorting word cards according to a variety of letter, sound, and conceptual criteria. They also provide a clear rationale and many teaching suggestions for using spelling to reinforce and extend the fluent recognition of words.

Ehri's theory and research directly offer important, practical teaching suggestions that will allow a more efficient recognition of these words and progress toward the development of fluency. High-frequency words often have been seen as a serious challenge because, they are, in the jargon of reading instruction, "phonically irregular." While acknowledging the phonic irregularities of high-frequency words, Ehri suggests that they contain many letter–sound regularities and that these regularities are the best mnemonics for developing accurate, instant recognition. For example, while the word *have* does not follow the generalization about the effect of a final *e* on a preceding vowel sound, the *h*, *v*, and *e* all behave as they should, and the *a* does represent a sound that it often represents. Ehri suggests that, in our reading instruction, we should point out the regular elements of "irregular" words in order to help children gain instant recognition of them. This practice is rarely mentioned by experts or used by teachers, but it might play a very important role in avoiding difficulty with such words and thus promoting the development of fluency.

Word parts and spelling patterns. Word parts and spelling patterns (also called rimes and phonograms) are combinations of letters such as *at*, *ell*, *ick*, and *op* that are found as units in many words that appear in beginning reading texts. Here again, P.M. Cunningham (2000) and Bear et al. (1996) are among the many resources that offer practical teaching suggestions, including a list of the most common word parts found in beginning reading materials.

Introducing students to multiple-letter units clearly moves students from the fully alphabetic to the consolidated alphabetic stage. However, Ehri's research and theory offer an important instructional suggestion— that students should first be introduced to and made cognizant of the individual letters and sounds that constitute the rime (a fully alphabetic approach) in order to better recall and identify the unit that they constitute (a consolidated alphabetic approach). For example, before introducing young children to the rime *at*, which in effect requires a consolidated alphabetic response, they should first be taught the short /a/ sound associated with the letter *a* and the sound associated with the letter *t*, and shown how blending them, a fully alphabetic response, results in the unit *at*. In addition to following a developmental sequence that will probably result in more efficient learning, the child has been taught one of the two letter–sound associations he or she will need for four other rimes—*an*, *ap*, *ack*, and *ash*—which are among a short list of only 37 rimes whose recognition will aid in the identification of some 500 words commonly found in beginning reading materials (Wylie & Durrell, 1970).

Decoding strategies. As suggested in the preceding discussion, words can be recognized or identified in print in several different ways: instantly as units; through recognition of and blending of phonic elements; through the context in which they appear, including language or sentence context and picture clues; and by checking the phonetic respellings of a dictionary or glossary. Ehri's theory is clear: The best way to recognize words is through instant recognition that drains no attention. This feature is critical for fluent reading to occur. All other approaches require attention. However, when a word is not instantly recognized, it is useful for readers to be strategic.

Ehri's theory suggests a strategic approach to dealing with words that are not instantly recognized. In kindergarten and the beginning of first grade, where the instructional emphasis for most young readers is upon moving them from the partial to the fully alphabetic stages of reading, their attention needs to be focused on the graphophonic characteristics of the word and on attending to more and more details of that word. They need to be encouraged to think about the letter–sound associations they have learned and are learning and to blend the sounds together to form meaningful words. Because some words are not completely phonically regular, students should then be encouraged to ask themselves if their use of phonics results in the identification of a word that makes sense—that it is a word they have heard before and that fits the context of what they are reading. Teachers working with end-of-kindergarten and with most beginning first-grade students can use the following strategy of Ehri's to help move students into the fully alphabetic stage:

1. Look at the letters from left to right.
2. As you look at the letters, think about the sounds for the letters.
3. Blend the sounds together to read the word.
4. Ask yourself: Is this a word I know? Does it make sense in what I am reading?
5. If it isn't a word I know or if it doesn't make sense, what other word is close to these sounds?

As children begin to move from the fully alphabetic to the consolidated alphabetic stage of development, in addition to using phonic elements, they should also be encouraged to look for word parts (chunks) and spelling patterns that they know, such as phonograms. The order of phonics and word parts *followed by* use of context appears to be the order that will be most effective for correctly and fluently identifying the word.

Use of context as the primary approach to identifying words has serious limitations. First, if the context is highly predictive of a word, it is likely that students will not pay attention to the graphic information of the word. Careful processing of the printed form is what eventually enables a reader to recognize that word instantly. Using a very heavy, artificial context to allow word identification is a major limitation of predictable texts. Second, context rarely leads to the correct identification of a specific word in naturally occurring text, particularly informational text. Ehri reviews research that suggests that the words in a text that carry the most meaning can be correctly identified by context only about 10% of the time. However, context and the other approaches to decoding words do play an important role in decoding—that of confirming the identification of words. As Ehri (1998) states,

> As each sight word is fixated, its meaning and pronunciation are triggered in memory quickly and automatically. However, the other word reading processes do not lie dormant; their contribution is not to identify words in text but to *confirm* the identity already determined. Knowledge of the graphophonic system confirms that the word's pronunciation fits the spelling on the page. Knowledge of syntax confirms that the word fits into the structure of the sentence. World knowledge and text memory confirm that the word's meaning is consistent with the text's meaning up to that point. (p. 11)

Language Skills Needed for Fluency

In addition to the graphophonic skills, Ehri's theory requires a foundation in language skills so that students are familiar with the syntax or grammatical function of the words and phrases they are reading and with their meanings. Developing the oral-language and vocabulary skills of children, particularly those who are learning English as a second language or those who spent their preschool years in language-restricted environments, is one of the greatest challenges facing us as educators. Many excellent, recently published resources exist for meeting this challenge. For example, Johnson (2001) offers excellent research insights into the way vocabulary develops and suggests many ways of building these skills through conversations and discussions. He offers detailed suggestions for using writing as a major vehicle for vocabulary expansion. Throughout the book he offers teachers resources for helping students to develop sensitivity to and interest in words, as well as devoting two full chapters to this aspect of vocabulary development. Beck, McKeown, and Kucan (2002) take the position that instruction must be *rich* and *robust* if word meanings are to be learned. They offer a wide range of teaching suggestions that span kindergarten through high school for helping students to carefully process word meanings and to relate the new words to their experiences in a meaningful way. They also present a very helpful way of thinking about various tiers of words to help teachers decide whether a word is worth spending the sizeable amount of classroom time that robust vocabulary instruction requires. Biemiller (1999) takes the position that whenever a group of vocabulary words are introduced, different children are going to learn different words from the group presented, and that any one child is likely to learn only a quarter to a third of the words. He therefore recommends introducing a larger number of words and offers helpful suggestions for teaching during both reading and listening activities. In a very recent publication, Graves (2006) outlines, in sufficient detail to be helpful to teachers, a comprehensive, research-based approach to vocabulary that focuses on promoting incidental learning of vocabulary, teaching individual words, teaching word-learning strategies, and making students more "word conscious."

Ehri shows that progress in reading beyond the beginning stages is dependent on oral-language development, pointing out that reading words, particularly reading them fluently, is dependent on familiarity with them in their oral form. If the syntactic and meaning aspects of the word are to be activated, they must be part of what the reader knows through oral-language development. For the word-recognition process as proposed in Ehri's theory to be complete, it must connect with meaning that has been developed as another aspect of language development. It takes mature readers much longer to arrive at a pronunciation of a word that both appears very infrequently in print and that is an unknown in meaning than a word, such as *zigzags*, that does appear very rarely in print (Carroll, Davies, & Richman, 1971) but is likely to be a word whose meaning is familiar. Unless a printed word can connect with both the phonological memory for the word and also with the syntactical and meaning aspects of the word, it cannot be fluently decoded or read. Unfortunately, many surface discussions of fluency fail to make the point that fluency is dependent on the reader's vocabulary as well as on his or her decoding skills.

This chapter, with its focus on fluency, does not begin to comprehensively address the area of language development, which is receiving what may be unprecedented attention by the reading community; the topic is just too broad and too complex. However, it does seem important, even here, to build a link between vocabulary instruction and the responsibility to build content knowledge as part of quality reading instruction. Perhaps it is another manifestation of a reduced need to dwell on phonemic awareness and phonics, but the need to integrate content areas into the teaching of reading seems, finally, to be receiving much-needed attention. Students' vocabularies, comprising the words for which students know the meaning, consist of labels for the things they know. It seems only reasonable that if we want students to expand their vocabularies, we need to help them to expand the amount they know. Hirsch (e.g., 2003) has long championed this position. More recently Moss (2005) has made a convincing case for the need to significantly improve the extent to which content area disciplines such as science, social studies, art, music, and so on are part of literacy instruction beginning in the elementary grades. Her analysis of the content of the journal *The Reading Teacher* also offers evidence that this need is being addressed more now than it had been in the past. The position taken in this chapter is that in order for students to develop high levels of *advanced* literacy, they will need to develop vocabulary and content knowledge that are highly related.

Developmental Fluency Through the Grades

The Importance of Preschool in Developing Fluency

From a developmental perspective, the foundations for fluency begin at birth. Thus, to overemphasize the importance of home influences on reading and general academic achievement, as well as overall success in life (Hart & Risley, 1985, 1989), would be difficult. The work of Hart and Risley is particularly impressive in documenting the development of language skills that ultimately and powerfully influence fluency. However, the focus of this chapter is on that which can be done in a school setting to build eventual fluency, so the emphasis of my developmental perspective begins with preschool.

Most children at the pre-K level can also be expected to be at the pre-alphabetic stage of development. Although most pre-K children will not be expected to read, an emerging literacy point of view, which I see as highly related to a developmental approach to fluency, suggests that there are critically important areas to develop. The National

Research Council (NRC) Committee on Preventing Reading Difficulties in Young Children (Snow, Burns, & Griffin, 1998) clearly states the importance of early literacy development in children:

> We recognize that reading related development can start in infancy and with toddlers. Many young children are surrounded by written language products and are exposed to the importance and functions of reading in society. A child's reading-related development is interwoven and continuous with development that will lead to expertise in other spheres of life. (p. 42)

The NRC Committee on Early Childhood Pedagogy (Bowman, Donovan, & Burns, 2000) likewise defines emerging literacy as follows:

> The idea that the acquisition of literary is best conceptualized as a developmental continuum with its origin early in the life of a child, rather than an all-or-none phenomenon that begins when children start school...suggesting that there is no clear demarcation between reading and prereading.... Emergent literacy includes the skills, knowledge and attitudes that are precursors to conventional forms of reading and writing. (p. 186)

One area that is vital to develop during this pre-alphabetic stage of development is **motivation**, a desire to read as well as positive attitudes toward books and reading. Evidence will be cited later that the more students read, the more likely they are to become fluent. Motivation to read is obviously needed for wide reading to take place. Certainly, opportunities abound at these very influential, formative pre-K years to begin developing motivation for reading.

A second vital area to develop at the pre-K level is an understanding of the **alphabetic principle**, the idea that in an alphabetic language such as English an orderly relationship exists between written symbols, letters, and the sounds that make up the language. This recognition of the link between letters and sounds of a language is necessary for movement from the pre- to partial alphabetic stage of development. However, developing an understanding of the alphabetic principle requires at least some understanding of what a letter is and what a sound is. This means that pre-K children should receive some instruction to make them familiar with letters and to increase their phonological awareness.

A third area vitally important for moving toward fluency is the extraordinarily broad area of **language and vocabulary development**.

Most pre-K children will have oral-language skills that are more advanced than the letter familiarity and phonological areas. Nevertheless, children at this level must expand in their language development, or they will have later difficulties with more advanced fluency, which is dependent on well-developed language and vocabulary skills.

The Role of Kindergarten and First Grade in Building Fluency

In the last decade, a clear shift in the role of kindergarten in the learning-to-read process has occurred. Earlier, the purpose of kindergartens focused on building social skills. The NRC (Snow et al., 1998) is clear about the importance of kindergarten for learning to read:

> Preparing children to read is the top priority of the kindergarten teacher's agenda. (p. 179)

> A strong message of this report is that a priority mission of every school district in the United States should be to provide good kindergarten literacy preparation to all children. (p. 195)

Children who have had rich home experiences or who have attended effective pre-K programs will probably enter kindergarten functioning at the partial alphabetic stage of reading development. Other kindergarten children, however, will probably still be pre-alphabetic. To move kindergarten children closer to becoming fluent, teachers should direct their efforts to move those children who are still pre-alphabetic to being partial alphabetic; some children can be expected to make progress toward becoming fully alphabetic.

Certainly at kindergarten, as at all levels, motivation for reading and language and vocabulary development should be an integral part of a comprehensive reading program. Most kindergarteners will not make progress toward fluency unless they increase their letter familiarity and phonological skills and begin to merge these two areas into the practical skill of phonics. This skill will allow developing readers to use what they know about the sounds that letters represent to independently decode words.

First and Second Grade: The Ungluing From Print

Chall (1983) uses the colorful yet insightfully descriptive phrase "ungluing from print" to describe that stage of development when children achieve some modicum of fluency. In Ehri's theory, this stage represents movement from the effective but laborious process of figuring out the pronunciation of newly encountered words in print to recognizing larger "chunks" of letters and whole words at sight. In first and second grade children should be moving from the fully to the consolidated alphabetic stages of development. Phonics instruction should be, for the most part, completed during these years; it is also a time when instruction in rimes and phonograms will encourage the processing of larger "chunks" of print. Systematic introduction of high-frequency words will allow children to rapidly recognize at sight those words that appear over and over in written language, thus promoting rapid recognition of words, or fluency. As these fundamental pieces of word identification develop, the young reader can effectively practice the reading of connected texts, which will strengthen the ability to rapidly and accurately recognize words. Throughout these grade levels, as at all stages of development, the teacher needs to maintain a strong emphasis on motivation and language and vocabulary development.

Third Grade and Beyond: Developing Advanced Fluency

If children are progressing well, by the end of second grade they will have developed the ability to quickly, accurately, in other words, fluently, recognize those words that occur over and over in our language—the high-frequency words, as well as many other words that are part of common language. Pikulski and Chard (2005) refer to this ability as "basic fluency." The graphophonic aspects of learning to read will have, for the most part, been developed. Words that will require the more time-and-attention draining process of sequentially decoding words, as is characteristic of the fully alphabetic stage of development, will be those words that students have never seen before in print and to which they cannot attach meaning. Instruction with larger units of print—morphological units such as prefixes, suffixes, and root words—is appropriate to further enhance the ability to recognize words fluently, but few letter–sound associations will need to be taught. It is the contention of this chapter that students who have reached this stage of development will profit most in fluency development from two major instructional activities: wide independent reading and building vocabulary and background knowledge.

Wide independent reading. The beneficial effects of wide reading appear to have been somewhat called into question by the *Report of the*

National Reading Panel (NICHD, 2000), which reached the following conclusion: "Based on the existing evidence, the NRP can only indicate that while encouraging students to read might be beneficial, research has not yet demonstrated this in a clear and convincing manner" (p. 3). It is important to keep in mind that the NRP used restrictive criteria for what they included as "research" and that it also clearly held out the possibility of beneficial effects for wide reading.

Other highly respected research syntheses have been far less restrained about the salutary effects of wide reading. In *Becoming a Nation of Readers,* Anderson and colleagues (1985) conclude,

> Research suggests that the amount of independent, silent reading that children do in school is significantly related to gains in reading achievement... Research also shows that the amount of reading students do out of school is consistently related to gains in reading achievement. (pp. 76–77)

In her critical review of beginning reading research, Adams (1990) concludes, "Children should be given as much opportunity and encouragement as possible to practice their reading. Beyond the basics, children's reading facility, as well as their vocabulary and conceptual growth, depends strongly on the amount of text they read" (p. 127).

Keith Stanovich and his colleagues (A.E. Cunningham & Stanovich, 1998; Nathan & Stanovich, 1991; Stanovich, 1986) present impressive research results and theoretical arguments for the value of wide reading. Their evidence and rationale, however, are that the positive relationship between reading achievement and wide reading may not be affected exclusively through the development of fluency but through the development of language and cognitive abilities as well.

Although a convincing body of *experimental* evidence may be lacking to support the efficacy of wide reading in promoting fluency and higher levels of reading achievement, other forms of evidence and scholarly reviews provide a sufficient basis for strongly advocating and recommending its promotion.

Building vocabulary and background knowledge. Previously in this chapter, I have held that a major consideration in fluent word recognition is whether that word is one the reader has heard before and for which she or he has some meaning. To build excellent, advanced fluency and improve overall reading achievement, we as teachers may find the greatest challenge facing us to be building vocabulary. Although many children do find the task of building graphophonic skills a challenging one, it is a relatively defined, limited domain of learning. An imperfect relationship between letters and sounds exists in English, but compensating for that relationship is a systematic, generally predictable pattern of the 40 to 44 sounds of American English mapped onto the 26 letters of the alphabet or some combination of them. Defining the domain of vocabulary building is much more difficult. One frequently offered estimate (e.g., Snow et al., 1998) is that during the elementary grades children need to add somewhere between 2,500 and 3,000 words to their vocabularies every year. The job of acquiring vocabulary appears dramatically more challenging than that of learning letter–sound associations. For this reason, this chapter maintains that vocabulary development is a vital part of reading instruction throughout the grades in developing advanced fluency. Waiting to emphasize vocabulary development until third grade will place serious limits on developing that fluency, as well as on developing high levels of reading achievement.

Although vocabulary and content knowledge are not exactly the same thing, few would deny that the two are highly related. Vocabulary is the way of naming the things we know about. Snow and colleagues (1998) point out, "[P]reviously 'unimportant' reading difficulties may appear for the first time in fourth grade when children are dealing more frequently, deeply, and widely with nonfiction materials in a variety of school subjects" (p. 79). The importance of background knowledge for reading comprehension is widely acknowledged and documented, but it also seems quite possible that the lack of familiarity with the vocabulary and a concomitant lack of background knowledge, particularly in content areas, also results in nonfluent reading. These factors may also play a role in the overall poor achievement of some students who perform relatively well in reading in the early grades and then encounter difficulty as they encounter the more challenging vocabulary and content of the middle and later grades.

Intervention for Developing Fluency in Nonfluent Students

In an ideal educational world, all students would receive sound, research-based, developmentally appropriate instruction in reading that would allow almost all of them to achieve fluency by the end of the primary grades. Clearly, it is not an ideal educational world. Not all children receive excellent reading instruction; likewise, a very small proportion of children who do receive excellent instruction still encounter difficulties in becoming fluent in reading. Therefore, teachers of second grade and beyond should be equipped to identify students who are lagging behind in fluency and to provide intervention instruction aimed at moving those students ahead. While a number of approaches may be suitable, there is a great deal of research support for recommending the use of repeated-reading procedures, a variety of procedures wherein students reread the same texts multiple times, often with initial support for and modeling of fluent reading.

The *Report of the National Reading Panel* (NICHD, 2000) is unequivocal in its support of repeated-reading procedures. The report references a range of procedures in sufficient detail to allow teachers to employ them with students who need extra support in developing fluency. These procedures include those described as repeated reading (Samuels, 1979), neurological impress (Heckelman, 1969), radio reading (Greene, 1979), paired reading (Topping, 1987), "and a variety of similar techniques" (p. 3-1). A review of these approaches suggests substantial differences in the procedures used and the amount of teacher guidance offered (Chard, Vaughn, & Tyler, 2002; Kuhn & Stahl, 2000). However, as noted, the panel concluded that all appeared to have merit.

In spite of the convincing evidence for the effectiveness of repeated-reading procedures for students who are not progressing well in reading, repeated readings of the same texts may not be as necessary for more able readers. Increasing the amount of reading these able readers do may be equally or more beneficial (Mathes & Fuchs, 1993). Moreover, if students are making adequate progress with fluency, wide reading rather than repeated readings may lead to greater improvements in vocabulary and comprehension. However, for less able readers experiencing particular difficulties with fluency, repeated readings remain an important approach to building fluency.

The Assessment of Fluency: Implications of a Developmental Approach

An extensive discussion of the assessment of fluency is beyond the scope of this chapter. However, if fluency is seen as developmental and rooted in the very earliest stages of reading and literacy instruction, then assessment should also be early and should continue through the advanced grades. The stage theory of Linnea Ehri outlined in this chapter offers suggestions for reasonable expectations at the various grades. The developmental theory and the definition of fluency proposed also strongly suggest that though the assessment of oral reading will offer important insights into a child's fluency development, oral-reading fluency without reading comprehension is of limited value; therefore, oral reading should always be assessed within the context of comprehension when a full understanding of fluency is the goal.

Conclusions

Although the construct of fluency may have been neglected in the past, it is receiving much-deserved attention presently. A strong research and theoretical base indicates that fluency is absolutely necessary for high levels of achievement, even though fluency in and of itself is not sufficient to ensure that achievement. If a reader has not developed fluency, the process of decoding words drains attention, and insufficient attention is available for constructing the meaning of texts; however, fluency also depends upon and typically reflects comprehension.

Fluency builds on a foundation of oral-language skills, phonemic awareness, familiarity with letter forms, and efficient decoding skills. Ehri's description of the stages of word recognition explains how readers come to recognize words by sight through carefully processing print.

Substantial research has also been conducted on how best to develop fluency for students who do not yet have it. In spite of the dearth of experimental research studies on developing fluency through increasing the amount of independent reading in which students engage, substantial correlational evidence shows a clear relationship between the amount students read, their reading fluency, and their reading comprehension. However, students who are nonachieving in reading are not in a position to engage in wide reading, and they may need more guidance and support in order to develop fluency. Research shows that a variety of procedures based on repeated readings can help readers to improve their fluency.

Little research is available to guide the assessment of fluency. Although the issues of adequate fluency rates at various grade levels and of judging the quality of oral reading need more research, good agreement currently exists about including measures of oral-reading accuracy, rate of oral reading, and quality of oral reading in the comprehensive assessment of fluency. Consensus is growing for assessing these dimensions of fluency within the context of reading comprehension. Fluency without accompanying high levels of reading comprehension is of very limited value.

Questions for Discussion

1. Linnea Ehri has developed a widely recognized "stage theory" of reading development that has direct implications for teaching and developing fluency. Given the grade level you teach, what does her theory suggest to you about the instructional approaches you might use for developing fluency? What does it suggest for helping you to make diagnostic observations about the progress your students are making in developing fluency?

2. As the principal of an elementary school concerned about the development of fluency, what does a developmental approach to fluency suggest to you that you should be looking for as you observe the reading instruction of the teachers of your school at the various grade levels?

3. Language and vocabulary development have long been seen as critical to reading comprehension but have not been strongly emphasized in most discussions of reading fluency. What role do language and vocabulary skills play in fluency development? Can you think of any ways in which fluency and language development are mutually reinforcing?

REFERENCES

Adams, M.J. (1990). *Beginning to read: Thinking and learning about print.* Cambridge, MA: MIT Press.

Adams, M.J., Foorman, B.R., Lundberg, I., & Beeler, T. (1998). *Phonemic awareness in young children.* Baltimore: Paul H. Brookes.

Anderson, R.C., Hiebert, E.H., Scott, J.A., & Wilkerson, I.A. (1985). *Becoming a nation of readers: The report of the Commission on Reading.* Washington, DC: National Institute on Education.

Bear, D.R., Invernizzi, M., Templeton, S., & Johnston, F. (1996). *Words their way.* Columbus, OH: Merrill.

Beck, I.L., McKeown, M.G., & Kucan, L. (2002). *Bringing words to life.* New York: Guilford.

Biemiller, A. (1999). *Language and learning success.* Cambridge, MA: Brookline Books.

Bowman, B.T., Donovan, M.S., & Burns, M.S. (Eds.). (2000). *Eager to learn: Educating our preschoolers.* Washington, DC: National Academy Press.

Carroll, J.B., Davies, P., & Richman, B. (1971). *The American Heritage word frequency book.* New York: Houghton Mifflin.

Chall, J.S. (1965). *Learning to read: The great debate.* New York: McGraw-Hill.

Chall, J.S. (1983). *Stages of reading development.* New York: McGraw-Hill.

Chall, J.S., & Jacobs, V.A. (1983). Writing and reading in the elementary grades: Developmental trends among low-SES children. *Language Arts, 60,* 617–626.

Chard, D.J., Pikulski, J.J., & McDonagh, S.H. (2006). Fluency: The link between decoding and comprehension for struggling readers. In T. Rasinski, C. Blachowicz, & K. Lems (Eds.), *Fluency instruction: Research-based best practices* (pp. 39–61). New York: Guilford.

Chard, D.J., Vaughn, S., & Tyler, B.J. (2002). A synthesis of research on effective interventions for building fluency with elementary students with learning disabilities. *Journal of Learning Disabilities, 35,* 386–406.

Cunningham, A.E., & Stanovich, K.E. (1998, Spring/Summer). What reading does for the mind. *American Educator, 22*(1&2), 8–15.

Cunningham, P.M. (2000). *Phonics they use.* New York: Longman.

Ehri, L.C. (1995). Stages of development in learning to read words by sight. *Journal of Research in Reading, 18,* 116–125.

Ehri, L.C. (1998). Grapheme-phoneme knowledge is essential for learning to read words in English. In J.L. Metsala & L.C. Ehri (Eds.), *Word recognition in beginning literacy* (pp. 3–40). Mahwah, NJ: Erlbaum.

Gough, P.B., Hoover, W.A., & Peterson, C.L. (1996). Some observations on a simple view of reading. In C. Cornoldi & J. Oakhill (Eds.) *Reading comprehension difficulties* (pp. 1–13). Mahwah, NJ: Erlbaum.

Graves, M.F. (2006). *The vocabulary book: Learning and instruction.* New York: Teachers College Press; Newark, DE: International Reading Association; Urbana, IL: National Council of Teachers of English.

Greene, F.P. (1979). Radio reading. In C. Pennock (Ed.), *Reading comprehension at four linguistic levels* (pp. 104–107). Newark, DE: International Reading Association.

Harris, T.L., & Hodges, R.E. (1995). *The literacy dictionary: The vocabulary of reading and writing.* Newark, DE: International Reading Association.

Hart, B., & Risley, T.R. (1985). *Meaningful differences in the everyday experiences of young American children.* Baltimore: Paul H. Brookes.

Hart, B., & Risley, T.R. (1989). *The social world of children learning to talk.* Baltimore: Paul H. Brookes.

Heckelman, R.G. (1969). A neurological-impress method of remedial-reading instruction. *Academic Therapy, 4,* 277–282.

Hirsch, E.D. (2003). Reading comprehension requires knowledge of words and of the world. *American Educator, 27,* 10–29, 44–45.

Johnson, D.D. (2001). *Vocabulary in the elementary and middle school.* Boston: Allyn & Bacon.

Kuhn, M.R., & Stahl, S.A. (2000). *Fluency: A review of developmental and remedial practices.* Ann Arbor, MI: Center for the Improvement of Early Reading Achievement.

LaBerge, D., & Samuels, S.J. (1974). Towards a theory of automatic information processing in reading. *Cognitive Psychology, 6,* 293–323.

Mathes, P.G., & Fuchs, L.S. (1993). Peer-mediated reading instruction in special education resource rooms. *Learning Disabilities Research & Practice, 8,* 233–243.

Moss, B. (2005). Making a case and a place for effective content area literacy instruction in the elementary grades. *The Reading Teacher, 59*, 46–55.

Nathan, R.G., & Stanovich, K.E. (1991). The causes and consequences of differences in reading fluency. *Theory Into Practice, 30*, 3, 176–184.

National Institute of Child Health and Human Development (NICHD). (2000). *Report of the National Reading Panel. Teaching children to read: An evidence-based assessment of the scientific research literature on reading and its implications for reading instruction* (NIH Publication No. 00-4769). Washington, DC: U.S. Government Printing Office.

No Child Left Behind Act of 2001, Pub. L. No. 107-110, 115 Stat. 1425 (2002).

O'Connor, R.E., Notari-Syverson, A., & Vadasy, P.F. (1998). *Ladders to literacy: A kindergarten activity book.* Baltimore: Paul H. Brookes.

Pikulski, J.J., & Chard, D. (2005). Fluency: The bridge between decoding and reading comprehension. *The Reading Teacher, 58*, 6, 510–521.

Pinnell, G.S., Pikulski, J.J., Wixson, K.K., Campbell, J.R., Gough, P.B., & Beatty, A.S. (1995). *Listening to children read aloud.* Washington, DC: Office of Educational Research and Improvement, U.S. Department of Education.

Reitsma, P. (1983). Printed word learning in beginning readers. *Journal of Experimental Child Psychology, 75*, 321–339.

Samuels, S.J. (1979). The method of repeated readings. *The Reading Teacher, 32*, 403–408.

Samuels, S.J. (2002). Reading fluency: Its development and assessment. In A.E. Farstrup & S.J. Samuels (Eds.), *What research has to say about reading instruction* (3rd ed., pp. 166–183). Newark, DE: International Reading Association.

Snow, C.E., Burns, M.S., & Griffin, P. (Eds.). (1998). *Preventing reading difficulties in young children.* Washington, DC: National Academy Press.

Stahl, S.A., & Heubach, K.M. (2005). Fluency-oriented reading instruction. *Journal of Literacy Research, 37*, 26–60.

Stanovich, K.E. (1986). Matthew effects in reading: Some consequences in individual differences in the acquisition of literacy. *Reading Research Quarterly, 21*, 360–407.

Stecker, S.K., Roser, N.L., & Martinez, M.G. (1998). Understanding oral reading fluency. In T. Shanahan & F.V. Rodriguez-Brown (Eds.), *47th yearbook of the National Reading Conference* (pp. 295–310). Chicago: National Reading Conference.

Strickland, D.S., & Schickendanz, J. (2004). *Learning about print in preschool: Working with letters, words, and beginning links with phonemic awareness.* Newark, DE: International Reading Association.

Topping, K. (1987). Paired reading: A powerful technique for parent use. *The Reading Teacher, 40*, 608–614.

Wylie, R.E., & Durrell, D.D. (1970). Teaching vowels through phonograms. *Elementary English, 47*, 787–791.

Chapter 5

Fluency: Still Waiting After All These Years

Richard L. Allington

Almost 25 years ago my article "Fluency: The Neglected Goal" (Allington, 1983a) was published. Fluency was a topic of interest for a while. A number of studies, most often measuring the effectiveness of some form of repeated reading on fluency, were published over the years, but fluency did not really become a focal point of educators' concerns again until it was identified as one of the evidence-based "pillars" of scientific reading by the National Reading Panel (National Institute of Child Health and Human Development [NICHD], 2000). Still, there remain a number of issues concerning fluency that have not been adequately sorted out.

Reading Efficiency Versus Fluency

One question we educators should ask is whether current popular measures of fluency are more accurately measures of word-reading efficiency than of fluency (Mathson, Solic, & Allington, 2006). I think fluency is reading in phrases, with appropriate intonation and prosody—fluency is reading with expression.

Phrasing, intonation, and prosody have long been considered components of fluent reading (Clay & Imlach, 1971; Schreiber, 1980, 1991); however, today we find measures of word- and nonword-reading efficiency and of reading rate being offered as measures of fluency (see, for instance, Dynamic Indicators of Basic Early Literacy Skills [DIBELS]; Good & Kaminski, 2002). But automaticity of isolated word recognition is a measure of something quite different from a measure of reading fluency as historically conceived. Although one's reading rate is most certainly related to fluency, if only because word-by-word reading is always slower than phrase reading, one can also read quickly but with little appropriate phrasing, intonation, or prosody (Rasinski, 2000).

What Research Has to Say About Fluency Instruction, edited by S. Jay Samuels and Alan E. Farstrup. © 2006 by the International Reading Association.

Dahl and Samuels (1977) demonstrated that training in rapid word identification did not improve reading fluency or comprehension of texts read. Buly and Valencia (2002) found that one of five students who failed a state fourth-grade reading proficiency test were automatic decoders who read accurately and quickly but with little comprehension. It is not that reading rate, or word-reading efficiency, is unimportant, but that it is something different from reading fluency (Schwanenflugel, Hamilton, Kuhn, Wisenbaker, & Stahl, 2004).

More problematic is the sight of struggling readers practicing speeded reading of lists of nonwords and words in the hopes of improving their DIBELS word-reading efficiency performances. Problematic because, as Schwanenflugel and her colleagues (2004) caution, several studies have convincingly demonstrated that such training simply does not improve text-reading performances. Perhaps this distortion of the notion of what fluency is and how it is developed has resulted in the DIBELS not proving a very reliable predictor of early reading difficulties. Carlisle, Schilling, Scott, and Zeng (2004) found that about half of the second and third graders who were predicted to be reading on level in the spring, based on fall DIBELS performances, were actually performing below the 50th percentile on the Iowa Test of Basic Skills (ITBS) Total Reading in the spring. Such students who prove to be false negatives, particularly on this scale, are of concern because of the implications for their access to needed instruction. Similarly, while DIBELS seems to measure word-reading efficiency fairly reliably, Pressley, Hilden, and Shankland (2005) evaluated DIBELS and found that "DIBELS mispredicts reading performance on other assessments much of the time, and at best is a measure of who reads quickly without regard to whether the reader comprehends what is read" (p. 1).

Fluency, reading in phrases with appropriate intonation and prosody, seems an important characteristic of effective reading. Word-reading efficiency also seems an important, but different, characteristic of effective reading. Although problems with decoding and word-reading automaticity can be linked to reading dysfluency (word-by-word reading) in some cases, several other explanations for children who can read accurately but not fluently will be discussed in the following section.

Sources of Reading Dysfluency

Dysfluent reading is the opposite of fluent reading. Dysfluent reading is most often rendered as a word-by-word reading of a text with little or no phrasing, intonation, or inflection. Dysfluent reading may also be reading in clumps of words but not reading phrases or reading fast and accurately but with no intonational variation, with little or no phrasing. Dysfluent reading simply sounds awkward.

The Role of Instruction

I think that word-by-word reading may be a learned adaptive response to a specific type of instructional setting (Allington, 1980, 1983b). Children read word-by-word when they have been trained to rely on an external monitor (the teacher, aide, or other students) rather than to self-regulate when reading aloud. So how is this dependence learned?

Several researchers have documented that teachers are more likely to have lower achieving readers read aloud than the better readers (Allington, 1983b; Chinn, Waggoner, Anderson, Schommer, & Wilkinson, 1993; Hiebert, 1983). Often this reading aloud occurs during a directed reading lesson when each child reads aloud a bit, in turn. In these lessons teachers are far more likely to interrupt the lower achieving readers than the higher achieving readers, to interrupt poor readers more quickly, and to have the interruption focus on "sounding words out" (Allington, 1980; Chinn et al., 1993; Hoffman et al., 1984). Teachers also allow other readers to interrupt struggling readers, while discouraging such interruptions when better readers read aloud (Eder & Felmlee, 1984). In other words, we have good evidence that teachers typically interact differently with students who differ in reading proficiency. They not only interact differently, but they also organize reading lessons differently.

The evidence indicates that struggling readers are more likely than better readers

- to be reading material that is difficult for them,
- to be asked to read orally,
- to have their attention focused on accuracy rather than comprehension,
- to be interrupted when they misread a word,
- to be interrupted more quickly,
- to pause while reading and wait for a teacher to prompt, and
- to be told to sound out a word.

And evidence also indicates that better readers are more likely than struggling readers

- to be reading material of an appropriate level of difficulty,
- to be asked to read silently,
- to be expected to self-monitor and self-correct,
- to have attention focused on understanding,
- to be interrupted only after a wait period or at end of sentence, and
- to be asked to reread or to cross-check when interrupted.

Given such different reading lessons, is it surprising that struggling readers begin to read differently, hesitantly? I describe the word-by-word reading as a learned behavior, a "checking the traffic" response (Allington, 2006). Given a steady stream of rapid, external interruptions, struggling readers begin to read with an anticipation of interruptions—reading word-by-word. In some classrooms, you can observe an audible "Um-huh" from the teacher after a struggling reader pronounces each word. In some severe cases, the struggling reader actually looks up from the text to check with the teacher after every word is read.

I will suggest that this hesitation is a trained behavior and not an indication of any skills deficit in particular. Some have argued that word-by-word reading indicates inadequate development of sight vocabulary or limited decoding proficiency. But a number of studies have indicated that older struggling readers—those dysfluent, word-by-word readers—often know more sight words and have more phonics skills when compared to younger better readers. At the same time, the younger better readers read more fluently and with better self-monitoring (Allington, 1983b). Other studies have shown that training struggling readers to recognize words faster had little positive effect on reading fluency or overall reading achievement (Dahl & Samuels, 1977; Kuhn & Stahl, 2003).

What does seem effective is providing struggling readers with lots of opportunity to develop self-monitoring skills and strategies (Kuhn, 2005a, 2005b; Samuels, 2002). Thus, teachers would offer lessons more like those offered better readers: Reading from appropriately difficult texts, more opportunities to read silently, and more opportunities to select texts they find interesting. When reading aloud teachers would reduce or delay interruptions when word recognition breaks down, focus student attention on self-monitoring and on understanding what was read. Although each of these shifts seems important, most are dependent on the first—providing appropriate texts.

The Role of High-Success Reading Experiences

I think some children fail to develop adequate fluency for another reason: They have had limited reading practice, particularly practice in high-success texts. High-success reading experiences are characterized by accurate, fluent reading with good understanding of the text that was read. It is this sort of reading that too often seems in short supply in the reading experiences of struggling readers. However, I know of no experimental research directly testing the hypothesis that a steady diet of too-hard texts fosters dysfluency. Designing such a study—at least one following the federal criteria for scientific research—would create some ethical concerns. That is, given the known power of placing children in appropriately difficult text, providing a steady diet of too-hard texts to some randomly selected children (control group) and a diet of appropriately difficult texts to other randomly selected children (experimental group) would seem to violate the basic ethical principle of "Knowingly, do no harm."

Nonetheless, the widespread evidence from natural experiments—studies of the naturally occurring variation that exists from classroom to classroom—that struggling readers typically read less and that they are often placed in texts that are too hard, as well as the commonness of fluency problems in these students, suggests that the "checking-the-traffic" and high-success reading practice hypotheses deserve consideration. I do know from my clinical experiences that providing children access with appropriately leveled texts and a noninterruptive reading environment typically produces profound changes in reading fluency and self-monitoring.

The Role of Reading Volume

Modifying the reading lessons so that there is a greater focus on self-regulating and on ensuring that struggling readers have texts they can read accurately, fluently, and with understanding is critical if we want to enhance fluency. But as I have suggested (Allington, 2006), another critical step in designing interventions for struggling readers begins with ensuring that these students engage in at least as much reading activity as their more successful peers. As Guthrie (2004) has noted, virtually every study of reading volume indicates that struggling readers engage in far less reading activity than do more successful readers. The work of Share and Stanovich (1995) and Stanovich and West (1989) suggests that it is extensive engagement in high-success reading activity that provides the opportunity for readers to consolidate the various skills and components of proficient reading. With little high-success practice, readers simply fail to develop the proficiencies that are essential for skilled, autonomous reading.

There exists support for an important role for reading volume in several studies of reading fluency, especially the studies of the repeated-reading technique. A bountiful supply of research on the positive effects of the repeated-reading procedure in fostering fluency exists (Kuhn & Stahl, 2003; NICHD, 2000). However, much of that research is fundamentally flawed because few studies had the control groups engaged in reading while the experimental students engaged in repeated readings of texts. As Kuhn and Stahl (2003) first noted, it may be the more extensive reading practice that fostered fluency rather than practice repeatedly reading the same texts. In the few studies that had the control groups engage in independent reading while the experimental students engaged in repeated reading, the two activities have produced comparable fluency and word-recognition gains (cf. Rashotte & Torgesen, 1985). Thus, simply increasing the volume of reading produced the same positive effects of reading fluency and word recognition as the repeated-reading technique. But little has been written about the role of reading volume in fostering fluency or broader reading proficiencies.

In addition, Kuhn (2005a, 2005b) found that extensive independent-reading activity produced comprehension gains that the repeated-reading technique did not. She notes that though fluency is important, fluent reading does not automatically ensure comprehension. Furthermore, a focus on simply reading fluently in repeated-reading interventions may bias students in a manner that undermines developing an intention to understand what is being read. Repeated-reading interventions would seem to benefit from a more viable comprehension component than has been typically provided.

Extensive engagement in high-success reading activity seems an essential factor in fostering proficient reading (Share & Stanovich, 1995). More-than-sufficient evidence illustrates the impacts of reading volume to seriously consider whether the fundamental problem faced by dysfluent readers is simply one of limited high-success reading practice (Guthrie, 2004). If struggling readers are typically engaged in far less reading activity (as virtually every study on the topic demonstrates) and substantially less high-success reading practice, then one does not have to invoke pseudoscientific explanations such as attention deficits, learning disabilities, or neurological damage or deficiencies to explain why few struggling readers ever become active, engaged, and proficient readers.

Looking at Struggling Readers in Your School

The importance of high-success reading activity has its own fairly extensive research base (Allington, 2006). But only the best readers in most schools actually engage in huge amounts of high-success reading. These are the children reading above grade level who have desks filled with grade-level texts, ones they can read accurately, fluently, and with strong comprehension. It is the average and struggling readers who more often consume a steady diet of less successful reading.

Consider a third grader in your school who reads at the early second-grade level. Does she have a third-grade–level basal reader, a third-grade core trade book, a third-grade science book, and a third-grade social studies book in her desk—and in her hands all day long? Do we really need a psychologist to explain why she is not making much progress in school? To explain why she reads dysfluently? With little comprehension? Why she seems unmotivated to read much voluntarily? Even if she participates in a supplemental intervention program that provides 30 minutes of daily lessons and practice in appropriately difficult texts, she returns to a classroom and her desk filled with books she cannot read successfully. And she still has 300 minutes of instruction every day in texts that are inappropriately difficult.

Too often, even participating in a supplemental intervention program does little to optimize matching struggling readers with appropriate texts. O'Connor and colleagues (2002) indicate that in many school systems the supplementary intervention lessons use the grade-level texts that are found in the struggling reader's desk. Their randomized field experiment demonstrated that providing daily intervention lessons using those grade-level texts was not nearly as successful as providing daily lessons using texts matched to the reading level of the struggling readers. Given that selecting texts that are of appropriate complexity for the learners is the first step in the design of effective instruction, O'Connor and colleagues wonder why anyone would think that matching intervention texts to readers would not also be the first step in planning effective intervention. I wonder also and likewise routinely observe support personnel attempting to drag some struggling reader through a text he or she should never have been given in the first place.

I have never encountered a theory that suggests that matching texts to kids is only important for achieving students but that struggling students will do well with too-hard texts. No empirical evidence supports such lesson design either. All readers need texts of appropriate complexity for their lessons and practice. But for some reason many schools seem to be enamored with providing too-hard texts for students, especially struggling readers; for example, consider the current antiscientific emphasis on placing all students in a grade-level reading program and providing whole-class lessons as a way to enhance reading achievement. Do struggling readers in your school have high-success texts in their hands all day long? For every subject area? Or do those struggling readers have mostly too-difficult texts in their desks and in their hands?

Adults prefer easy, high-success, reading. No adult has ever decided not to read the new John Grisham novel because the last one was "too easy"—with too few hard words or with too few passages that required several rereadings to comprehend. If adults preferred hard reading, you would not be able to sell *People* magazine, *Entertainment Weekly*, or *The National Enquirer*. Instead, adults would be purchasing *Scientific American*, *The Economist*, and the *Financial Times*.

Learning to read requires huge amounts of highly successful and engaging practice (Guthrie, 2004; Share & Stanovich, 1995). We might begin to redesign our reading lessons (and our science and social studies lessons) in ways that ensure that all students have easy, frequent access to texts that provide high-success practice, engaging content (Guthrie & Humenick, 2004), and opportunities for literate conversation about those texts (Johnston, 2004).

Conclusions

I do believe reading with fluency is important. But I also believe that many, if not most, students who exhibit dysfluent reading are but products of poorly designed instructional environments. Too often these are children who sit all day in classrooms and rarely have texts in their hands they can read accurately, fluently, and with understanding. These are too often children whose dysfluency is but a signal that they have been routinely given the wrong texts, texts that are too difficult. They often then avoid even trying to read these texts, but when they do read them they struggle. And then they are subjected to almost continuous external interruptions and corrections until the instructional environment has disabled them.

The intervention that I would propose is straightforward. Provide these children with high-success reading experiences all day long. Fill their desks with books that they can read accurately, fluently, and with understanding. Once a day we might give them slightly harder texts in a guided-reading setting. Guided reading that uses shared-book experiences (Reutzel, Hollingsworth, & Eldredge, 1994), for instance, can help ease students into high-success reading of those texts. Provide a few minutes of explicit and powerful demonstrations of useful decoding, self-regulating, and comprehension strategies. Make sure the classroom has a huge supply of interesting texts at levels of complexity that will allow these students to engage in extended independent reading (Guthrie, 2004).

I might make some short-term use of strategies such as repeated reading. But only in the short term (say two to three weeks). My goal with repeated readings would be to help dysfluent readers begin to understand what fluent reading feels like. But these repeated-reading lessons should also focus on understanding what is being read (Kuhn, 2005a; Stayter & Allington, 1991). After years of reading word by word, some students may need repeated-reading training to begin to break a long-standing habit brought on by poorly designed instruction and poorly thought-out reading curriculum (whole-class lessons in a grade-level reading series, for instance).

After a few weeks, I would drop repeated reading and concentrate on ensuring that struggling readers read more each day than my normally developing readers (a necessity if they are ever to close the gap). Furthermore, even while I was having the two weeks of 15–20 minutes of repeated reading each day, I would work to enhance the volume of reading across the school day for the struggling readers. How much time should be spent reading during the school day? That is a question yet to be answered experimentally. But the research available from natural experiments suggests 90–120 minutes of daily high-success reading activity in school is a minimal target (Allington, 2006; Guthrie, 2004). So we should work to ensure that the design of reading lessons for struggling readers, both classroom and intervention lessons, ensures this minimal volume of successful practice.

Reading fluency is once again a topic of interest. But much remains to learn about the role of reading fluency in reading acquisition, how to best foster reading fluency, and how to ensure that fostering reading fluency also enhances reading comprehension, motivation, and proficiency. We also need to better understand how our instructional interactions might undermine self-regulation and agency and create readers who read dysfluently, with little understanding and little motivation to read voluntarily. We know a little about fluency, but a little knowledge can be a dangerous thing.

Questions for Discussion

1. If you selected 10 struggling readers in your school, how many would have a desk full of texts they could read accurately, fluently, and with understanding?

2. If you observed 10 reading lessons offered to struggling readers, how many lessons would provide support for developing self-regulation while reading? How many lessons would be characterized by immediate and frequent interruptions of struggling readers' performances?

3. How many second-grade–level books does the typical fourth-grade classroom have for struggling fourth-grade readers to read? Is it less than 100 books?

4. How many struggling readers actually read more than the better readers every day in school? How many read less? Much less?

REFERENCES

Allington, R.L. (1980). Teacher interruption behaviors during primary grade oral reading. *Journal of Educational Psychology, 72,* 371–377.

Allington, R.L. (1983a). Fluency: The neglected goal. *The Reading Teacher, 36,* 556–561.

Allington, R.L. (1983b). The reading instruction provided readers of differing abilities. *The Elementary School Journal, 83,* 548–559.

Allington, R.L. (2006). *What really matters for struggling readers: Designing research-based programs* (2nd ed.). Boston: Allyn & Bacon.

Buly, M.R., & Valencia, S.W. (2002). Below the bar: Profiles of students who fail state reading assessments. *Educational Evaluation & Policy Analysis, 24,* 219–239.

Carlisle, J.F., Schilling, S.G., Scott, S.E., & Zeng, J. (2004). *Do fluency measures predict reading achievement? Results from the 2002–2003 school year in Michigan's Reading First schools.* Ann Arbor: University of Michigan.

Chinn, C.A., Waggoner, M., Anderson, R.C., Schommer, M., & Wilkinson, I. (1993). Situated actions during reading lessons: A microanalysis of oral reading error episodes. *American Educational Research Journal, 30,* 361–392.

Clay, M.M., & Imlach, R.H. (1971). Juncture, pitch, and stress as reading behavior variables. *Journal of Verbal Learning and Verbal Behavior, 10,* 133–139.

Dahl, P.R., & Samuels, S.J. (1977). An experimental program for teaching high-speed word recognition and comprehension skills. In J. Button, T. Lovitt, & T. Rowland

(Eds.), *Communications research in learning disabilities and mental retardation* (pp. 33–65). Baltimore: University Park Press.

Eder, D., & Felmlee, D. (1984). The development of attention norms in ability groups. In P.L. Peterson, L.C. Wilkinson, & M. Hallinan (Eds.), *The social context of instruction: Group organization and group process* (pp. 171–193). New York: Academic.

Good, R.H., & Kaminski, R.A. (Eds.). (2002). *Dynamic Indicators of Basic Early Literacy Skills* (6th ed.). Eugene, OR: Institute for the Development of Educational Achievement.

Guthrie, J.T. (2004). Teaching for literacy engagement. *Journal of Literacy Research, 36,* 1–28.

Guthrie, J.T., & Humenick, N.M. (2004). Motivating students to read: Evidence for classroom practices that increase motivation and achievement. In P. McCardle & V. Chhabra (Eds.), *The voice of evidence in reading research* (pp. 329–354). Baltimore: Paul H. Brookes.

Hiebert, E.H. (1983). An examination of ability grouping for reading instruction. *Reading Research Quarterly, 18,* 231–255.

Hoffman, J.V., O'Neal, S., Kastler, L., Clements, R., Segel, K., & Nash, M.F. (1984). Guided oral reading and miscue focused verbal feedback in second-grade classrooms. *Reading Research Quarterly, 19,* 367–384.

Johnston, P.H. (2004). *Choice words: How our language affects children's learning.* York, ME: Stenhouse.

Kuhn, M.R. (2005a). A comparative study of small group fluency instruction. *Reading Psychology, 26,* 127–146.

Kuhn, M.R. (2005b). Helping students become accurate, expressive readers: Fluency instruction for small groups. *The Reading Teacher, 58,* 338–344.

Kuhn, M.R., & Stahl, S.A. (2003). Fluency: A review of developmental and remedial practices. *Journal of Educational Psychology, 95,* 3–21.

Mathson, D.V., Solic, K.L., & Allington, R.L. (2006). Hijacking fluency and instructionally informative assessment. In T. Rasinski, C. Blachowicz, & K. Lems (Eds.), *Fluency instruction: Research-based best practices* (pp. 109–116). New York: Guilford.

National Institute of Child Health and Human Development. (2000). *Report of the National Reading Panel. Teaching children to read: An evidence-based assessment of the scientific research literature on reading and its implications for reading instruction* (NIH Publication No. 00-4769). Washington, DC: U.S. Government Printing Office.

O'Connor, R.E., Bell, K.M., Harty, K.R., Larkin, L.K., Sackor, S.M., & Zigmond, N. (2002). Teaching reading to poor readers in the intermediate grades: A comparison of text difficulty. *Journal of Educational Psychology, 94*(3), 474–485.

Pressley, M., Hilden, K., & Shankland, R. (2005). *An evaluation of end-of-grade 3 Dynamic Indicators of Basic Early Literacy Skills (DIBELS): Speed reading without comprehension, predicting little.* East Lansing: Michigan State University Literacy Achievement Research Center.

Rashotte, C.A., & Torgesen, J.K. (1985). Repeated reading and reading fluency in learning disabled children. *Reading Research Quarterly, 20,* 180–189.

Rasinski, T.V. (2000). Speed does matter in reading. *The Reading Teacher, 54,* 146–151.

Reutzel, D.R., Hollingsworth, P.M., & Eldredge, J.L. (1994). Oral reading instruction: The impact on student reading development. *Reading Research Quarterly, 29,* 40–65.

Samuels, S.J. (2002). Reading fluency: Its development and assessment. In A.E. Farstrup & S.J. Samuels (Eds.), *What research has to say about reading instruction* (3rd ed., pp. 166–183). Newark, DE: International Reading Association.

Schreiber, P.A. (1980). On the acquisition of reading fluency. *Journal of Reading Behavior, 12*, 177–186.

Schreiber, P.A. (1991). Understanding prosody's role in reading acquisition. *Theory Into Practice, 30*, 158–164.

Schwanenflugel, P.J., Hamilton, A.M., Kuhn, M.R., Wisenbaker, J.M., & Stahl, S.A. (2004). Becoming a fluent reader: Reading skill and prosodic features in the oral reading of young readers. *Journal of Educational Psychology, 96*, 119–129.

Share, D.L., & Stanovich, K.E. (1995). Cognitive processes in early reading development: Accommodating individual differences in a model of acquisition. *Issues in Education, 1*, 1–57.

Stanovich, K.E., & West, R. (1989). Exposure to print and orthographic processing. *Reading Research Quarterly, 26*, 402–429.

Stayter, F., & Allington, R.L. (1991). Fluency and comprehension. *Theory Into Practice, 33*, 143–148.

Chapter 6

Building Reading Fluency: Cognitive, Behavioral, and Socioemotional Factors and the Role of Peer-Mediated Learning

Keith J. Topping

This chapter explores different definitions of fluency and offers a model to show how different aspects and types of fluency might relate to each other—a model that also offers practitioners guidance for setting progressive teaching and learning goals. Next the chapter considers the difficulties of measuring fluency, relevant to evaluating whether teaching has been successful or whether it needs adapting. Practical interventions to enhance fluency are briefly reviewed and set in the context of peer-mediated learning. Repeated reading (RR) and paired reading (PR) are two of the most widely used interventions. The latter is an example of a peer-mediated learning method, and the former can be used in this way. Both are defined with some care, and evidence for effectiveness is discussed. I wrote this chapter out of the related convictions that fluency is extremely important for student progress and life beyond school, fluency is all too often imperfectly understood and somewhat neglected by busy teachers under pressure to "cover the curriculum," and peer-mediated learning holds great potential to enhance fluency if well implemented.

What Is Fluency?

Fluency is not an entity, a benchmarkable competence, or a static condition. Fluency is an adaptive, context-dependent process that can operate at a number of layers or levels (this is also true of comprehension). Even expert readers will show dysfluency when confronted with a text on an unfamiliar topic that provides challenge greatly beyond their independent reading level, however high that level might be. Fluency is of little value in itself—its value lies in what it enables.

What Research Has to Say About Fluency Instruction, edited by S. Jay Samuels and Alan E. Farstrup. © 2006 by the International Reading Association.

For silent reading, fluency is defined by this author as the extraction of maximum meaning at maximum speed in a relatively continuous flow, leaving spare simultaneous processing capacity for other higher order processes. This definition assumes the text is at an appropriate level of difficulty for the reader. For reading out loud, the task—and therefore the definition—is more demanding because among the higher order processes, the reader must have an awareness of audience needs and the capability to manage the prosodic demands for expressiveness (varying phrasing, stress, intonation, pitch, rhythm, loudness, pauses, etc.).

Already, two context-specific definitions of fluency have been implied, and it becomes more complex. Fluency often means different things to different people and can be defined at different levels of complexity. Simple assumptions can prove misleading. Thus, a simple definition of fluency in terms only of speed of word recognition appears to assume that reading faster is always reading better. However, just reading faster might actually result in reduced accuracy. Fast reading, even if accurately decoded, does not always automatically result in good comprehension (although it is in general positively correlated with good comprehension). Students who assume that just because they can read words fast and accurately they are "fluent" readers may be on dangerous ground. Some so-called measures of fluency in widespread use reinforce this damaging fallacy by measuring only speed of accurate word recognition.

A number of factors interact with each other in the area of fluency. This chapter attempts to map these factors in the model of fluency presented in the following section. All of this has implications for how we might effectively intervene to enhance fluency and how we might usefully measure it. This chapter thus asserts a fluid definition of fluency conceptualized within an information-processing or resource-allocation model, while mapping the many varieties of fluency and the consequently varied implications for intervention and measurement. Socioemotional factors are given equal prominence with cognitive aspects.

The Deep Processing Fluency (DPF) Model

The model of fluency presented in this section groups various relevant factors into four sequentially arranged sectors: (1) predisposing factors (entry skills and conditions that facilitate fluency), (2) surface fluency (speed of accurate and automatic word recognition), (3) strategic fluency (control of speed of reading to yield comprehension and expression at the optimal level required for a specific purpose), and (4) deep fluency (control of speed of reading to maximize comprehension, expression, and deep reflection for specific purposes, enhancing explicit awareness and self-regulation of these processes). (See Figure 6.1.)

This grouping suggests further definitional complexity—three different kinds of fluency. Additionally, even the apparent linearity of the DPF model is beguiling because there are feedback loops, including from "end" to "beginning." Actually the model is circular or recursive.

Predisposing Factors

Predisposing factors facilitating the development of fluency ("entry skills" if you prefer) include the following:

- **Management of text difficulty.** Fluency is not likely to be developed on material that is much too hard or easy. Have teachers matched the readability level of the texts to the reading ability of the students and taught students readability self-checking strategies?

- **Time exposed, time on task, and time engaged.** Simply allocating silent-reading time is not enough. Have teachers ensured that allocated time is spent actually effectively engaged with the task?

- **Vocabulary (listening or reading).** Have teachers, parents, and peers engaged students in increasingly complex dialogue? Have they had students listen to stories to develop their receptive vocabulary and facilitate decoding when these words are encountered in print?

- **Memory.** Both visual and verbal, short- and long-term memory are needed. Teachers can help develop memory, but avoid abstract games that might have no effects generalized to reading.

- **Motivation (individualization and ownership).** Have teachers considered individual student reading preferences and offered balanced access to fiction and nonfiction to tap existing motivation? Have they treated multiple and gendered literacies and home cultures with respect? Have they sought to bridge discontinuity between home, community, and school interests and competences, rather than promote only "schooled" literacy experiences?

- **Confidence (self-efficacy and resilience).** Have teachers created a classroom ethos free of a fear of failure, shame at error, and obsession with "the right answer," where strategic risk taking is seen as normal? Have they avoided abstract self-esteem building exercises that might not generalize to reading? Remember that too much

Figure 6.1. The Deep Processing Fluency (DPF) model

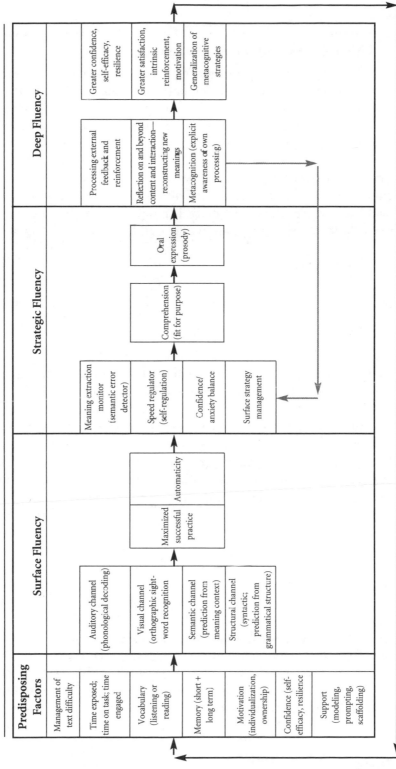

confidence is almost as unhelpful as too little—students benefit from high but realistic expectations.

- **Support (modeling, prompting, and scaffolding).** Have teachers made available a variety of supports for those attacking texts above their current independent readability level, such as assistants, volunteers, or peers, with modeling of fluent reading, prompting while reading, and other forms of scaffolding such as audiotapes?

Even if a highly energetic teacher were able to provide all these, different students will always have different profiles of strengths and weaknesses across these factors. With luck and good management, they will make the best of what they have available as they seek to develop fluency.

Surface Fluency

In developing surface fluency (speed of accurate and automatic word recognition), different students will also have different profiles of strengths and weaknesses in the four major channels for extracting meaning: (1) the auditory channel (phonological decoding), (2) the visual channel (orthographic sight-word recognition), (3) the semantic channel (prediction from meaning context), and (4) the structural channel (syntactic; prediction from grammatical structure).

Stanovich (1984) describes this model as "interactive-compensatory." Of course, some written languages and some specific texts or parts of texts are intrinsically more accessible through particular channels (e.g., Finnish through the auditory channel, Mandarin through the visual channel). Unfortunately for our students, English is a complex, mongrel language requiring some capability in all channels.

Nonetheless, given reasonable availability of predisposing factors and reasonable competence in most, if not all, of the channels, students who have substantial practice at reading will over time develop automaticity in extracting meaning. The process will become less effortful, require less concentration, and use up less mental resources—until, of course, the difficulty of the book increases, when the student has to start trying hard all over again. Some students prefer to avoid this never-ending struggle for self-improvement and might at the age of 7 decide that they can read ("fluently") and coast along reading at that level for the rest of their lives. In fact, it is not "practice that makes perfect," but *successful* practice *at an appropriate level of difficulty* that yields wider automaticity. Consequently, teachers need to monitor not only volume of student practice in and out of school, but also its quality, its challenge level in relation to student ability, and the successfulness of that practice in leading to high-quality comprehension.

Notwithstanding these difficulties, many students do achieve a reasonable degree of surface fluency, albeit in some cases almost accidentally; that is, given a book at their independent readability level, they can read it reasonably accurately, at a reasonable speed, and with reasonable continuity. Unfortunately, some students see this level as the end of the road. In fact, this automaticity gives them spare processing capacity that can be deployed to move on to the next stage of fluency development—strategic fluency.

Strategic Fluency

Moving on, however, requires more focused strategy on the part of the reader. Strategic fluency is control of speed of reading to yield comprehension and expression at the optimal level required for a specific purpose. Some readers try to apply their strongest surface-fluency channel to all words, on a "one-size-fits-all" basis. Given the nature of the English language, this is only likely to be effective and efficient a quarter of the time. Some readers apply their strongest surface-fluency channel to all words first, then quickly revert to their second strongest if that proves ineffective, and so on. Some readers apply any channel that comes to mind, hoping for the best from random chance. However, the most capable readers tend to analyze the nature of the problem word and choose a channel they judge most likely to maximize success for that word. Such surface strategy management does not necessarily operate at an explicit level—it might have developed inductively or intuitively and been automatized without ever having been made explicit, much as how to ride a bicycle is rarely made explicit. It is typically done at considerable speed.

Furthermore, moving on also requires awareness that greater speed might result in reduced accuracy, and greater accuracy might result in reduced speed. It requires a balancing act in the child's brain between meaning-extraction checking and speed regulation. The balance must suit the purpose of the reading task in hand. The spare processing capacity available has to be able to handle two competing processes at the same time—and to do so at some speed. The well-known U-shaped relationship between anxiety and performance is also relevant here. If the student regards the book as easy, anxiety will be low and confidence high, and the speed regulator will be dominant—the student will read fast but possibly not accurately, even though the book is easy. If the student regards the book as hard, anxiety will be high and confidence low, the meaning monitor will be dominant—and the student will read accurately but very slowly. Of course, if speed becomes very slow, the interaction with memory becomes important—by the time the last word in the sentence has been decoded, the student might have forgotten the first words.

If the student manages this balancing act with reasonable success, good comprehension will result. Remember that there were no guarantees that surface fluency would lead to good comprehension—only rapid and accurate decoding, which might be little more than "barking at print." In strategic fluency, however, good comprehension is a requisite. Of course, defining exactly what good comprehension is leads to many interesting questions. Comprehension is a layered concept. Does it mean extracting every last drop of meaning the author put in there? Was the author aware of all the meaning that might be in there? Can any text mean exactly the same to all readers? How *good* the comprehension has to be might vary according to the purposes and intentions of the reader—which might change as the individual is reading the text.

Leaving such complexities aside for the moment, we now behold a generally strategically fluent silent reader who is a "good comprehender." The next step requires even more spare processing capacity—moving to fluent oral reading with expression (prosody). As previously noted, this step requires all of the foregoing skills, and in addition the reader must be able to manage text complexities and respond to the audience's prosodic demands for expressiveness (varying phrasing, stress, intonation, pitch, rhythm, loudness, speed, pauses, etc.).

Deep Fluency

Having mastered all of these skills to a greater or lesser extent, our strategic reader has good reason to feel pleased—but the final stage of deep fluency beckons (control of speed of reading to maximize comprehension, expression, and deep reflection for specific purposes, enhancing explicit awareness and self-regulation of these processes).

Deep fluency requires even more spare processing capacity. At this stage, readers not only have excellent comprehension of text content but also have spare capacity to go beyond it in personal reflection on content—reconstructing new meanings. They are also able to process and reflect upon external feedback and reinforcement, such as audience responses to a read-aloud. Perhaps most important, they have spare capacity to begin to develop metacognition (explicit awareness of the nature of their own processing, most and least effective strategies in specific contexts, and their relative strengths and weakness). Such explicit awareness is a prerequisite for more effective self-regulation of deeply fluent reading, and the DPF model shows a feedback loop returning to surface strategy management (refer to Figure 6.1 on page 109). Pikulski and Chard (2005) have also discussed the difference between surface and deep fluency.

From these developments, powerful socioemotional effects stem, not the least of which are greater confidence, self-efficacy, and resilience as a reader (and perhaps as a learner in general). The reader feels greater satisfaction, and the intrinsic reinforcement and motivation that is associated with learner autonomy. Additionally, the metacognitive awareness gained in the area of reading might generalize spontaneously or deliberately to other subjects or other aspects of the student's life.

Measuring Fluency

Fluency has typically been measured by individually administered (and therefore time-consuming) criterion-referenced or norm-referenced tests that require the reader to read lists of single words or (better) continuous text out loud both accurately and quickly. However, some students can read accurately and fast but fail to comprehend at even minimal levels. At best, such measures only give a measure of surface fluency, and then only if the interaction between accuracy and speed is carefully studied. Additionally, fluent silent reading is easier than fluent oral reading, so the test is likely to underestimate the former. And what of the predisposing factors? Is the student motivated to read this alien text? Are they confident in the test situation? Is the text consistently of a level of difficulty appropriate to them? How long is it—will their memory last out and will fatigue set in? Is the vocabulary familiar to them and the content culturally appropriate? If they have been used to receiving support through modeling, prompting, or scaffolding, how does the sudden absence of these aids affect them?

With regard to strategic fluency, measuring accuracy and speed only makes sense if the interaction with quality of comprehension is considered simultaneously. Words decoded accurately per minute is an even poorer proxy for reading. Words accurate per minute irrespective of error rate? Words accurate per minute for how many continuous minutes? Words and minutes are easily counted, but they have validity problems as metrics. But meaning extraction (comprehension) is not easily segmented or counted. Students cannot be strategic if they are not told what the aim of their strategy should be. Therefore, any test of fluency should be introduced as seeking to measure how well the student can balance accuracy of reading and speed of reading in order to achieve good comprehension. But this can only be specified at a given level of text difficulty. Developing readers with reasonable motivation, sensing their increasing fluency, are likely to respond by seeking out the challenge of more difficult texts—on which they will again appear dysfluent. The difficulties of measuring fluency naturalistically when readers are likely to respond to an increasing sense of competence by selecting texts of higher challenge are considerable.

Parallel tests of silent-reading fluency and oral-reading fluency will be needed. Although tests of oral-reading fluency probably still require time-consuming personal interaction, tests of silent-reading fluency may not. The latter may therefore lend themselves more readily to computer-based tests of fluency, and indeed such tests are starting to appear.

Turning to deep fluency, the key components of reflection and metacognition do not lend themselves readily to assessment by some simple test. If you want to know what your students are thinking, ask them (which will mean thinking up some intelligent questions, but try to avoid making yet another written task). Or have them ask each other (they might be more inclined to accurately record each other's responses). In general, teachers would be ill advised to rely solely on tests, which might have adequate internal reliability but doubtful external validity, and which might fail to address more than surface fluency. Teacher naturalistic observation and informal formative assessment are powerful when informed by appropriate frameworks, and the DPF model can be used as such a checklist for individual children.

Methods to Promote Fluency

Various interventions to enhance fluency have been promoted, and some of these have been evaluated. All are relative to text difficulty for the individual because most students are "surface fluent" at some readability level, even if only reading their own names. (Indeed, some teachers advocate having students read and reread texts below their independent readability level, with the intention of "boosting their confidence.") Some of these methods seeking to build component skills are construed as contributing to fluency in a rather linear way "from the bottom upward." Others are more holistic and offer the reader alternative pathways to fluency. Yet others aim to give the reader a "virtual" experience of being fluent so that they see what it means, why they should want to get there, and indeed that it is possible to get there. These methods give the student a "higher altitude" or more "top-down" view of reading and usually involve some form of support to boost the reader's limited processing capacity.

Repeated Reading

Repeated reading (RR) is a well-known method aimed at enhancing automaticity by many readings of the same text. LaBerge and Samuels (1974) identified the importance of automaticity many years ago. The instructional implications were then outlined in Samuels (1979). Students were required to read a 100-word passage out loud to an adult, and then they reread the passage silently repeatedly, with occasional further oral readings to check speed and accuracy, until they reached the criterion rate of 100 words per minute (wpm). As students worked their way through a story doing 100-word segments at a time, results demonstrated that they were learning because each new segment led to increased starting speed and fewer repetitions needed to reach the criterion speed.

Dahl and Samuels (1979) compared RR to other strategies with second-grade struggling readers and found it effective in increasing reading speed and other aspects of reading. Carver and Hoffman (1981) and Dahl and Samuels (1979) found gains in comprehension on texts read repeatedly, but no generalization to new texts. However, Young, Bowers, and MacKinnon (1996) found transfer effects in reading comprehension on new passages. Dowhower (1987, 1989, 1994) found RR had effects on prosodic features. Rashotte and Torgesen (1985) compared different variations of RR, but found no effect for any of them. Mathes and Fuchs (1993) compared RR on easy and difficult materials and found no difference in effects. Homan, Klesius, and Hite (1993) found no difference in outcome between repeatedly reading few texts or singular reading of more texts, suggesting simple engagement with print was the main underlying factor. Taking these studies together, it seems that RR can enhance reading speed, comprehension, and expression, but this enhancement is not guaranteed, and generalization of these improvements to new texts is not automatic. The latter might be especially problematic where the new texts contain few or none of the words practiced, and the new words require the redeployment of a range of word-recognition skills.

In some of these studies, questions of implementation integrity arose (e.g., concerns about whether the text passages used were appropriately adjusted for difficulty for each child, and concerns about prescribing a set number of readings rather than meeting a performance criterion—"intervention drift"). Kuhn and Stahl (2003) reviewed 15 controlled studies of the effects of RR on fluency. In seven of these, RR outperformed controls (although in one case without transfer effects to new text). The type of control condition varied: Some were no-intervention controls; others read equivalent amounts of text without repeating (i.e., effectively an alternative treatment, but one controlling for exposure to print, albeit not necessarily successful exposure to print). Where Kuhn and Stahl found a difference in fluency, they also found an increase in comprehension.

Considering the Samuels version of RR and the variants in relation to the model of fluency, the original version appears to address the predisposing factors better than the variants. However, the RR method appears to address only increases in reading speed (surface fluency), and any transfer to strategic or deep fluency is left to chance or teacher judgment (as reflected in the reported uncertainty of transfer to new texts). Of course, some elaboration to ensure that such connections are made could be added. One issue that seems little addressed in the literature is student motivation to repeatedly read brief texts that are not of their choosing— hardly an "authentic" literature experience. Another is whether any preteaching of passage vocabulary takes place. Yet another is whether the rationale for these procedures is explained to students (the analogy with sports practice is useful here), or the procedures merely "done to" them— which would be likely to affect student ownership and confidence.

Teachers wishing to try out RR should perhaps use Samuels's (1979) original version in the first instance, implement it carefully, ensure the texts are of some intrinsic interest to the students, and consider how they can connect it to other activities to ensure transfer of fluency to comprehension of new texts.

Alternative Methods

A number of other methods involving various kinds of support for reading have been developed, and many of these seem likely to have positive effects on fluency. They usually involve some combination of modeling, practice, prompting, scaffolding, and feedback. They include neurological impress method (NIM); reading-while-listening (RWL); Prime-O-Tec; ARROW; talking books; and forms of assisted reading such as the lap method, shadow reading, and duet reading (details follow of those that are more widely known and/or better evaluated). These approaches can be characterized by components present or absent with respect to the model of fluency.

NIM involves student and instructor reading aloud together in unison. The instructor leads the reading, sitting a little behind the student and speaking directly into the student's right ear while moving a finger along under the word(s) being read. No corrections are made during or after the reading. NIM is intended to be multisensory and to provide a model of accurate and fluent reading. Evaluation evidence is limited (often to case studies), but Heckelman (1969, 1986) did report use with 24 delayed readers from 7th to 10th grade who showed gains in fluency and comprehension (no control group).

RWL was a development of NIM, involving practicing reading while listening to an audiotape recording of a fluent reading of the material and pointing at the words. It has been positively evaluated (Schneeberg, 1977). Hollingsworth (1978) used a mass-production version of this method; fourth- to sixth-grade delayed readers who were wired up to hear the same passage simultaneously showed significant gains in comprehension after 62 sessions compared to a control group (but leaving questions about the monitoring demands and quality). Prime-O-Tec is a similar method, which was designed for use with adult disabled readers, as reported in Meyer (1982).

NIM has the advantage of applicability to any text that might be of interest to the reader and of appropriate difficulty, while the texts available for RWL will be limited. However, it is difficult to see how either method could enhance fluency beyond surface fluency unless additional components or activities were added. More comprehensive is the ARROW (aural-read-respond-oral-written) technique, involving young children listening to their own recorded voices as a continuous prompt while reading, writing, or responding orally (Lane & Chinn, 1986). However, all of these are somewhat costly in professional time, preparation, and materials.

Carbo (1978) reported work in supporting reading development through talking books—audiotape recordings of real books. For struggling readers, the problem with many commercially available audio books is that they are *too* fluent; they are spoken fast at a speed designed for listening rather than simultaneously following the text, and they offer a model of fluency so far removed from the student's starting point that the gulf seems enormous and impossible. Carbo made tapes especially for the purpose, stressing phrases and cuing page turnover. Teacher monitoring was much lighter than in the previously described methods, which presumably raises concern about student engagement. Small groups of reading-delayed students made greater-than-normal gains in word recognition (Carbo, 1978), but no control group of any sort was measured. Dowhower (1987) compared RR to audio-supported reading with second graders and found some gains with both methods, although audio support had more impact on prosodic features. Rasinski (1990) replicated this finding with third graders.

The term *assisted reading* has been applied to a number of different methods, some of them not well defined (Hoskisson, 1975). All involve some element of synchronous reading with a more expert helper on difficult words.

Peer-Mediated Learning

Several of the previously described methods might be suitable for deployment via peer-mediated learning. Fluency building via peer-mediated learning has also been directly researched, and effectiveness is claimed for most reported interventions of this type. Peer-mediated strategies might have considerable advantages in practical viability given professional time-resource constraints.

Hoskisson and Krohm (1974) evaluated a combination of audio-supported story exposure with the opportunity subsequently to read the stories to a peer. This method was connected to a home reading program. This early study was notable for its attention to motivational and ecological aspects, as well as its careful adjustment of reading levels and speed of audio narration to individual student needs. Participating students made gains, but there was no control group. Koskinen and Blum (1986) deployed peer-mediated RR with reading-delayed third graders. Students selected their own texts. The experimental group outperformed an alternative activity group.

Eldredge and Quinn (1988; Eldredge, 1990) tested out a modified version of NIM with more fluent peers as the leaders for second-grade delayed readers, compared to a control group using basal readers and controlling readability to slightly above the tutee's independent readability level. Experimental students outperformed controls on tests of reading comprehension. What benefits or disbenefits accrued to the tutors is unknown, although doubtless this would be of interest to the parents of those tutors.

Kouzekanani et al. (2000) provided eight classrooms of third graders ($n = 111$) and their teachers with two intervention strategies: a partner-reading intervention designed to enhance fluency or a collaborative strategic reading designed to enhance comprehension. Over time, both interventions demonstrated statistically significant effects on *rate of reading* for low- to average-achieving students and students with reading disabilities. Again, questions remain about whether volume of text exposure was an underlying variable.

King and colleagues (2001) researched the effectiveness of a peer-assisted learning strategy (PALS) intervention to develop fluency in beginning readers with and without disabilities. Pairs of students completed phonically based activities and then repeated readings of a shared text. Evaluation indicated that the peer-mediated RR promoted both reading fluency *and* reading comprehension.

Echoing Hoskisson and Krohm (1974), Griffith and Rasinski (2004) reported peer modeling of fluent reading by class preview and rehearsal of scripts for class theater productions. This method ensured purposeful RR and peer accountability; however, these features were not evaluated as separate components.

Kuhn (2004) compared four groups: (1) one had oral and choral (simultaneous oral) RR of whole stories with both teacher and peers, (2) one had peer choral reading of an equivalent volume of text without repetition, (3) one had students listening to reading, and (4) one had students receiving regular class teaching only. Twenty-four second graders operated in groups of four to six students. The intervention was brief (18 sessions over six weeks). The first, or RR, group read six trade books overall; the second, or non-RR, group, read 18. Both of these experimental reading groups improved more in word recognition, word recognition per minute, and expert ratings of fluency than the third and fourth groups who were the comparison groups, but only the choral nonrepetitive group showed improved comprehension. This finding echoes that of Homan, Klesius, and Hite (1993).

Paired Reading

A method specifically designed for peer-assisted learning, paired reading (PR), is also widely used by parents, classroom assistants, and volunteer tutors. It features many of the desirable components in the DPF model. Unfortunately, over the years other workers have applied the name for this structured and well-evaluated method to vaguely similar or quite dissimilar practices that have not been evaluated. Consequently, the structured and evaluated method was renamed "duolog reading" in an attempt to establish a name that was more distinctive (this name was chosen by 100 teachers in Texas). However, we will use the original name under a strict definition in the following sections.

Definition of paired reading. PR is a straightforward and generally enjoyable way for more able readers to help less able readers develop better reading skills (i.e., a form of cross-ability tutoring). The method is adaptable to any reading material, and tutees select texts that are of intrinsic interest to them but a little above their independent readability level (otherwise, the support of PR is pointless). This might include newspapers, magazines, community literature, or texts in electronic environments. The texts must be within the independent readability level of the tutor, but a relatively modest differential in reading ability is recommended if the hope is to improve the reading of the tutor as well as the tutee. The pair might use the five-finger test of readability:

1. Open a page at random.
2. Spread five fingers on one hand.
3. Place fingertips on the page at random.
4. Tutor attempts to read the five words.
5. Repeat on another four pages.

If the tutor has struggled on more than one or two words, the book is too hard. This is not perfectly scientific but gives the pair a ritual to remind them to think about readability. Additionally, if the tutee has a fanatical interest in one topic that is not shared by the tutor, further negotiation about text choice is needed.

Encouragement to read "little and often" is usual. Pairs commit themselves to read at least three times per week for at least 10 minutes per session for at least six weeks. This frequency is needed in order to develop automaticity (fluency, even) with the technique and give it a fair test. At the end of six weeks, pairs consider if they wish to continue; if so, they can opt for greater or lesser frequency, perhaps new partners, or adapting or emphasizing some aspect of the method.

The PR technique has two main aspects. First, tutor and tutee read out loud simultaneously in close synchrony. This is termed "reading together." The tutor adjusts his or her reading speed to the tutee's pace as necessary. The tutee must read all the words out loud correctly. The tutor corrects any errors by again giving a perfect example of how to read the error word and ensuring that the tutee repeats it correctly. Then the pair continues reading.

Second, when the tutee feels confident enough to read a section of text unsupported, the tutee signals by a knock, nudge, or other nonverbal signal for the tutor to be silent. The tutee then engages in reading alone (independent reading), with the tutor listening and ready to help when necessary. The tutor praises the tutee for taking this initiative and subsequently praises the tutee regularly, especially for mastering difficult words or spontaneously self-correcting.

When the tutee makes an error while reading alone, the tutor corrects this as before (by modeling and ensuring perfect repetition), and then joins back in reading simultaneously. Any word not read correctly within a pause of four seconds is treated as an error—the tutee is not left to struggle. (However, tutors often have difficulty learning to give the tutee this time to self-correct—without which they will never learn to self-correct.) Throughout, a great deal of emphasis is placed on praising the tutee for correct reading and pausing from time to time to discuss the meaning of the text. Figure 6.2 describes the flow of PR.

Initially, much reading is usually done simultaneously, but as the tutee improves and makes more appropriate choices of reading materials, more and more independent reading occurs (until the tutee becomes more ambitious and chooses harder books). Any tendency to rush on the part of the pupil is usually resolved by consistent use of the correction procedure (although sometimes a shorter pause is needed initially) or visually "pacing" the reading by the reader pointing to each word as it is to be pronounced (usually only on harder texts with smaller print and closer spacing).

With emergently literate students, teachers sometimes use PR in an RR mode. Highly motivating books are reread at the student's request, perhaps starting with a complete reading to the student, who merely listens. In subsequent rereadings, more reading together emerges, and then reading alone begins to emerge and eventually predominate.

Young readers sometimes assume that they are expected to read more and more alone as they get better at reading. In fact, this is only true if they stick to books of just the same difficulty. It is probably more advantageous that as they get better, they tackle harder and harder books and, therefore, still need a good deal of support from reading together.

Figure 6.2. Flow of paired reading

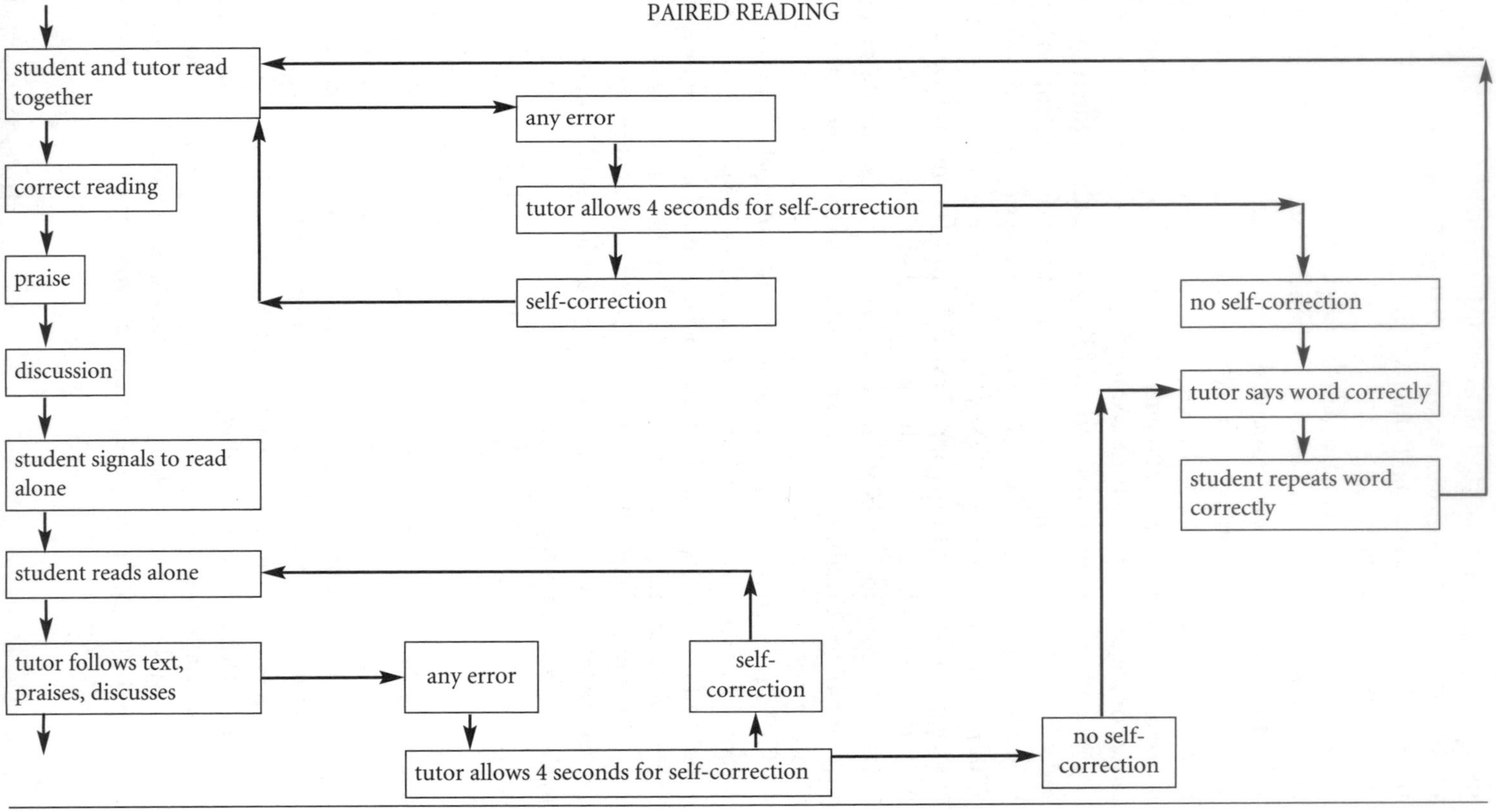

Some readers regard silent reading as the "grown-up" way of reading and might be resistant to reading together, especially if its benefits are not made clear to them and they do not use it to attack texts beyond their independent readability level.

PR can do a lot of good, but equally important, it seems to do little harm and to be widely ideologically acceptable. PR at home works in parallel with a school reading curriculum based on look-and-say, phonics, language experience, pictograms, precision teaching, direct instruction, or any other kind of approach. (Those who wish to read more about the theoretical underpinnings of PR and its connections with the wider literature on how children learn to read should see Topping & Lindsay, 1992c.)

You now know that *paired reading* is a specific name for a specific technique. It is *not* any old thing that two people feel like doing together with a book. Unfortunately, the name has become too widely misused. You will often meet people who say, "Oh, yes, we do that paired reading." When you actually *look* at what they are doing, you often find that it is nothing like the specific method described in this chapter. Further details of the method will be found in the sources listed in Table 6.1, including specimen leaflets for peer and parent tutors, checklists for monitoring implementation integrity, and so on. Topping (2001) gives detailed organizational advice for planning and operating a good-quality implementation.

PR touches on many components of the DPF model. Additionally, an extended version of the technique, paired reading and thinking (PR&T), provides a specific methodology to bridge students into strategic fluency and deep fluency.

Effectiveness of paired reading. PR is a well-evaluated method, the focus of a great many studies over the years. The English government included PR in its review of what works in literacy interventions (Brooks, 2002) and now recommends it as part of the national literacy strategy. Importantly, PR has been shown to work both in carefully controlled research studies and in naturalistic, large-scale field trials. It has been used as an intervention for students with reading delay and also as a broad-spectrum mainstream method deployed inclusively for all students. (The method tends to show larger effects with students with reading delay, although it shows good effects for students with no delay.) Gains in reading comprehension as well as reading accuracy are very commonly reported. The PR research literature has been reviewed by Topping and Lindsay (1992a) and Topping (1995, 2001).

Table 6.1. Paired-reading resources

Brooks, G. (2002). *What works for children with literacy difficulties? The effectiveness of intervention schemes* (Research Report No. 380). London: Department for Education & Skills. Available at http://www.dfes.gov.uk/research/data/uploadfiles/RR380.pdf

International Reading Association PR video pack. Available at http://www.reading.org

Read On Project. Information available at http://www.dundee.ac.uk/fedsoc/research/projects/readon

Renaissance Learning video pack. Available at http://www.renlearn.com (search under *duolog reading*)

Topping, K.J. (2000). *Peer assisted learning: A practical guide for teachers.* Cambridge, MA: Brookline.

Topping, K.J. (2001). *Thinking reading writing: A practical guide to paired learning with peers, parents & volunteers.* New York: Continuum. Resources available at http://www.dundee.ac.uk/fedsoc/research/projects/trw

Topping, K.J. (2001). *Tutoring by peers, family and volunteers.* Geneva, Switzerland: International Bureau of Education, United Nations Educational, Scientific, and Cultural Organization (UNESCO). [Online; also in translation in Chinese, Spanish, Portuguese, and Catalan]. Available at http://www.ibe.unesco.org/International/Publications/EducationalPractices/prachome.htm

Topping, K.J. (2002). *Peer- and parent-assisted learning in reading, writing, spelling, and thinking skills.* Scotland: The SCRE Centre, University of Glasgow. Available at http://www.scre.ac.uk/spotlight/spotlight82.html

Topping, K.J. (2003). *The adventures of Natividad and Toledo* [Online text for paired reading and thinking]. Available at http://www.dundee.ac.uk/fedsoc/staff/kjtopping/highplaces/nandt.htm

Topping, K.J., & Ehly, S. (Eds.). (1998). *Peer assisted learning.* Mahwah, NJ: Erlbaum.

Topping, K.J., & Hogan, J. (1999). *Read on: Paired reading and thinking video resource pack.* London: BP Educational Services. Available from Data Control Centre, ODL, Buchanan House, 63 Summer Street, Aberdeen AB10 1SJ, Scotland, UK.

For further evidence of the effectiveness of PR see Cupolillo, Silva, Socorro and Topping (1997), Murad and Topping (2000), Topping (1987, 1992a, 1992b), Topping and Lindsay (1992b), and Topping and Whiteley (1990, 1993). Research on the use of PR with adults of restricted literacy was reported in Scoble, Topping, and Wigglesworth (1988). The most recent wave of research in the United Kingdom developed PR into PR&T—moving even further into strategic and deep fluency territory. McKinstery and Topping (2003) found PR&T very effective in high school settings, and Topping and Bryce (2004) found that PR&T added value in thinking skills when compared with standard PR in elementary school.

Paired reading and fluency. As previously discussed in this chapter, finding a measure of fluency that is more than superficial is difficult; therefore, directly researching the impact of PR on fluency in a way consistent with the DPF model of fluency is a tough assignment. However, some studies (often small scale) have explored aspects of the model in relation to PR. More detail of these studies can be found in Topping (1995); just the main findings are summarized in this section.

These studies (Topping, 1995) found only small correlation coefficients between reading accuracy and comprehension and time spent reading during a PR project, so PR does not work merely by increasing time spent on reading, although it does that as well. The general pattern of PR results is fewer refusals (greater confidence), greater fluency, greater use of the context, and a greater likelihood of self-correction, as well as fewer errors (greater accuracy) and better phonic skills. This pattern has implications for all stages of the DPF model.

Conclusions

Fluency is an adaptive, context-dependent process that can operate at a number of levels of complexity. Given that fluency is complex, measuring fluency in a reliable and valid way has many difficulties. Various methods have been proposed to enhance fluency. RR is possibly the best known of these, but evaluation studies have often tested variants rather than the original method, yielding mixed results. A variety of other methods include NIM, RWL, and talking books. Some weak evidence supports the effectiveness of NIM; somewhat stronger evidence supports the other methods. Researchers have evaluated a number of peer-mediated strategies to enhance fluency from 1974 onward. The quality of study varied, but outcomes were almost all positive. PR (also known as duolog reading) is a well-evaluated method for peer-mediated learning or use by other tutors. PR has implications for all stages of the DPF model of fluency and has now been broadened into PR&T, extending higher order reading skills.

For the future, we need researchers, practitioners, managers, and policymakers to become more aware of the importance and complexity of fluency and to work together to develop more comprehensive, reliable, valid, and cost-effective ways of measuring student development in these complexities. These stakeholders also need to be more aware of the existing research evidence (or lack of it) on interventions in fluency, and this should inform their onward actions. Intervention methods need more precise specification, and "intervention drift" should be actively avoided. Interventions also need better evaluation, both formatively at classroom and student levels, and summatively at school, district, and national levels. However, such evaluations should be connected to over-arching theoretical models of fluency such as the one provided here; otherwise they will prove difficult to synthesize and interpret.

Peer-mediated learning appears to hold considerable potential but, like all methods, needs careful planning and good quality implementation if it is to be successful. The extension of PR into PR&T holds particular promise for building higher order fluency, but further replications and more rigorous studies are needed.

Questions for Discussion

1. Arguably, students understand fluency not so much from the way we define it to them but from the way we teach it and assess it. How have you taught and assessed fluency in the past? What messages have you sent to students in this way? How might you now do things differently?

2. Do all your students understand that fluency is not just one static thing, condition, or state—but should operate dynamically at different levels in different contexts for different purposes? How can you help them understand this more complex idea—verbally, visually, gesturally, interactively?

3. Would you be interested in trying repeated reading in your classroom? How exactly would you do it? How would you know whether it had worked?

4. Do any methods for peer-mediated enhancement of fluency appeal to you? Which? Why? What do you think might be the advantages and disadvantages?

5. If you tried paired reading with your students, would you go for parent, peer, assistant, or volunteer tutoring—or a mixture? Which? Why? If peer tutoring, what might be the relative advantages and disadvantages of same-age and cross-age tutoring? How would you organize it to ensure the peer tutors gained as well?

REFERENCES

Brooks, G. (2002). *What works for children with literacy difficulties? The effectiveness of intervention schemes* (Research Report No. 380). London: Department for Education & Skills.

Carbo, M. (1978). Teaching reading with talking books. *The Reading Teacher, 32,* 267–273.

Carver, R.P., & Hoffman, J.V. (1981). The effect of practice through repeated reading on gain in reading ability using a computer-based instructional system. *Reading Research Quarterly, 16,* 374–390.

Cupolillo, M., Silva, R.S., Socorro, S., & Topping, K.J. (1997). Paired reading with Brazilian first-year school failures. *Educational Psychology in Practice, 13*(2), 96–100.

Dahl, P.R., & Samuels, S.J. (1979). An experimental program for teaching high speed word recognition and comprehension skills. In J.E. Button, T. Lovitt, & T. Rowland (Eds.), *Communications research in learning disabilities and mental retardation* (pp. 33–65). Baltimore: University Park Press.

Dowhower, S.L. (1987). Effects of repeated reading on second-grade transitional readers' fluency and comprehension. *Reading Research Quarterly, 22,* 389–406.

Dowhower, S.L. (1989). Repeated reading: Theory into practice. *The Reading Teacher, 42,* 502–507.

Dowhower, S.L. (1994). Repeated reading revisited: Research into practice. *Reading & Writing Quarterly, 10,* 343–358.

Eldredge, J.L. (1990). Increasing the performance of poor readers in the third grade with a group-assisted strategy. *Journal of Educational Research, 84,* 69–77.

Eldredge, J.L., & Quinn, W. (1988). Increasing reading performance of low-achieving second graders with dyad reading groups. *Journal of Educational Research, 82,* 40–46.

Griffith, L.W., & Rasinski, T.V. (2004). A focus on fluency: How one teacher incorporated fluency with her reading curriculum. *The Reading Teacher, 58,* 126–137.

Heckelman, R.G. (1969). A neurological-impress method of remedial-reading instruction. *Academic Therapy, 4,* 277–282.

Heckelman, R.G. (1986). N.I.M. revisited. *Academic Therapy, 21,* 411–420.

Hollingsworth, P.M. (1978). An experimental approach to the impress method of teaching reading. *The Reading Teacher, 31,* 624–626.

Homan, S., Klesius, P., & Hite, S. (1993). Effects of repeated readings and non-repetitive strategies on students' fluency and comprehension. *Journal of Educational Research, 87,* 94–99.

Hoskisson, K. (1975). The many facets of assisted reading. *Elementary English, 52,* 312–315.

Hoskisson, K., & Krohm, B. (1974). Reading by immersion: Assisted reading. *Elementary English, 51,* 832–836.

King, S., Yoon, E., Jernigan, M., Jaspers, J., Gilbert, T., Morgan, P., et al. (2001). Developing first-grade reading fluency through peer mediation. *Teaching Exceptional Children, 34*(2), 90–93.

Koskinen, P.S., & Blum, I.H. (1986). Paired repeated reading: A classroom strategy for developing fluent reading. *The Reading Teacher, 40,* 70–75.

Kouzekanani, K., Linan-Thompson, S., Tyler, B., Coleman, M., Bryant, D.P., Chard, D.J., et al. (2000). Fluency and comprehension interventions for third-grade students. *Remedial & Special Education, 21*(6), 325–335.

Kuhn, M. (2004). Helping students become accurate, expressive readers: Fluency instruction for small groups. *The Reading Teacher, 58,* 338–344.

Kuhn, M.R., & Stahl, S.A. (2003). Fluency: A review of developmental and remedial practices. *Journal of Educational Psychology, 95*(1), 3–21.

LaBerge, D., & Samuels, S.J. (1974). Toward a theory of automatic information processing in reading. *Cognitive Psychology, 6,* 293–323.

Lane, C.H., & Chinn, S.J. (1986). Learning by self-voice echo. *Academic Therapy, 21,* 477–482.

Mathes, P.G., & Fuchs, L.S. (1993). Peer-mediated reading instruction in special education resource rooms. *Learning Disabilities Research & Practice, 8,* 233–243.

McKinstery, J., & Topping, K.J. (2003). Cross-age peer tutoring of thinking skills in the high school. *Educational Psychology in Practice, 19,* 199–217.

Meyer, V. (1982). Prime-O-Tec: A successful strategy for adult disabled readers. *Journal of Reading, 25,* 512–515.

Murad, C.R., & Topping, K.J. (2000). Parents as reading tutors for first graders in Brazil. *School Psychology International, 21*(2), 152–171.

Pikulski, J.J., & Chard, D.J. (2005). Fluency: Bridge between decoding and reading comprehension. *The Reading Teacher, 58,* 510–519.

Rashotte, C.A., & Torgesen, J.K. (1985). Repeated reading and reading fluency in learning-disabled children. *Reading Research Quarterly, 20,* 180–188.

Rasinski, T.V. (1990). Effects of repeated reading and Listening-While-Reading on reading fluency. *Journal of Educational Research, 83,* 147–150.

Samuels, S.J. (1979). The method of repeated readings. *The Reading Teacher, 32,* 403–408.

Schneeberg, H. (1977). Listening while reading: A four year study. *The Reading Teacher, 29,* 629–635.

Scoble, J., Topping, K.J., & Wigglesworth, C. (1988). Training family and friends as adult literacy tutors. *Journal of Reading, 31,* 410–417.

Stanovich, K.E. (1984). The interactive-compensatory model of reading: A confluence of developmental, experimental, and education psychology. *Remedial and Special Education, 5*(3), 11–19.

Topping, K.J. (1987). Peer tutored paired reading: Outcome data from ten projects. *Educational Psychology, 7,* 133–145.

Topping, K.J. (1992a). The effectiveness of paired reading in ethnic minority homes. *Multicultural Teaching, 10*(2), 19–23.

Topping, K.J. (1992b). Short- and long-term follow-up of parental involvement in reading projects. *British Educational Research Journal, 18,* 369–379.

Topping, K.J. (1995). *Paired reading, spelling and writing: The handbook for teachers and parents.* London: Cassell.

Topping, K.J. (2001). *Thinking reading writing: A practical guide to paired learning with peers, parents and volunteers.* New York: Continuum.

Topping, K.J., & Bryce, A. (2004). Cross-age peer tutoring of reading and thinking: Influence on thinking skills. *Educational Psychology, 24,* 595–621.

Topping, K.J., & Lindsay, G.A. (1992a). Paired reading: A review of the literature. *Research Papers in Education, 7,* 199–246.

Topping, K.J., & Lindsay, G.A. (1992b). Parental involvement in reading: The influence of socio-economic status and supportive home visiting. *Children and Society, 5,* 306–316.

Topping, K.J., & Lindsay, G.A. (1992c). The structure and development of the paired reading technique. *Journal of Research in Reading, 15*, 120–136.

Topping, K.J., & Whiteley, M. (1990). Participant evaluation of parent-tutored and peer-tutored projects in reading. *Educational Research, 32*(1), 14–32.

Topping, K.J., & Whiteley, M. (1993). Sex differences in the effectiveness of peer tutoring. *School Psychology International, 14*(1), 57–67.

Young, A.R., Bowers, P.G., & MacKinnon, G.E. (1996). Effects of prosodic modeling and repeated reading on poor readers' fluency and comprehension. *Applied Psycholinguistics, 17*, 59–84.

Chapter 7

Reading Fluency: Critical Issues for Struggling Readers

Joseph K. Torgesen and Roxanne F. Hudson

S everal findings from recent research have stimulated our interest in reading fluency as a topic for theoretical analysis and research. The first set of findings includes the powerfully converging data on the relationship between simple measures of oral-reading rate and performance on measures of reading comprehension (Chard, Vaughn, & Tyler, 2002; Fuchs, Fuchs, & Maxwell, 1988; Fuchs, Fuchs, Hosp, & Jenkins, 2001; Jenkins, Fuchs, van den Broek, Espin, & Deno, 2000, 2003). For students at all levels—but particularly for students at beginning stages of learning to read—oral-reading rate is strongly correlated with students' ability to comprehend both simple and complex text.

The relationship between individual differences in reading fluency and successful performance on measures of reading comprehension is dramatically illustrated in a recent study of the reading portion of the Florida Comprehensive Assessment Test (FCAT), which is used to monitor progress in reading in grades 3–10. In this study (Schatschneider, Buck, et al., 2004), the researchers gave a two-hour battery of reading, language, and cognitive ability tests to approximately 200 students at 3rd, 7th, and 10th grades. The goal of the study was to determine which dimensions of reading, language, or cognitive ability were most important in accounting for individual differences in reading comprehension performance at each grade level. The FCAT is a criterion-based test that requires students to read lengthy passages (passages are approximately 325 words in 3rd grade, 820 in 7th grade, and 1,000 in 10th grade) and then answer a variety of types of questions based on the content of the passages. The percentage of questions that assess higher order thinking skills increases from approximately 30% at third grade to 70% at 10th grade. Performance on the FCAT is categorized in five levels (1–5), with Level 3 being considered grade-level performance. Students must perform at Level 2 or higher on the FCAT to be eligible for promotion from 3rd to

What Research Has to Say About Fluency Instruction, edited by S. Jay Samuels and Alan E. Farstrup. © 2006 by the International Reading Association.

4th grade, and they also must attain a given level of proficiency on the test in order to be eligible for a regular high school diploma.

At third grade, oral-reading rate was the dominant factor in accounting for individual differences in performance on the FCAT, with the fluency factor accounting for 56% of the variance, the verbal knowledge and reasoning factor accounting for 44%, and the nonverbal reasoning and working memory factors accounting for 25% and 14% of the variance, respectively. At seventh grade, fluency and verbal knowledge and reasoning were equally dominant in accounting for variance on the FCAT; at 10th grade, verbal knowledge and reasoning was the dominant factor (52% of the variance), with fluency being second (32% of the variance) and the other variables being less important.

The sample used in this study was representative of the overall demographics of the student population in Florida at each of the three grade levels. Table 7.1 presents the average performance levels on a number of the tests for third-grade students who performed at each of the levels on the FCAT. The most striking finding from Table 7.1 is the extremely low performance of students at Level 1 on measures of reading fluency. When the students were asked to read FCAT-level passages orally, Level 1 students read them at half the rate of students who performed at the average level on the FCAT, and they achieved an average reading fluency score at the 6th percentile on a nationally standardized

Table 7.1. Average performance of third-grade students on measures of reading and verbal ability who achieved different levels of proficiency on the FCAT

Skill/Ability	FCAT Performance Level (N)				
	1 (47)	2 (26)	3 (54)	4 (63)	5 (17)
WPM on FCAT	54	92	102	119	148
Fluency percentile[1]	6th	32nd	56th	78th	93rd
Phonemic decoding[2]	25th	45th	59th	74th	91st
Verbal knowledge/reasoning[3]	42nd	59th	72nd	91st	98th

[1]Fluency was measured with the Gray Oral Reading Test (Wiederholt & Bryant, 2003).
[2]Phonemic Decoding Efficiency was measured with the Test of Word Reading Efficiency (Torgesen, Wagner, & Rashotte, 1999).
[3]Verbal knowledge/reasoning were measured with the Vocabulary and Similarities subtests of the Wechsler Abbreviated Scale of Intelligence (Wechsler, 1974).

measure of reading fluency. In 2004, 22% of Florida's third-grade students achieved Level 1 performance on the FCAT. If the reading fluency scores of these students are well represented by the sample in our study, this means that about 45,000 students in the state may be struggling on the FCAT primarily because they have not yet become fluent readers by the end of third grade.

Another reason for our interest in reading fluency is that reading fluency is one of the more difficult aspects of reading skill to remediate in older struggling readers. For example, in one highly successful intervention study with third- to fifth-grade students (Torgesen, Alexander, et al., 2001), intensive remedial interventions produced large gains in reading ability in a group of students who began the study with very impaired reading skills. During the eight-week intervention period, the students went from the 2nd to the 39th percentile in phonemic decoding accuracy, from the 4th to the 23rd percentile in text-reading accuracy, and from the 13th to the 27th percentile in reading comprehension. However, their reading fluency scores only went from the 3rd to the 5th percentile. When these same students were followed up two years after the intervention, their scores for phonemic decoding, text-reading accuracy, reading comprehension, and reading fluency were at the 29th, 27th, 36th, and 4th percentile, respectively. Although the students in this study were able to substantially "close the gap" with average readers in phonemic decoding, reading accuracy, and reading comprehension, the gap in reading fluency remained essentially unaffected by the intervention.

We would hasten to add that the students in this study did become more fluent readers in an absolute sense. For example, before the study began, students read the most difficult passage they were exposed to on the Gray Oral Reading Test-III (GORT-III; Wiederholt & Bryant, 1992) at a rate of 38 words per minute with 10 errors. At the two-year follow-up, the students read passages of similar difficulty at 101 words per minute with 2 errors. Similarly, rate for the next most difficult passage they read increased from 42 to 104 words per minute. Thus, for passages that had a constant level of difficulty, the children's reading rate more than doubled from pretest to the end of the follow-up period. Although the students clearly became more fluent readers, they were not able to "close the gap" with their average reading peers, because their peers were also growing rapidly in reading fluency during this period in their lives. This relative difficulty with "closing the gap" in reading fluency in older struggling readers has been replicated in other studies using a variety of instructional methods (Torgesen, 2005), and we will offer an explanation for it later in this chapter.

Finally, our interest in reading fluency has been further piqued by recent studies of reading-disabled students who are learning to read in languages in which grapheme–phoneme relationships are more consistent than they are in English. Most of this research has been conducted in Germany and reported by Heinz Wimmer (Wimmer & Mayringer, 2001). The basic finding is that children with severe reading difficulties in Germany tend to have far less severe problems with phonemic decoding and reading accuracy than dyslexic students in the United States, but they do have substantial difficulties with reading fluency. A longitudinal study with Dutch children (de Jong & van der Leij, 2003) similarly found that sixth-grade dyslexic and normally reading groups were very different on their reading speed or reading level but had considerable overlap on decoding accuracy. This relative dissociation between reading accuracy and reading fluency among dyslexic students learning to read languages with more transparent orthographies is interesting when compared to the difficulties we have just described in "closing the gap" in reading fluency with older children with reading disabilities. In both cases, after effective instruction, students with reading disabilities are more similar to average readers in their phonemic decoding and reading accuracy scores than they are in reading fluency. Why is it so difficult for them to become fluent readers?

Reading Fluency: A Definition

Fluent reading comprises three key elements: (1) accurate reading of connected text, (2) at a conversational rate, (3) with appropriate prosody (Hudson, Mercer, & Lane, 2000). A fluent reader can maintain this performance for long periods of time, retains the skill after long periods of no practice, and can generalize across texts. A fluent reader is also not easily distracted and reads in an effortless, flowing manner.

Word-reading *accuracy* refers to the ability to recognize or decode words correctly. Strong understanding of the alphabetic principle, the ability to blend sounds together (Ehri & McCormick, 1998), the ability to use other cues to the identity of words in text (Tunmer & Chapman, 1995), and knowledge of a large bank of high-frequency words are required for word-reading accuracy.

Reading *rate* comprises both fluent identification of individual words and the speed and fluidity with which a reader moves through connected text. As children practice in learning to read, they come to recognize larger and larger numbers of words "by sight," which means they can read them without having to sound them out or guess at their identity from contextual cues (Ehri, 2002; Share & Stanovich, 1995). Well-practiced words are recognized automatically (Kuhn & Stahl, 2000; LaBerge & Samuels, 1974), which implies that recognition occurs quickly and with little cognitive effort. The automaticity with which a reader can recognize words is almost as important as word-reading accuracy. It is not enough to get the word right if a great deal of cognitive effort is required to do so, because the effort and attention involved in phonemically decoding words or in guessing at words from context distract the reader's attention from building a coherent representation of the meaning of the text (Schwanenflugel, Hamilton, Kuhn, Wisenbaker, & Stahl, 2004). Most educators quantify rate in terms of reading speed—either the number of words read correctly per minute or the length of time it takes for a reader to complete a passage.

Prosody is a linguistic term that describes the rhythmic and tonal aspects of speech: the "music" of oral language. Prosodic features are variations in pitch (intonation), stress patterns (syllable prominence), and duration (length of time) that contribute to expressive reading of a text (Allington, 1983a; Dowhower, 1991; Schreiber, 1980, 1991). These elements signal question, surprise, exclamation, and other meanings beyond the semantics of the words being spoken. When these features are present and appropriate in oral reading, the reader is reading prosodically or "with expression." Struggling readers are often characterized as reading in a monotone without expression or with inappropriate phrasing.

One of the most interesting current questions in research on fluent reading concerns the role of prosody in the definition. The role of accuracy and rate seem central to the notion of fluent reading, but what role does prosody play? Perhaps the most straightforward reason to include prosody as part of the definition of fluency is that it may reflect the reader's understanding of the meaning of the passage being read. Reading fluency is more than just the ability to read text fast; it includes an understanding of the message being conveyed by the text. In this sense, prosody is a sign or an index that the reader is actively constructing the meaning of the passage as the words are being identified and pronounced.

Another, and less obvious, reason to include prosody as part of the definition of fluent reading is that prosodic reading may serve as an aid to comprehension itself. This view of prosody in relation to comprehension is expressed in the following statements from a recent widely disseminated introduction to the assessment of reading fluency written for teachers and other school professionals (Rasinski, 2004):

> Just as fluent musicians interpret or construct meaning from a musical score through phrasing, emphasis, and variations in tone and volume, fluent readers use cognitive resources to *construct meaning through expressive interpretation of the text.* (p. 4, italics added)

> Expressive reading happens once a degree of automaticity is established, and *expression is one way in which a reader constructs meaning while reading.* (p. 14, italics added)

The idea that prosody may be reciprocally related to comprehension is expressed within the same text in the following passages:

> When readers embed appropriate volume, tone, emphasis, phrasing, and other elements in oral expression, they are *giving evidence of actively interpreting or constructing meaning* from the passage.... (p. 4, italics added)

> This embedding of prosody shows that the reader is *trying to make sense of or comprehend the text....* (p. 14, italics added)

The following question has obvious instructional implications: Do children need to read prosodically to improve their comprehension, or is prosody in reading an index that comprehension has occurred? While it is clear that prosody in reading may be an important aid in understanding to the individual who is *listening* to someone read, it is less clear that prosody is used by the *reader* to help construct meaning.

Schwanenflugel et al. (2004) report a recent investigation in which this question was directly addressed. These investigators administered measures of isolated word-reading efficiency, prosody in reading, and reading comprehension to a sample of 120 second-grade students. The standard for prosodic reading on selected passages was first established by recording the tonal inflections, pauses, and so forth of a sample of adult readers. Then, the acoustic profiles of child and adult readers were compared using digital recording and comparison techniques. Children's prosody scores depended on the extent to which their acoustic profiles matched those of the adult profile. This study found that, although prosody was strongly related to individual differences in word-reading efficiency, individual differences in prosody did not have a strong or consistent relationship with reading comprehension by themselves. In other words, students who were able to read individual words rapidly and accurately showed more adult-like prosodic features in their reading, and these students also showed stronger reading comprehension. However, once the effect of single-word-reading efficiency was controlled, individual variations in prosody did not make a meaningful contribution to comprehension of the text. The investigators also found little evidence that prosody in oral reading provides additional evidence about reading comprehension above and beyond that provided by simple measures of single-word-reading efficiency.

In addition to ambiguities in the role of prosody as a central feature of fluent reading that contributes to comprehension or that can provide an independent assessment of comprehension, the prosodic features of oral reading are also more difficult to reliably assess than are the features of accuracy and rate. Only when prosody-rating measures include an assessment of rate do they approach reasonable levels of reliability for purposes of individual assessment (Rasinski, 2004). For all of these reasons, the most widely used current assessments for reading fluency do not typically include measures of prosody but appropriately focus on accuracy and rate to assess growth on this dimension of reading skill. The assessment of rate and accuracy is done using samples of oral reading because measures of silent-reading rate are much less reliable than those in which the examiner actually listens to the child read each word in the passage (Jenkins, Fuchs, Espin, van den Broek, & Deno, 2000).

Factors That Strongly Influence Reading Fluency

One of the goals of this chapter is to contribute to understanding of the factors that may be most critical to the reading-fluency problems of students with reading difficulties. The following discussion suggests which factors may underlie individual differences in text-reading fluency as we have defined it.

1. **Proportion of words in a passage that can be recognized "by sight."** As Ehri (2002) and others point out, words in text can be recognized in several ways. The reader can use letter–sound relationships to "sound out" the word, guess the word from a sense of the context, or recognize the word from memory. Adult readers rely mostly on the third strategy, and this is one of the things that allows them to achieve high levels of reading fluency. Asking a student to read a passage in which a relatively high proportion of the words

must be decoded analytically or identified by contextual inference will have an obvious impact on his or her reading fluency. Thus children, such as those in our intervention studies with older students, might appear to be relatively fluent on a "second-grade" level passage but relatively dysfluent on a "fifth-grade" level passage. When reading passages at the higher level, children simply see too many words that are not part of their "sight-word vocabulary" and that cannot be decoded without some kind of analytic or inferential process that takes more time than simple recognition.

2. **Variations in speed with which "sight words" are processed.** Because speed of word recognition increases directly with practice (Levy, Abello, & Lysynchuk, 1997), variability in the number of times a reader has previously recognized a word in text may cause individual differences in speed, as may fundamental differences in processing speed among individuals. We know, for example, that processing rate on cognitive tasks is a relatively stable and general characteristic on which individuals differ from one another (Kail, 1988). Differences in processing speed that might have a biological or constitutional basis would likely extend to reading fluency, which is itself a complex cognitive task. Within this latter category of constitutionally based differences in speed of processing, we would include (a) more central word-identification processes that would influence both oral- and silent-reading rates and (b) more peripheral processes, such as articulation rate, that might most heavily influence oral-reading rate. An interesting question for research would be to determine whether the reading-fluency problems of disabled readers are primarily the result of limitations in the range of words they can recognize "by sight" or in the rate at which they identify words within their sight-word vocabularies in text. The answer to this question is not likely to have an either/or answer, but answers to questions about the relative impact of these two factors would have important implications for intervention methods for students struggling with reading fluency.

3. **Speed of decoding processes used to identify unknown words (decoding fluency).** When words are not read by sight, they must be identified analytically. This may be through phonemic decoding, use of analogy, or guessing from context. Decoding is a sequentially executed process where the reader blends sounds to form words from their parts by blending individual phonemes

(beginning decoding) or phonograms (a more advanced form of decoding; Ehri, 2002). To decode unknown words fluently, readers need to develop at least the following knowledge and skills to a fluent level: knowledge of sound–symbol relationships, blending of sounds into words, recognition of reoccurring patterns across words (phonograms), and coordination of phonemic–orthographic and meaning information to determine exactly the right word. If any of the analytic or knowledge-retrieval processes that are required for decoding unknown words in text operate slowly or inaccurately, this slowness or imprecision should have a noticeable impact on both the speed and accuracy of text processing.

4. **Use of context to speed word identification.** Words are consistently read faster when they occur in a meaningful context than when they are read in isolated word lists (Jenkins et al., 2003; Stanovich, 1980). Although some studies suggest that passage context plays a much larger role in supporting word-reading fluency and accuracy for students with poor word-reading skills than for skilled readers (Stanovich & Stanovich, 1995), other research has reported relatively consistent effects of context for both good and poor readers (Bowey, 1985). A consistent finding, however, is that context does provide useful support for younger and poor readers (Ben-Dror, Pollatsek, & Scarpati, 1991; Pring & Snowling, 1986). There may be important differences among young children and poor readers in ability to use context that are related to individual differences in reading fluency. One thing that may underlie differences in the ability of poor readers to use context as an aid to increasing their word-reading fluency is the extent of their vocabulary and background knowledge. Children more adept at constructing meaning because of a larger knowledge base may experience a stronger beneficial effect of context on reading fluency than those who are less able to construct the meaning of a passage. The child's sense of the context can improve word-reading accuracy and fluency in at least two ways: (1) it can provide slight improvements in the speed with which "sight words" are identified (Share & Stanovich, 1995), and (2) it can be combined with phonemic information about words to help children identify previously unknown words in text (Ehri, 2002).

5. **Speed with which word meanings are identified.** As long as children are under obligation to be actively thinking about the mean-

ing of what they are reading, speed of identification of word meanings may play a role in limiting oral-reading fluency. On a test like the GORT-III, children know they will be expected to answer comprehension questions following their reading of the passage. Thus, differences in rate may be partially the result of individual variation in the speed with which students can access the meaning of words in text (Wolf, 2001b).

6. **Speed with which overall meaning is constructed.** Again, if students know they must answer questions about meaning after a passage is read, they may devote varying amounts of attention and spend varying amounts of time in identifying and rehearsing the major meaning elements of a passage as they are reading. For example, students may pause for varying amounts of time while reading a passage in order to consolidate or integrate the meaning of a sentence that has just been read. Other processes involved in reading comprehension that require attentional resources that might vary in their fluency across children include making connections between words and sentences, relating textual meaning to prior knowledge, and making inferences. These processes could potentially limit the reading fluency of readers, depending on how much of their attentional resources they use and how quickly the processing takes place.

7. **Differences in the relative value a child places on speed versus accuracy in reading.** On almost any task in which both speed and accuracy of performance are measured, rate of responding can be influenced by the value a reader sets on speed versus accuracy. For example, some students may be so concerned about making errors when reading orally that they unnecessarily slow their rate to provide an extra measure of insurance against mistakes. In contrast, other students may place a premium on getting through the text quickly, and as a result they make more errors than they would have if they allowed themselves to read at a little slower rate. On measures of oral-reading rate, the best performance will be achieved by students who pick the right balance between speed and accuracy, one that allows them to read as fast as possible while keeping errors to a minimum. Another possibility for some struggling readers may be that they rely on a "reliable and safe" strategy for reading words, such as phonemic decoding, when they could actually read most of the words through simple recognition processes. Teachers sometimes report that students are dysfluent

readers because they continue too long to rely on phonemic decoding strategies, but no reliable evidence supports that this problem is widespread among dysfluent readers. A more likely explanation for older struggling readers' use of analytic procedures to identify words in text is that they have not had enough correct learning trials to be able to identify the words by sight.

The foregoing analysis of the factors that might contribute to individual differences in reading fluency clearly demonstrates that these differences are likely to be multiply determined. However, if one of our goals is to develop effective interventions for struggling readers, and our time to intervene is limited (as it always will be), then we should start with interventions that will have the biggest payoff. They should focus on the factors that actually account for the most variance in fluency among children with reading disabilities, as long as those factors are amenable to instructional interventions. In an earlier analysis (Torgesen, Rashotte, & Alexander, 2001), we provided substantial evidence that the single most important factor in accounting for individual differences in reading fluency among students with reading disabilities was the speed with which individual words are recognized. In other words, when students with reading disabilities are compared to one another on a measure of text-reading fluency, the most important predictor of variability in reading fluency was a measure that assessed both speed of recognition for individual words and the range of words that could be recognized by sight. In this analysis, we examined the relationships between a standardized measure of oral-reading fluency and students' knowledge and skill in a number of areas, including the following four:

1. **Sight-word reading efficiency** was a direct measure of both the size of a child's sight-word vocabulary and the speed with which individual words could be recognized. This measure (Torgesen, Wagner, & Rashotte, 1999) required students to rapidly identify words that increase rapidly in difficulty from simple high-frequency words like *it*, *look*, and *hot* to less frequent, more complex words like *question*, *horizon*, and *inquire*. Thus, a child's score on the test was a function of both the speed with which "sight words" could be identified (words like *it*, *look*, and *hot* were likely to be in the sight-word vocabulary of most of the students in these samples) and the extent and range of the child's sight-word vocabulary itself (students with larger sight-word vocabularies would have been able to go fur-

ther in the list because they could recognize more of the difficult words by sight). A child's total score was the number of words that can be correctly recognized within 45 seconds.

2. **Phonemic decoding efficiency** was a measure of how fluently and accurately the children could pronounce regularly spelled non-words that increased gradually in difficulty from words containing two phonemes to words containing seven phonemes.

3. **Size of vocabulary** was not a direct measure of speed of access to word meanings, but was a reasonable proxy, because there is good evidence that speed of verbal processing is substantially correlated with measures of verbal knowledge (Hunt, Lunneborg, & Lewis, 1975). A reasonable assumption is that children with more extensive vocabularies have had more exposures to a broader variety of words than other children (Cunningham & Stanovich, 1998), and thus may be relatively more fluent in identifying word meanings within text.

4. **General naming speed**, or speed of processing, was measured by assessing how rapidly students could name a series of randomly repeated digits that were visually presented in an array on a single page.

Although these measures do not encompass all of the variables identified as potentially important in explaining individual differences in reading fluency, they do assess several of the most important ones. Torgesen, Rashotte, and Alexander (2001) examined relationships between these variables and reading fluency in five samples of students. For purposes of our discussion in this chapter, it is sufficient to know that one of the samples (longitudinal) was randomly selected and represented a cross section of students of all reading abilities, two samples (Remedial I and Remedial II) consisted of students ages 10–12 who had received relatively intensive reading interventions, and the last two samples were of students who had received preventive reading interventions because they were identified as "at risk" in kindergarten or first grade. The intervention implemented in Prevention I extended from kindergarten through second grade, and the students were followed up at the end of fourth grade. Prevention II involved an intervention that lasted during first grade, and the students were followed up in second grade.

Table 7.2 clearly shows that our assessment of the size of children's sight-word vocabularies and speed of recognition for individual words (sight-word efficiency) had the strongest and most consistent relationships with text-reading fluency across these five samples. Remarkably,

Table 7.2. Correlations between text-reading rate and component reading skills, processing speed, and general vocabulary knowledge

	Longitudinal (5th grade)	Remediation I (5th–7th grade)	Remediation II (3rd–6th grade)	Prevention I (4th grade)	Prevention II (2nd grade)
Nonword Efficiency	.75**	.55**	.73**	.87**	.81**
Sight-Word Efficiency	.82**	.71**	.81**	.88**	.89**
Rapid Naming	.44**	.28	.53**	.66**	.63**
Vocabulary	.62**	.13	.33*	.44**	.07
Text-Fluency Range[1]	55–145	55–95	55–115	55–140	70–130

*p<.05
**p<.01

[1]This is the range of standard scores on the reading rate measure from the Gray Oral Reading Test-Revised. Standard scores were transformed to a mean of 100 and standard deviation of 15.
Adapted from Torgesen, J.K., Rashotte, C.A., & Alexander, A. (2001). Principles of fluency instruction in reading: Relationships with established empirical outcomes. In M. Wolf (Ed.), *Dyslexia, fluency, and the brain* (pp. 333–355). Timonium, MD: York Press.

given the number of factors that might potentially influence reading fluency, four of the five correlations approach the theoretical maximum possible correlation that can be obtained between two tests whose reliabilities are not perfect. Because all the predictor variables in this table are correlated with one another, we performed another set of analyses to determine which variables helped to explain variance in reading fluency beyond that explained by sight-word efficiency. The results were as follows:

1. **Longitudinal sample.** Sight-word efficiency (SWE) accounted for 67% of the variance. Nonword efficiency explained an additional 1% of the variance, and vocabulary an additional 6%. The combination of variables that explained the most variance was SWE and vocabulary (73%).

2. **Remediation Study I.** None of the variables explained significant variance in reading fluency beyond that explained by sight-word efficiency.

3. **Remediation Study II.** Nonword efficiency explained an additional 2% of the variance, and in combination with sight-word efficiency, they explained 68% of the variance in reading fluency.

4. **Prevention I.** Nonword efficiency explained an additional 2% of the variance, and rapid naming of digits explained an additional

1%. The combination that explained the most variance was sight-word efficiency and nonword efficiency (80%).

5. **Prevention II.** Nonword efficiency explained an additional 1% of the variance, and rapid naming of digits explained an additional 1%. The combination that explained the most variance was sight-word efficiency and nonword efficiency (83%).

These results indicate that the additional contribution made by the other variables to explaining individual differences in reading fluency was quite small. One potentially interesting variation in the results across samples was the relatively substantial independent contribution of vocabulary knowledge to individual differences in reading fluency in the random sample of fifth-grade students (longitudinal sample). Among these students, fluency scores covered the full range from extremely dys-fluent to extremely fluent. Evidence suggests that within this sample the richness of a child's semantic network (vocabulary) may be uniquely important to text-reading fluency only in older children at higher ranges of fluency. For example, when children with above-average fluency scores are eliminated from this sample, the correlation between verbal ability and fluency was cut in half (.62 to .31), and verbal ability no longer explained unique variance in text-reading rate. In this same sample with restricted range of fluency scores, the correlation between sight-word efficiency and fluency remained a relatively robust .74.

The idea that verbal and comprehension processes may be more important in explaining individual differences in fluency among more fluent than less fluent readers is consistent with the findings from a recent study by Jenkins et al. (2003). Using a sample of students with a full range of reading ability, these authors found that individual differences among students in their ability to read isolated words was the most important factor accounting for differences in reading fluency at low levels of fluency. In contrast, individual differences among students in their reading comprehension skill accounted for the largest share of variance in reading fluency among the more fluent readers in the sample. One possible interpretation of these findings is that fast-spreading processes of semantic activation produce a word "priming" effect that leads to increasingly higher levels of fluency in students once they attain some threshold of word-reading ability and comprehension. For these students, comprehension processes themselves enable words that are related to the overall meaning of the passage to be read more rapidly, because they are "primed" to be read by their semantic relationship to the central meanings or themes of the passage. Until students reach this theoretical threshold for word-recognition fluency and comprehension, however, it is differences in the size of students' sight-word vocabularies that appear to be most important in explaining individual differences in fluency. A remaining ambiguity in the analyses reported by Torgesen, Rashotte, and Alexander (2001) arises from the nature of the sight-word efficiency measure that was used. As explained earlier, individual differences in performance on this measure probably arise from two different sources. One of the sources is simple pronunciation speed for individual words, and the other is the range of words that can be recognized by sight. In one of the samples (Remediation I), we were able to more directly study the impact that the size of the students' sight-word vocabulary had on their reading fluency.

In this sample, reading fluency was assessed using the GORT-III. This test provides a "standard score" for reading fluency that is based on performance of students in a national standardization sample, with a score of 100 being average. We examined the rate at which children would have to read the passages of the GORT-III to achieve an average score on the test. To achieve a standard score of 100 for fluency, students ages 10 years, 6 months, to 10 years, 11 months, would have to read at 137–150 words per minute (wpm) on each of the first seven stories.

We then examined the speed of reading for students in our remediation study on the GORT-III story just prior to the last story on which they reached a ceiling (because of too many word-reading errors). At the posttest in this study, maximum story levels ranged from Story 4 to Story 9. The average reading rate for the group was 78.3 correct wpm. Clearly, the students were reading at a rate well below expectations. These passages were difficult for the children, and the average number of errors indicated that they were at their instructional rather than independent reading level. If we were to examine reading rate on passages where the children were reading at an independent level (2 errors or less), would the rate still be slow and halting, or would it approach more normal fluency levels? Using the same subjects, but using the most difficult passage on which there were 2 or less errors (average story level was 4), we found an overall reading rate of 122 wpm. This finding suggests that when the students were familiar with the words in a story, their fluency approached that of an average reader, although it did not quite reach average levels. However, when they encountered words that they had to decode phonemically, or by some other conscious process, their overall fluency rate quickly declined. Because students are given 10 seconds to decode words on the GORT-III before the examiner provides the word, it is easy to see how difficulty with just a few words could significantly influence reading rate.

Difficulty in Remediation of Fluency Problems in Older Struggling Readers

As mentioned at the beginning of this chapter, one of the consistent findings in our remedial research for children who begin the intervention with moderate or serious impairments in word-reading ability is that the interventions have not been sufficient to close the gap in reading fluency. Although the students increase in fluency in an absolute sense (they become more fluent within passages of the same level of difficulty), the interventions do not bring the students to average levels of fluency for students their age, nor are students' percentile or standard scores for fluency nearly as high as they are for accuracy.

When teachers or other researchers see these results, they think immediately that the interventions we have studied must be faulty. Perhaps the interventions have emphasized phonics too much, perhaps they focus on accuracy too much, or perhaps they do not provide enough practice in reading fluency itself. We do not entirely discount these possibilities, but we also have considerable evidence that the problem may lie in the nature of reading fluency itself, particularly for students who are struggling with very low levels of fluency.

First, in one study with severely impaired readers (Torgesen, Alexander, et al., 2001), one of the instructional interventions invested 50% of instructional time in reading connected text, while the other invested only 5%. Nevertheless, we found no difference in fluency outcomes between the two methods. Second, we have reported a series of interventions with students who had moderate (10th percentile) or mild (30th percentile) impairments in word-level reading skills, and which focused considerable instructional time in text-reading activities with an emphasis on both modeling and practicing fluent reading (Torgesen, Rashotte, Alexander, Alexander, & MacPhee, 2003). Again, the students who began the intervention with moderate level (10th percentile) word-reading difficulties showed only small improvement in their age-based percentile ranking for fluency, although they increased substantially in other dimensions of reading skill.

Third, and probably most important, we have not obtained the same differences in outcomes between reading fluency and reading accuracy in our prevention studies as we have in the remedial studies. Figure 7.1 shows the percentile scores (a score of 50 is average) for reading accuracy and fluency outcomes for four samples of 9- to 12-year-old children with severe (below 2nd percentile) to moderate (10th percentile) word-level reading difficulties. Each sample is identified by its reading accuracy percentile at the beginning of the intervention. The left-most data are from Torgesen, Rashotte, and Alexander (2001); next is from a severely impaired sample in Torgesen, Rashotte, et al. (2003) that received 133 hours of intervention; next is from a moderately impaired sample that received 51 hours of intervention from Torgesen, Rashotte, et al. (2003); and next is the moderately impaired sample that received 100 hours of intervention reported in the same paper.

Outcomes for text-reading fluency and accuracy from two prevention studies are presented on the right side of Figure 7.1. The most ob-

Figure 7.1. Outcomes for reading accuracy and reading rate from remedial and preventive studies of children with reading disabilities

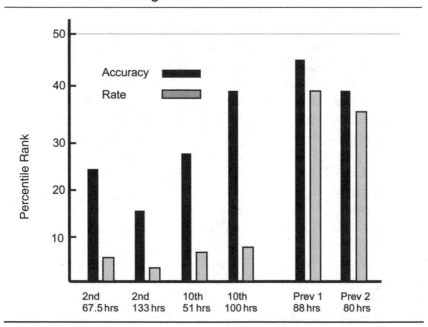

vious difference between the outcomes from the prevention and remediation studies is that the gap between reading fluency and reading accuracy is not nearly as large for the prevention studies as for the remediation studies. The first prevention study (Torgesen, Wagner, Rashotte, et al., 1999) provided 2$^1/_2$ years of instruction to children in 20-minute sessions four days a week from the second semester of kindergarten through second grade. The children were identified as the 10% most at risk for reading failure because of low scores in phonemic awareness and letter knowledge in the first semester of kindergarten. The data in Figure 7.1 show the performance of children in the most effective instructional condition at the end of fourth grade, two years after the intervention was concluded. The children's scores for both reading accuracy and fluency are solidly in the average range.

The second study (Torgesen, Wagner, Rashotte, & Herron, 2003) provided preventive instruction during first grade to children identified at the beginning of first grade as the 20% most at risk for reading failure. The children were taught in small groups using a combination of teacher-led and computer-assisted instruction in 50-minute sessions, four days a week from October through May. The data in Figure 7.1 show the performance of the children from the most-effective condition at the end of second grade, one year after the intervention concluded. Again, both reading accuracy and fluency scores are solidly within the average range, and the gap between these scores is very small.

We have proposed elsewhere (Torgesen, Rashotte, & Alexander, 2001) several possible explanations for the difficulty we have experienced in helping older children to "close the gap" in reading fluency after they have struggled in learning to read for several years. The most important factor appears to involve difficulties in making up for the huge deficits in accurate reading practice the older children have accumulated by the time they reach late elementary school. These differences in reading practice emerge during the earliest stages of reading instruction (Allington, 1983b; Biemiller, 1977/1978) and they become more pronounced as the children advance across the grades in elementary school. Reading practice varies directly with the severity of a child's reading disability, so that children with severe reading disabilities receive only a very small fraction of the total reading practice obtained by children with normal reading skills (Cunningham & Stanovich, 1998).

One of the major results of this lack of reading practice is a severe limitation in the number of words the children with reading disabilities can recognize automatically, or at a single glance (Ehri, 2002; Share & Stanovich, 1995). This limitation of "sight word" vocabulary is a principle characteristic of most children with reading disabilities after the initial phase in learning to read (Rashotte, MacPhee, & Torgesen, 2001; Torgesen, Alexander, et al., 2001; Wise, Ring, & Olson, 1999). The limitation arises because children must read specific words accurately a number of times before they can become part of their sight vocabulary (Reitsma, 1983; Share & Stanovich, 1995). As Ehri (2002) points out, "sight words include any word that readers have practiced reading sufficiently often to be read from memory" (p. 10).

We have already provided evidence in this chapter that inefficiency in identifying single words is the most important factor in accounting for individual differences in text-reading fluency in samples of children with reading disabilities. These findings, combined with the fact that the number of less frequent words (words children are less likely to have encountered before in text) increases rapidly after about third-grade level (Adams, 1990), make it easy to see why closing the gap in reading fluency with their normally achieving peers is so difficult for children who have failed in reading for the first three or four years of school. If successively higher grade-level passages include increasing numbers of less frequent words, and normal readers are continually expanding their sight vocabularies through their own reading behavior, it should be very difficult for children, once significantly behind in the growth of their sight-word vocabulary, to close the gap in the number and extent of words they can read from memory. Such "catching up" would seem to require an extensive period of time in which the reading practice of the previously disabled children was actually *greater* than that of their peers. Even if word-reading accuracy is dramatically increased through the more efficient use of analytic word-reading processes, reliance on analytic processes will not produce the kind of fluent reading that results when most of the words in a passage can be recognized at a single glance.

Other Factors That May Limit Fluency in Children With Reading Disabilities

Maryanne Wolf (Wolf, 2001a; Wolf & Bowers, 1999) and Patricia Bowers (Bowers, Golden, Kennedy, & Young, 1994; Bowers & Wolf, 1993) have proposed that some children with reading difficulties may experience unique problems forming the orthographic representations that are the basis for recognizing words from memory. In their conceptualization, this problem exists independently from the common problems that most children with reading disabilities have in becoming accurate readers through the use of alphabetic reading skills. Children with this second type of processing deficit perform extremely poorly on measures of rapid automatic naming, which require them to name series of familiar digits or letters as rapidly as possible when they are presented in visual arrays. In their conceptualization of the processes common to both rapid naming and fluent word reading, Wolf and Bowers (1999) focused on the need for a "precise timing mechanism" that is important in the formation of the visually based representations of words that allow them to be recognized as whole units in text. They hypothesized that "slow letter (or digit) naming speed may signal disruption of the automatic processes which support induction of orthographic patterns, which, in turn, result in quick word recognition" (Bowers & Wolf, 1993, p. 70). If this conceptualization is correct, it means that, even after students with this second type of deficit become accurate readers, they will still struggle with reading fluency because it is much more difficult for them to learn to recognize words by sight than for other children.

Linnea Ehri (2002) recently developed a compelling theory of the way that sight-word representations are formed that does not require a "double deficit" to explain the special difficulties that some students with reading disabilities may have in learning to recognize words from memory. Her theory also helps to explain the lingering problems with reading fluency experienced by dyslexic students in Germany, even after they have become relatively accurate readers. In developing this theory, Ehri sought to understand how children are able to acquire very large numbers of precise orthographic representations (representations in memory that contain information about a word's spelling) so rapidly.

Ehri (1998, 2002) suggested that to understand the speed with which children form orthographic representations for previously unknown words, we need a "mnemonically powerful" system. One of the central ideas of her theory of sight-word development is that "readers learn sight words by forming connections between letters seen in spellings of words and sounds detected in their *pronunciations already present in memory*" (Ehri, 2002, p. 11, italics added). In other words,

> readers learn to process written words as phonemic maps that lay out elements of the pronunciation visually. Beginners become skilled at computing these mapping relations spontaneously when they read new words. This is the critical event for sight word learning. Grapho-phonemic

connections provide a powerful mnemonic system that bonds written words to their pronunciations in memory along with meanings. Once the alphabetic mapping system is known, readers can build a vocabulary of sight words easily. (p. 12)

To use a word's phonology as a mnemonic for helping to remember its orthography, children need to be able to fluently apprehend the phonological structure of words as they compute the "mapping relations" between the letters and sounds in words. Thus, children with highly fluent and easily applied phonemic-segmentation skills (skill in identifying all the individual phonemes in words) should be able to form orthographic representations more easily than children who are less phonemically fluent. This relationship suggests that individual differences in the fluency and accuracy of phonemic-segmentation processes should be related to the development of sight-word representations and reading fluency.

The current research literature, however, does not consistently support this relationship. For example, a recent longitudinal study by Schatschneider, Fletcher, Francis, Carlson, and Foorman (2004) examined the relative importance of phonemic awareness, rapid naming of letters, rapid naming of objects, letter naming, letter–sound knowledge, vocabulary, and visual discrimination measured in kindergarten in predicting reading accuracy, fluency, and comprehension at the end of first and second grades. The combination of phonemic awareness, rapid naming of letters, letter naming, and letter–sound naming was a strong and significant predictor of all three outcomes at both grades. However, in this study, as in others (e.g., reviewed in Allor, 2002), rapid naming of letters was a stronger predictor of fluency than was phonemic awareness when the variables were considered separately.

A number of studies have directly compared the predictive power of phonemic awareness and rapid automatic naming speed, and some have suggested that the importance of individual differences in phonemic awareness may diminish because other factors become more important in predicting reading fluency as reading skills develop (e.g., Allor, Fuchs, & Mathes, 2001; Bowers & Wolf, 1993; Catts, Gillispie, Leonard, Kail, & Miller, 2002; Sprugevica & Hoien, 2004; Sunseth & Bowers, 2002). Allor's (2002) review of 16 studies that included both phonemic awareness and rapid-naming measures found mixed results as to whether both contributed uniquely with the other in the predictive model. Findings varied based on whether reading was measured as single-word-reading accuracy, comprehension, or fluency. In general, however, rapid automatic-naming tasks were found to be better predictors of reading fluency than were measures of phonemic awareness.

One unexamined possibility in these longitudinal predictive studies is that rapid automatic-naming tasks may be better predictors of reading fluency than measures of phonemic awareness because they assess the *fluency* of fundamental cognitive processes required for construction of sight-word representations, whereas measures of phonemic awareness have measured only the accuracy of these processes. The model of sight-word development considered in this chapter would predict strong relationships between measures of rapid automatic naming for letters (assuming that speed of identifying letter names is highly correlated with speed of identifying letter sounds) and reading fluency. Rapid computation of mapping relationships between the orthographic and phonological structure of words would require highly automatic associations between letters and the sounds they typically represent. However, the model would also predict a strong relationship between individual differences in fluent access to the phonological structure of words and individual differences in the speed and ease with which orthographic representations are formed. A more complete test of this hypothesis must await the development of reliable and valid measures of fluency of access to the phonological structure of words.

Let us now return to the findings mentioned in the introduction to this chapter that children with reading disabilities in Germany and other countries with regular orthographies have more serious problems with reading fluency than they do with reading accuracy. In the context of Ehri's (2002) theory of the way sight-word representations are formed, it is interesting that Landerl, Wimmer, and Frith (1997) found their sample of German dyslexic students to perform equivalently to a sample of American dyslexic students on a difficult measure of phonemic awareness, in spite of the stronger decoding skills of the German students. This finding mirrors that of de Jong and van der Leij (2003), who found that Dutch fourth-grade children with significant reading fluency problems had average decoding skill and performed competently on relatively easy measures of phonemic awareness, but were impaired relative to grade-level control students on a more difficult phonemic-awareness measure. These authors view these results as suggesting that in regular orthographies, subtle deficits in phonemic awareness may not influence older students' decoding skill, but such deficits still might have an effect on their reading fluency. The link from these findings to Ehri's theory depends on whether deficits on the more difficult tests of phonemic awareness (as opposed to simpler tests) signal a remaining deficit in the fluency of the phonological processes required in mapping the relations between the phonological and orthographic structure of words when they are first encountered in text.

Conclusions

The basic premise of this chapter has been that the reading fluency problems of children with reading difficulties occur primarily as the result of their difficulties forming large vocabularies of words that they can recognize "by sight" or at a single glance. Without powerful early interventions to support the development of independent and accurate reading skills, these students do not read accurately or extensively enough to learn to recognize thousands of words from memory. Thus, when they are asked to read a passage at grade level, two kinds of problems are likely to occur. First, they will not be able to instantly, or automatically, recognize as many of the words in the text as average readers. They will stumble on, guess at, or attempt to "sound out" many words. Second, their attempts to identify words they do not immediately recognize will produce many errors. They will not be efficient in using letter–sound relationships (phonics) in combination with context to identify unknown words.

If older students with these types of word-level reading problems receive powerful and appropriately focused interventions, many of them can become accurate readers, and their reading comprehension improves as a result of being able to correctly identify more of the words in text (Torgesen, 2005; Torgesen, Rashotte, & Alexander, 2001). However, when compared to average readers of the same age, the sight-word vocabulary of these students will still remain severely restricted because sight words must be acquired one at a time through multiple correct reading trials over time. Because average-level readers are adding new words to their sight-word vocabulary through reading practice almost every day, it is very difficult for reading-disabled students, even if they begin reading more accurately, to close the enormous gap between them and their same-age peers in the numbers and extent of words that can be read fluently from memory. Thus, it is not easy for these students to become "fluent readers" if the standard of reading fluency is based on the ability to fluently identify almost all of the words in *text appropriate for their age.* This difficulty in recovering the "lost ground" in the development of sight-word vocabulary that results from several years of minimal and inaccurate reading is the simplest current explanation for the enduring reading-fluency problems of students even after they become more accurate readers through strong reading interventions.

We have also considered the possibility that many students with reading disabilities may have special difficulties acquiring fully developed orthographic representations, even after they become accurate readers. Although the precise nature of the underlying difficulty associated with this problem is not clear at this point, the problem itself would mean that these students would require even more accurate practice trials than normal readers to create reliable orthographic representations. They also may require different kinds of instructional support, particularly support that makes the phonological structure and grapheme-phoneme connections in unfamiliar words more explicit.

In this chapter, we have said nothing about effective instruction for reading fluency, anticipating that other chapters in this volume will cover this topic. What should be clear from the analysis presented here, however, is that effective interventions for students struggling with reading fluency must substantially increase the number of opportunities these students have to accurately practice reading previously unknown words. Both techniques that provide reading practice in connected text (Hudson, Lane, & Pullen, 2005; Meyer & Felton, 1999) and those that provide practice in reading words in isolation (Levy, 2001; Levy, Abello, & Lysynchuk, 1997; Tan & Nicholson, 1997) have been shown to improve reading fluency in struggling readers. Another possible avenue for the development of more powerful interventions in the future lies in the use of "engineered" text that provides systematic and frequent exposures to high-utility words as a way to help build children's sight-word vocabularies (Hiebert, 2004). Finally, it may be useful to experiment with ways to enhance students' awareness of the match between the orthography and phonology of unknown words as a way to stimulate the use of the words' phonology as a mnemonic for their orthography (Ehri, 2002).

Questions for Discussion

1. What is the most powerful argument presented in this chapter for the value of working to prevent early reading difficulties in young students?

2. A remedial specialist indicates that, over the past six months of remedial work, she has seen significant improvement in the level of

text that her students with learning disabilities can read with 95% accuracy. However, she has not seen a correspondingly dramatic increase in the level of text the student can read with acceptable levels of fluency. How does the information presented in this text help to understand this problem?

3. What appears to be the major factor that limits the reading fluency of older struggling readers?

4. Many teachers consider "sight words" to be just those words that they teach to students directly using flashcards. How is the conception of "sight words" presented in this chapter different from that idea?

5. What are some of the factors that are likely to create differences among a group of fifth-grade students in the fluency with which they can read fifth-grade–level text?

REFERENCES

Adams, M.J. (1990). *Beginning to read: Thinking and learning about print.* Cambridge, MA: MIT Press.

Allington, R.L. (1983a). Fluency: The neglected reading goal. *The Reading Teacher, 36,* 6, 556–561.

Allington, R.L. (1983b). The reading instruction provided readers of different reading abilities. *The Elementary School Journal, 83,* 549–559.

Allor, J.H. (2002). The relationships of phonemic awareness and rapid naming to reading development. *Learning Disability Quarterly, 25,* 47–57.

Allor, J.H., Fuchs, D., & Mathes, P.G. (2001). Do students with and without lexical retrieval weaknesses respond differently to instruction? *Journal of Learning Disabilities, 34,* 264–275.

Ben-Dror, I., Pollatsek, A., & Scarpati, S. (1991). Word identification in isolation and in context by college dyslexic students. *Brain and Language, 40,* 471–490.

Biemiller, A. (1977/1978). Relationships between oral reading rates for letters, words, and simple text in the development of reading achievement. *Reading Research Quarterly, 13,* 223–253.

Bowers, P.G., Golden, J., Kennedy, A., & Young, A. (1994). Limits upon orthographic knowledge due to processes indexed by naming speed. In V.W. Berninger (Ed.), *The varieties of orthographic knowledge: Theoretical and developmental issues* (Vol. 1, pp. 173–218). London: Kluwer Academic.

Bowers, P.G., & Wolf, M. (1993). Theoretical links among naming speed, precise timing mechanisms and orthographic skill in dyslexia. *Reading and Writing: An Interdisciplinary Journal, 5,* 69–85.

Bowey, J.A. (1985). Contextual facilitation in children's oral reading in relation to grade and decoding skill. *Journal of Experimental Child Psychology, 40,* 23–48.

Catts, H.W., Gillispie, M., Leonard, L.B., Kail, R.V., & Miller, C.A. (2002). The role of speed of processing, rapid naming, and phonological awareness in reading achievement. *Journal of Learning Disabilities, 35*, 510–525.

Chard, D.J., Vaughn, S., & Tyler, B.J. (2002). A synthesis of research on effective interventions for building reading fluency with elementary students with learning disabilities. *Journal of Learning Disabilities, 35*, 386–406.

Cunningham, A.E., & Stanovich, K.E. (1998). What reading does for the mind. *American Educator, 22*(1–2), 8–15.

de Jong, P.F., & van der Leij, A. (2003). Developmental changes in the manifestation of a phonological deficit in dyslexic children learning to read a regular orthography. *Journal of Educational Psychology, 95*, 22–40.

Dowhower, S.L. (1991). Speaking of prosody: Fluency's unattended bedfellow. *Theory Into Practice, 30*(3), 165–175.

Ehri, L.C. (1998). Grapheme-phoneme knowledge is essential for learning to read words in English. In J.L. Metsala & L.C. Ehri (Eds.), *Word recognition in beginning literacy* (pp. 3–40). Mahwah, NJ: Erlbaum.

Ehri, L.C. (2002). Phases of acquisition in learning to read words and implications for teaching. In R. Stainthorp & P. Tomlinson (Eds.), *Learning and teaching reading* (pp. 27–42). London: British Journal of Educational Psychology Monograph Series II.

Ehri, L.C., & McCormick, S. (1998). Phases of word learning: Implications for instruction with delayed and disabled readers. *Reading & Writing Quarterly, 14*(2), 135–163.

Fuchs, L.S., Fuchs, D., Hosp, M.K., & Jenkins, J.R. (2001). Oral reading fluency as an indicator of reading competence: A theoretical, empirical, and historical analysis. *Scientific Studies of Reading, 5*, 239–256.

Fuchs, L.S., Fuchs, D., & Maxwell, L. (1988). The validity of informal reading comprehension measures. *Remedial and Special Education, 9*(2), 20–28.

Hiebert, E. (2004, May 5). *Effects of daily reading of information text on young reader's fluency.* Paper presented at the International Reading Association annual convention, Reno, NV.

Hudson, R.F., Lane, H.B., & Pullen, P.C. (2005). Reading fluency assessment and instruction: What, why, and how? *The Reading Teacher, 58*, 702–714.

Hudson, R.F., Mercer, C.D., & Lane, H.B. (2000). *Exploring reading fluency: A paradigmatic overview.* Unpublished manuscript. University of Florida, Gainesville.

Hunt, E., Lunneborg, C., & Lewis, J. (1975). What does it mean to be high verbal? *Cognitive Psychology, 7*, 194–227.

Jenkins, J.R., Fuchs, L.S., Espin, C., van den Broek, P., & Deno, S.L. (2000, February). *Effects of task format and performance dimension on word reading measures: Criterion validity, sensitivity to impairment, and context facilitation.* Paper presented at Pacific Coast Research Conference, San Diego, CA.

Jenkins, J.R., Fuchs, L.S., van den Broek, P., Espin, C., & Deno, S.L. (2003). Sources of individual differences in reading comprehension and reading fluency. *Journal of Educational Psychology, 95*, 719–729.

Kail, R. (1988). Developmental functions for speeds of cognitive processes. *Journal of Experimental Child Psychology, 45*, 339–364.

Kuhn, M.R., & Stahl, S.A. (2000). *Fluency: A review of developmental and remedial practices.* Ann Arbor, MI: Center for the Improvement of Early Reading Achievement.

LaBerge, D., & Samuels, S.J. (1974). Toward a theory of automatic information processing in reading. *Cognitive Psychologist, 6,* 293–323.

Landerl, K., Wimmer, H., & Frith, U. (1997). The impact of orthographic consistency on dyslexia: A German-English comparison. *Cognition, 63,* 315–334.

Levy, B.A. (2001). Moving the bottom: Improving reading fluency. In M. Wolf (Ed.), *Dyslexia, fluency, and the brain* (pp. 357–382). Timonium, MD: York Press.

Levy, B.A., Abello, B., & Lysynchuk, L. (1997). Transfer from word training to reading in context: Gains in reading fluency and comprehension. *Learning Disabilities Quarterly, 20,* 173–188.

Meyer, M.S., & Felton, R.H. (1999). Repeated reading to enhance fluency: Old approaches and new directions. *Annals of Dyslexia, 49,* 283–306.

Pring, L., & Snowling, M. (1986). Developmental changes in word recognition: An information-processing account. *Quarterly Journal of Experimental Psychology: Human Experimental Psychology, 38,* 395–418.

Rashotte, C.A., MacPhee, K., & Torgesen, J.K. (2001). The effectiveness of a group reading instruction program with poor readers in multiple grades. *Learning Disability Quarterly, 24,* 119–134.

Rasinski, T.V. (2004). *Assessing reading fluency.* Honolulu, HI: Pacific Resources for Education and Learning.

Reitsma, P. (1983). Printed word learning in beginning readers. *Journal of Experimental Child Psychology, 36,* 321–339.

Schatschneider, C., Buck, J., Torgesen, J.K., Wagner, R.K., Hassler, L., Hecht, S., et al. (2004). *A multivariate study of factors that contribute to individual differences in performance on the Florida Comprehensive Reading Assessment Test* (Technical Report No. 5). Tallahassee: Florida Center for Reading Research.

Schatschneider, C., Fletcher, J.M., Francis, D.J., Carlson, C.D., & Foorman, B.R. (2004). Kindergarten prediction of reading skills: A longitudinal comparative analysis. *Journal of Educational Psychology, 96,* 265–282.

Schreiber, P.A. (1980). On the acquisition of reading fluency. *Journal of Reading Behavior, 7*(3), 177–186.

Schreiber, P.A. (1991). Understanding prosody's role in reading acquisition. *Theory Into Practice, 30*(3), 158–164.

Schwanenflugel, P.J., Hamilton, A.M., Kuhn, M.R., Wisenbaker, J.M., & Stahl, S.A. (2004). Becoming a fluent reader: Reading skill and prosodic features in the oral reading of young readers. *Journal of Educational Psychology, 96*(1), 119–129.

Share, D.L., & Stanovich, K.E. (1995). Cognitive processes in early reading development: Accommodating individual differences into a model of acquisition. *Issues in Education: Contributions From Educational Psychology, 1,* 1–57.

Sprugevica, L., & Hoien, T. (2004). Relations between enabling skills and reading comprehension: A follow-up study of Latvian students from first to second grade. *Scandinavian Journal of Psychology, 45,* 115–122.

Stanovich, K.E. (1980). Toward an interactive-compensatory model of individual differences in the development of reading fluency. *Reading Research Quarterly, 16,* 32–71.

Stanovich, K.E., & Stanovich, P. (1995). How research might inform the debate about early reading acquisition. *Journal of Research in Reading, 18*(2), 87–105.

Sunseth, K., & Bowers, P.G. (2002). Rapid naming and phonemic awareness: Contributions to reading, spelling, and orthographic knowledge. *Scientific Studies of Reading, 6*, 401–429.

Tan, A., & Nicholson, T. (1997). Flashcards revisited: Training poor readers to read words faster improves their comprehension of text. *Journal of Educational Psychology, 89*, 276–288.

Torgesen, J.K. (2005). Recent discoveries from research on remedial interventions for children with dyslexia. In M. Snowling & C. Hulme (Eds.), *The science of reading* (pp. 521–537). Oxford, England: Blackwell.

Torgesen, J.K., Alexander, A.W., Wagner, R.K., Rashotte, C.A., Voeller, K., Conway, T., et al. (2001). Intensive remedial instruction for children with severe reading disabilities: Immediate and long term outcomes from two instructional approaches. *Journal of Learning Disabilities, 34*, 33–58.

Torgesen, J.K., Rashotte, C.A., & Alexander, A. (2001). Principles of fluency instruction in reading: Relationships with established empirical outcomes. In M. Wolf (Ed.), *Dyslexia, fluency, and the brain* (pp. 333–356). Timonium, MD: York Press.

Torgesen, J.K., Rashotte, C., Alexander, A., Alexander, J., & MacPhee, K. (2003). Progress towards understanding the instructional conditions necessary for remediating reading difficulties in older children. In B. Foorman (Ed.), *Preventing and remediating reading difficulties: Bringing science to scale* (pp. 275–298). Timonium, MD: York Press.

Torgesen, J.K., Wagner, R.K., & Rashotte, C. (1999). *Test of word reading efficiency.* Austin, TX: Pro-Ed.

Torgesen, J.K., Wagner, R.K., Rashotte, C.A., & Herron, J. (2003). *Summary of outcomes from first grade study with Read, Write, and Type and Auditory Discrimination In Depth instruction and software with at-risk children* (Technical Report No. 3). Tallahassee: Florida Center for Reading Research.

Torgesen, J.K., Wagner, R.K., Rashotte, C.A., Rose, E., Lindamood, P., & Garvan, C. (1999). Preventing reading failure in young children with phonological processing disabilities: Group and individual responses to instruction. *Journal of Educational Psychology, 91*, 579–593.

Tunmer, W.E., & Chapman, J.W. (1995). Context use in early reading development: Premature exclusion of a source of individual differences? *Issues in Education, 1*, 97–100.

Wechsler, D. (1974). *Wechsler Intelligence Scale for Children: Revised.* New York: Psychological Corporation.

Wiederholt, J.L., & Bryant, B.R. (1992). *Gray Oral Reading Test* (3rd ed.). Austin, TX: Pro-Ed.

Wiederholt, J.L., & Bryant, B.R. (2003). *Gray Oral Reading Fluency Test* (4th ed.). Austin, TX: Pro-Ed.

Wimmer, H., & Mayringer, H. (2001). Is the reading-rate problem of German dyslexic children caused by slow visual processes? In M. Wolf (Ed.), *Dyslexia, fluency, and the brain* (pp. 333–355). Timonium, MD: York Press.

Wise, B.W., Ring, J., & Olson, R.K. (1999). Training phonological awareness with and without explicit attention to articulation. *Journal of Experimental Child Psychology, 72,* 271–304.

Wolf, M. (2001a). *Dyslexia, fluency, and the brain.* Timonium, MD: York Press.

Wolf, M. (2001b). A provisional, integrative account of phonological and naming-speed deficits in dyslexia: Implications for diagnosis and intervention. In M. Wolf (Ed.), *Dyslexia, fluency, and the brain* (pp. 5–21). Timonium, MD: York Press.

Wolf, M., & Bowers, P.G. (1999). The double-deficit hypothesis for the developmental dyslexias. *Journal of Educational Psychology, 91,* 415–438.

Chapter 8

Perspectives on Fluency: English-Language Learners and Students With Dyslexia

Theresa J. Palumbo and Jennifer R. Willcutt

Fluent reading looks easy. Skilled readers hardly think about reading; they just do it. They look at a page filled with print or glance up at a billboard on the roadside and read it. For those to whom reading comes easily, reading is often a skill they take for granted. For them, reading happens without much effort. Effortless reading, however, is in reality a complex process that for certain populations of readers is exceedingly difficult. Students with dyslexia and English-language learners (ELLs) are two populations that tend to struggle with fluency. New evidence from neuro-imaging studies, along with growing sensitivity to multiculturalism and individual differences among learners, has led to a greater awareness and interest on the part of researchers and teachers about why reading with fluency is difficult for these learners, and they want to know what can be done about it.

The goal of this chapter is to explain why ELLs and students with dyslexia struggle by connecting fluency research to instruction to better understand how fluent reading is taught and learned, and how to inform instruction regarding the particular needs of these two groups. This chapter will define fluency, provide relevant background information about these two groups, and explain how fluency skills differentially affect these groups. Finally, we will suggest techniques and assessments that address challenges for these groups of learners.

Defining Fluency

Teaching children to read fluently is now a primary focus of reading instruction. Fluency recently became a focus when the U.S. Congress assigned the National Reading Panel (NRP) to outline effective reading-

What Research Has to Say About Fluency Instruction, edited by S. Jay Samuels and Alan E. Farstrup. © 2006 by the International Reading Association.

instruction techniques based on a thorough analysis of the research literature (National Institute of Child Health and Human Development [NICHD], 2000). Among its findings, the NRP report states that "the fluent reader is one who can perform multiple tasks—such as word recognition and comprehension—at the same time" (p. 3-8). To be considered fluent, the reader must decode and comprehend simultaneously.

Fluent readers have had so much experience with decoding and comprehending that every new encounter with text requires less cognitive processing. When the words in a text can be decoded with ease, this leaves more cognitive resources available for the task of comprehension. This explanation of how fluent readers process text is derived from automaticity theory (LaBerge & Samuels, 1974). As beginning readers encounter greater numbers of high-frequency words, these words no longer need to be decoded letter-by-letter but can be processed as holistic, meaningful units. These words can then be decoded automatically, and cognitive resources can be directed toward comprehension.

In today's information age, our concept of literacy has broadened. Concepts other than reading and writing, such as critical thinking, logical reasoning, and technology use, constitute essential literacy skills that ELLs, students with dyslexia, and all students need to be taught (Secretary's Commission on Achieving Necessary Skills, 1991, as cited in Spangenberg-Urbschat & Pritchard, 1994). If ELLs and students with dyslexia are to become competitive in today's educational system and later in tomorrow's marketplace, literacy skill is essential.

Previously, research in the area of reading fluency focused on the average reader. Now, researchers are interested in more fully understanding the ways in which readers differ in fluency ability. Traditional definitions and measures of fluency have not yet considered readers from different language backgrounds. Because the evaluation of teacher performance under the No Child Left Behind Act of 2001 (NCLB, 2002) is based on the achievement of all students, and because students need to acquire fluency to be proficient in many careers, it is necessary to determine what challenges ELLs and students with dyslexia encounter as they strive to become fluent.

Fluency Challenges

Students learning English and students with dyslexia are two groups of readers for whom fluency is difficult. Their reading is likely to be slower, choppier, and to lack expression, but for different reasons. Not having appropriate command of English vocabulary is often the cause of ELLs' reading difficulties. To comprehend while decoding, the decoded word must hold meaning. Once a meaning is found for a new word, ELLs must also have a place to fit that meaning within a mental framework, or schema for representing that meaning with associated concepts. For students who are just starting to learn English, English words they decode may not yet hold meaning for them. They will need to increase their English vocabulary and their familiarity with English story grammars, text structure, and perhaps new concepts before they will begin to decode and comprehend at a productive pace. ELLs' fluency problems stem from having a different spoken language and a lack of English vocabulary, and sometimes a mismatch between the culture of the home and the culture of the classroom.

Educators recognize several levels of dyslexia, such as deep dyslexia and surface-level dyslexia, and we may end up adopting the concept of a "dyslexia-spectrum" (Snowling, 2000). One approach for identifying a student with a reading problem is to use the discrepancy method. In this method, a teacher identifies a student by noticing the student is having difficulty learning to read despite having adequate instruction and intelligence. A student has a reading difficulty if his or her reading attainment is significantly below what his or her IQ predicts (Snowling, 2000). According to Snowling, this definition is useful for diagnosing a reading difficulty and accessing appropriate instruction and resources. Some debate exists regarding the use of a discrepancy definition, however, because this definition may underidentify readers with severe reading difficulties. Having such stringent criteria makes it difficult for many students to be eligible for additional instructional services that they need. Some have suggested using a definition that is not so exclusionary, such as identifying students who are not making adequate progress. In other words, key indicators of dyslexia are slowed development of learning to read and lack of mastery of spelling skills.

Students with dyslexia experience fluency difficulties because of processing differences in the brain. *Dyslexia,* the term used in medicine for reading disability, is a reading problem that persists despite adequate intelligence and opportunity to learn to read. Dyslexia is essentially characterized by difficulty decoding words. Some students with dyslexia do reverse letters, reading *d* instead of *b* and *p* instead of *q*, although this is not the only characteristic of dyslexia. Students with dyslexia will often switch the words *and* and *the* while reading, and will frequently substitute *of*, *for*, and *from* for each other. Sometimes students with dyslexia will substitute a word that has the same meaning for the word they are substituting for, even starting with the same letter, although it will be a completely different word with no other shared letters (Ehri & McCormick, 1998). Sometimes the words *no* and *not* will be missed or put in the wrong spot, which can result in comprehension difficulties. Some students with dyslexia also experience phonics difficulties. The process of translating written symbols into the correct combination of sounds to create a meaningful word is challenging for students with dyslexia. The fluency problem for these students is not a lack of relevant background knowledge or meaningful vocabulary, but it is the decoding piece of the definition of fluency (simultaneous decoding and comprehension) that makes fluency difficult. Decoding is the biggest roadblock to fluency for these students; thus their resulting oral reading is halting and choppy. Comprehension will suffer further as a result of lack of fluency because reading with adequate speed aids retention. If the student must read slowly because of difficulty decoding, he or she may not be able to remember what happened at the beginning of the sentence. This lack of adequate speed can hinder comprehension, even though these students are familiar with the meanings of all of the words on the page and have the necessary background knowledge.

Research currently focuses on whether and under what conditions students with dyslexia become fluent readers. Students with dyslexia that master reading in certain highly specialized content areas have employed compensatory strategies to overcome their decoding difficulties. Research with successful dyslexics (Fink, 1995/1996, 2002, 2006) has been informative for the development of fluency because it bridges two seemingly distinct ideas—dyslexia and fluency. In interviews, "successful dyslexics"— individuals considered experts in their fields, some of which include highly specialized areas requiring heavy reading such as medicine, law, literature, and science—revealed how they had come to be successful despite persistent difficulty decoding words. Research in this area suggests that achieving fluency is possible for this population of readers.

Fluency Factors

To understand what disrupts fluency and how each group of students is affected, this chapter discusses reading factors on which building fluency depends. Examining the role each factor plays in fluency represents a place to focus research and instruction.

Lack of Reading Readiness

Many students come to school without any concept of print. Concepts of print include knowing what a book is, what a book is for, what a book looks like, the direction print is read (from left to right, top to bottom), that print represents meaning, that words are groups of letters surrounded by spaces, and that letters correspond to sounds. The Hmong language, for example, was only recently transcribed into a written form, and only recently developed its own dictionary. Therefore, teaching Hmong children concepts of reading and written language is one example of the need to directly instruct concepts of print. Other languages, such as Arabic or Hebrew, have concepts of print in which reading is performed from right to left. By orienting a student to the task and the text, basic literacy concepts support fluency development. Gaining basic text navigation skills is one of the necessary foundations for fluency instruction.

Culture

Many ELLs and their families do not share a U.S. cultural background; thus, these students find it difficult to derive meaning from distinctly U.S. cultural concepts or expressions. For instance, a person from a different culture asks a friend from the United States to go to lunch and receives the reply, "You don't have to twist my arm." Even a proficient English speaker who is unfamiliar with Anglo-American culture would have no idea how twisting an arm could relate to having lunch. A person can acquire this type of linguistic knowledge by being exposed to the social use and idiomatic expressions of language in a particular culture. Simply decoding the language is a formidable task, so deriving meanings from figures of speech without the aid of cultural background can make the task of comprehension more difficult.

Oral Language

Oral-language skills influence the ability to map spoken language onto print. If students come to school with only minimal exposure to English, students will find reading challenging when entering the English-dominant classroom. Speakers of different languages come to school with different ideas of language structure (syntax), of how words are built (morphology), of sound systems (tones and phonology), of the variety of words from which to choose (lexicon), of the multiple meanings that a word can have (polysemy), and of written symbols (orthography). When the child's language does not match the language of the school, children will use the best strategy they have, which is to match their native spoken language to written English. Students' native languages have differing degrees of overlap with English (Graves, Juel, & Graves, 2004). For example, Spanish has a great deal of overlap with English syntax, morphology, and orthography, whereas Vietnamese letters do not overlap with English letters. Certain sounds in English do not exist in other languages, such as the /r/ and /l/ sound for Japanese speakers. Because of differing degrees of overlap, ELLs do not acquire English as a result of mere exposure. Thus, for many students it is not adequate to simply immerse English learners in conversation and English literature. Research indicates that it takes ELLs from six to eight years to reach the oral-skill level of their English-speaking peers (Collier, 1987). Evidence of this nature suggests that developing oral-language skills can enhance fluency.

The level of oral and written skills from a student's first language facilitates the acquisition of reading fluency in English: "Accomplished readers in their first language tend to use many of the same strategies that successful native English-language readers do—skimming, guessing in context, reading for the gist of a text—when they are reading in a second language" (Drucker, 2003, p. 22). So if ELLs have strong language skills in their first language they are more likely to develop strong English skills. If, however, the ELLs are beginning readers, it is often useful to give them instruction in oral-language skills. Building children's oral English skills to help them succeed in matching new sounds and words to print is essential (Graves et al., 2004). Because learning to read develops as early as kindergarten through third grade, English-language instruction for ELLs early in their academic career is essential.

Vocabulary

Vocabulary is critical to developing reading skills for all learners. Often ELLs are accurate decoders, but once the code is deciphered, the words hold no meaning for them. Vocabulary knowledge is necessary for comprehending text. Students with dyslexia often understand the meaning of a word when it is spoken to them, but they may not be able to decode the word in print. Many words in English are polysemous (that is, they have multiple meanings), and it is important for teachers to help their students become aware that many English words have several meanings. If vocabulary words can enter the ELL's oral-language repertoire and can be spoken with meaning, it is more likely that the student will understand them when they are encountered during reading. Because a reader is not considered fluent unless they comprehend as they read, mastery of the meanings of new words is essential to developing fluency.

Neurophysiology

Brain imaging has helped researchers and students with dyslexia to understand reading disability as a processing difference due to neurophysiology. Before researchers had the technology to image the brain as it reads, students with dyslexia wondered why they had this difficulty while others did not. Often students with dyslexia felt that they were not intelligent. On the contrary, many students with dyslexia have average or above-average intelligence. Studies have shown that their reading difficulties are due to inadequacies in the way their brains process print. Poor readers who were given an intensive reading intervention increased their reading fluency, and functional magnetic-resonance imaging (fMRI) studies have shown that intervention caused the brains of children who read poorly to begin to function like the brains of good readers. This successful reading intervention program included individual tutoring that focused on teaching children phonics, letters, and combinations of letters that represent discrete sounds in speech. FMRI revealed that the activity in the brains of the previously poor readers demonstrated increased activation in left hemisphere regions, including the inferior frontal gyrus and the middle temporal gyrus, the areas of the brain used by good readers (Shaywitz et al., 2004). Evidence from fMRI studies helps us understand why decoding can give students with dyslexia additional difficulty. Students with dyslexia have more trouble than the average reader when trying to decode texts, but if the appropriate reading instruction is presented and the proper resources are available, many students can overcome their difficulties. Whether or not these students become truly fluent is a researchable question that has yet to be answered.

Methods for Reading-Fluency Instruction

Based on the findings of the National Reading Panel (NICHD, 2000), certain instruction methods increase reading fluency. Although the findings of the panel hold true for all readers, additional techniques can be used to increase reading fluency for ELLs and students with dyslexia.

To achieve fluency for all students, three steps are necessary: (1) Basic reading skills must be taught until the students are accurate at word recognition. (2) Once accuracy is achieved, providing practice time is essential for students to go beyond accuracy to fluency. (3) Because the first two tasks are hard, students often want to quit before the task is mastered. Therefore, motivation is essential to keep them on task until they become fluent. This progression of strong basic skills, practiced to overlearning, and sustained motivation are necessary for all fluency instruction methods to be effective.

Repeated Oral Reading

Repeated reading increases fluency by having children reread a short meaningful passage several times until satisfactory levels of word-recognition accuracy, speed, and comprehension are achieved (Dowhower, 1987; NICHD, 2000; O'Shea, Sindelar, & O'Shea, 1985, 1987; Samuels, 1997). Repeated reading was initially designed for developmentally disabled students and was so successful that it is now also used with typically developing students (Kuhn & Stahl, 2000). To help students master repeated reading, computer-based instruction programs have been developed based on repeated reading research. Current repeated-reading software incorporates technology that models reading. The model at first provides a slow pace so students can follow along. It then adjusts to a medium speed. Next, students listen to fluent reading at normal speed that is done with expression. After that, students read into a tape recorder. Students then self-monitor by listening to their own reading and assessing these recordings. Goal setting is a stage in which the computer takes students' original rate of reading and sets a modest increase in reading speed as the goal for the students. Last, a comprehension component helps to ensure that students are not only reading fast but also understanding the material. These programs assist teachers in tracking improvement in students' reading fluency. Students read the text over and over until a level of proficiency has been reached. ELLs benefit from this task because they gain a unique perspective when they hear their own reading off the tape recorder. At this stage, they are not concentrating on producing the words and sentences, so they can reserve attention for listening to how their reading sounds. They can self-monitor their readings in this manner and compare their renditions to the modeled fluent reader. Listening and comparing provide a clear picture of where they are and where they would like to be, or what the reading "should" sound like. Because ELLs often benefit from additional exposure and repetition, repeated reading is especially helpful for this group of students.

Assisted Reading

To become good readers, ELLs, students with dyslexia, beginning readers, and students reading below grade level can benefit from assisted reading. As they gain in proficiency, they can move on to independent reading. Several different kinds of assisted reading can be used: In **echo reading**, the teacher reads a few words and the students immediately read them again, "echoing" the teacher's expression. In **shared reading**, the students read some of the words and the teacher reads the rest. In **choral reading**, everybody reads together. Regardless of which kind of reading is used, it is important that students get enough practice to move beyond word-recognition accuracy to fluency.

Independent Reading

Independent reading aids fluency in a variety of ways. Although the National Reading Panel (NICHD, 2000) found a lack of experimental research on independent reading, a wealth of correlational evidence supports the value of independent reading (Taylor, Frye, & Maruyama, 1990; Stanovich, 1986).

Students may get little exposure to reading because they may not be encouraged to read at home or parents may be unable to assist them. For some younger students, the only exposure to reading they receive may be at school. For some older students, many only read when they are forced to complete assignments. This does not challenge students to read fluently but instead only requires them to seek individual facts. Independent reading is important for developing reading fluency because it allows students to gain practice while learning to enjoy reading for its own sake or as an avenue to pursue students' own interests.

Recreational reading is a type of independent reading. Reading at the "recreational level" means that students can decode and comprehend approximately 90% of the words they encounter. Students should be encouraged to read many books at their recreational reading level. When students read extensively, they encounter the same high-frequency words over and over again in numerous contexts. As the students see the same words repeatedly, they develop the ability to recognize them as discrete, holistic units. Furthermore, as students read books independently, they learn the spelling patterns of words, which enhances word recognition. Holistic processing is characteristic of fluent readers (Samuels, LaBerge, & Bremer, 1978). When students read books independently, teachers should encourage them to read carefully for understanding. The students should know that it is a priority to read deeply for good comprehension, not to read numerous books at a shallow level. If children do not read books that have an appropriate level of difficulty for their reading ability, they may never acquire a love of reading or become fluent readers.

To read books at the recreational level, students must know what their recreational level is and be able to acquire books at their level. Teachers can help students determine their reading level. Finding books at the correct readability level is a great challenge, and ELL parents should be encouraged to get help from librarians. It would be ideal if a universal reading level could be established so there would be consistency between publishers as to the readability level assigned to books. In addition, it would help if all the books in libraries that students use were to have readability levels assigned to them (Palumbo, 2005). It is also important to acquire books that are at the correct interest level. A 12th grader reading at an 8th-grade level wants books at the interest level of a 12th grader. Schools should send books home with students that are at the correct readability *and* interest level as frequently as possible. Often students choose books that are too hard for them to read, and the result is that they become frustrated and do not read them.

Read to Students

Reading to young children in English exposes them to various types of literature, provides background knowledge, and introduces students to English grammar and prosody such as proper expression and pitch. In addition, asking children to retell the story and asking guiding questions to enhance the lesson is a great way to train children to be active participants in the reading process. Each of these is an important element in comprehension. Parents who do not speak English at home may not be equipped to help their children learn to read stories written in English. If a parent is unable to help a child traverse this course due to a language barrier, children will need to acquire this background knowledge in a different way. If students read to themselves at the recreational level, the level where most words in the passage can be decoded and comprehended quickly, they will build the skills necessary to read fluently. Also, they will build background knowledge needed to make inferences, a skill that is necessary for quick, thorough comprehension.

Mentoring

Successful students with dyslexia usually have a mentor, or at least one person who takes an interest in their educational achievement and encourages their efforts at reading (Fink, 2002). This idea is consistent with the literature on resilience in that the factor that is most predictive of resilient children who overcome great difficulties in life is that they usually have at least one person who cared deeply about their educational achievement during their formative years. A close relative, reading tutor, or coach could act as that mentor figure for the emergent dyslexic reader. When reading does not come easily and is a chore, individuals with dyslexia need the caring support of an interested and engaged mentor to encourage their hard work and point out their successes.

An ELL may encounter different problems. Parents may be highly encouraging of their children's English acquisition because they know it will help them navigate American culture, but the parents may lack the skills to help with reading activities. These parents are still an active force in mentoring their children to study and work hard, showing they care about their children and their children's future.

Materials for Reading Fluency

Literature and Trade Books

Full participation in U.S. society requires certain basic English skills, and English is fast becoming the foremost language in global commerce. Language skills are not only for reading street signs, books, manuals, or voting, but they also provide access to status, power, and voice in the community. Not only must students learn English at school, they must also learn the language of instruction, or what *word* means, what *paragraph* means, and what *sentence* means. Technical words used in instruction such as *word*, *sentence*, and *paragraph* must be taught if the students are to learn from instruction, and teachers should not assume that students understand these words. Incorporating a balanced-literacy approach to instructing ELLs may give them more options and pathways to learning the language. Although learning decoding skills is important, focusing only on decoding instruction will underexpose students to the variety of literacy activities they can experience. Therefore, it is important to expose students to different genres of reading material to keep them interested and motivated. For example, ELLs will be captivated by a storybook that is read fluently to them and that they can read along with the teacher or other reader in their own copy.

Occasionally, in U.S. public schools, one of the hurdles in ELLs' ability to read fluently is that reading fluency is considered an advanced reading skill and viewed as an unnecessary ideal. Instead of developing reading skills to the level of fluency, considerable instructional time is allocated toward building accuracy in word recognition and the survival skills such as how to read traffic signs, fill out forms and applications, make a doctor's appointment, and pass citizenship tests. These goals, while important, often shortchange the student's exposure to fluency-development activities, such as building vocabulary and engaging in extensive independent reading. By the time students with dyslexia are in high school, they have often been tracked into a lower reading course and the curriculum is different than that of the higher placed students. Sometimes students graduate from high school without ever reading and comprehending a complete book. Although having realistic expectations is warranted, having high expectations for ELLs and dyslexic students is important.

Authentic texts should extend beyond literature to include all types of texts that students encounter inside and outside school, including content texts and occupationally relevant texts, such as trade journals and nonfiction. Literacy instruction, particularly with students in the intermediate grades and up, can begin with the reading of materials in mathematics or science, both of which can be presented with highly contextualized language through visuals and demonstrations. The students' initial success in recognizing and using authentic content area materials can provide strong motivation for further reading activities.

Picture Dictionaries and Word Sorts

The limited vocabulary of ELLs is a hindrance in their development of fluency. If the word *bacon* is a new word and also a new idea, then ELLs will not be able to comprehend this word because it is not part of their oral vocabulary or even their culture. Presenting new vocabulary with graphics simultaneously will aid in supplying the missing link between foreign words and familiar objects or ideas. ELLs sometimes have trouble applying the vocabulary they have memorized to the correct context. Many words have multiple meanings. For example, students may know only the dominant form of the word *bank*. When they read the sentence, "The pilot banked the plane as he flew over the river bank," students think that the pilot put the plane in a bank where they keep money. Help students start a picture dictionary and have them add to it regularly. After students master a word, have them put the word into a special box called their "treasure box." The treasure box is a place students can go to find words that they know. In this way, students can build their confidence with words and review words to build vocabulary. Encourage students to keep their treasure box with them as often as possible.

Another activity to encourage the oral-language development of ELLs is the use of a chart of everyday, high-frequency English words in one column and the equivalent words from the native languages represented in the classroom in the following columns. Also, a variety of word-sort activities can be used with all students to help them understand patterns in language. In word sorts, students actively manipulate and organize words on index cards. Either the teacher or the student can define the task, asking a student to arrange the words on a table according to a predetermined category. Some examples of different word sorts might be alphabetization (arranging words in alphabetical order), spelling patterns (sorting by *-eigh* or *-ay*, as in *weigh* or *way*), parts of speech (noun, adjective, verb), or meaning categories (birds, plants, places). Students can quiz each other with new words to drill vocabulary; students can build new words adding suffixes and prefixes to root words.

Incorporating Vocabulary Into Texts

Instructional materials that include definitions of challenging words can help students comprehend difficult texts. Repeated oral-reading instructional software packages, such as Fluent Reader or Read Naturally, provide this type of guidance. The computer provides fast access to definitions for vocabulary that students find difficult. As the students read along, they can click on the word that they have trouble decoding or comprehending, and its definition will appear. This modeled repeated oral-reading method performed with the benefit of the computer enhances reading fluency. One drawback to using a traditional dictionary, according to Yeung (1999), is that

> given a separate glossary, when readers encounter an unfamiliar word, they need to leave the text, turn to the vocabulary list, temporarily store

its meaning, and then revert to the text and try to incorporate the meaning into the text. (p. 197)

Yeung found that when definitions are placed next to the difficult words, these words become more readily understood. He suggested that in this integrated format, students' attention is not split, and the cognitive load is lowered. Attention is precious, and switching attention can distract from comprehension.

Two Texts on the Same Subject

One strategy for retaining various reading levels within the same classroom is to have two groups read about the same topic but with differentially challenging materials. The more skilled readers' text has more difficult words, phrase structures, and concepts, while the less skilled readers have texts on the same topic but the text is easier to read. In addition, some texts are purposefully designed to be complex, such as mysteries. Thus, the better readers will read stories that are more difficult and the associated comprehension questions will also be more challenging.

Passionate-Interest Reading Leads to Narrow Reading

According to Fink's (2002) work, successful dyslexics had a passionate interest that was so consuming that they read deeply in a narrow interest area, despite difficulties in decoding. This narrow interest area allowed them to practice various texts several times on the same topic, which created repeated exposure with certain keywords, phrases, and technical jargon. The pursuit of a passionate interest allows a reader to scaffold his or her reading experience through an overlearning of words that come up often. For example, when a dyslexic reader is driven by a passionate interest in the solar system or in romance novels, reading lots and lots of books about the solar system or romance taps the student's intrinsic motivation and helps the student to experience success. Not only does the student become more confident in his or her abilities, but the student also begins to become familiar with the words that will appear frequently, which leads him or her to encounter fewer new words. The student will also become highly familiar with the common structure, or "lay of the land," of texts in his or her interest area. Harnessing the power of students' passionate interests can also be powerful for developing reading skill for ELLs. Newspaper stories, magazine articles, books, novels, and the Internet are various sources that can be used on a topic of interest so that repeated exposure to related vocabulary is promoted (Schmitt & Carter, 2000).

Comprehension

Checking During and After Reading

Checking comprehension during reading is important to help students develop fluency skills. One way to do this is to help the student draw predictions from illustrations and titles. Judging a book by its cover is important in this instance: The reader can gather clues about what is likely to occur in the book and whether this book is likely to be of interest to the reader. Asking the student leading questions, such as "What does the table of contents suggest?" "Is this a story or a how-to guide?" "Is this a book that fits our purpose?" "Will we learn something or be entertained?" Making these reading goals explicit may seem obvious to an instructor, but readers sometimes skip this step, which may lead to misunderstanding. Encourage students to summarize after each page. The more this is practiced, the easier and more automatic it becomes. At first it tends to slow down the reader, but with practice it becomes very beneficial.

To get the most out of independent reading, students should be encouraged to summarize what they have read either in writing or in a verbal summary. These summaries are useful because reconstructing the information from reading is an excellent way to remember something (Craik & Lockhart, 1972). The two benefits of the summary are a focus on comprehension and a means of assessing whether or not the independent reading was done carefully.

Prior Knowledge

Teaching English as a second language is becoming a hot topic in reading instruction. With the demands on classrooms to have all students reading proficiently, more attention is being given to the nonnative English speaker in the context of learning to read. What can we do to instruct ELLs? First, we need to recognize children's strengths. We can make children feel accepted by incorporating culturally familiar experiences into the curriculum. For example, it is useful to have books available featuring children from multiple cultural backgrounds. This requires identification and understanding of students' cultural background and experiences. Another technique that is helpful in working with students who come from different cultures is to try to get them to relate what they know about to that which is new. Suppose that we are reading a story to our students about a wedding in a foreign country where the customs are different than in the United States. What we can do to help them understand the new wedding customs is to ask the students what happens at a wedding in the United States. For example, who decides who will get married and which guests will be invited, will there be an exchange of money, and where will the bride and groom live? Then, having discussed these details about marriage in the United States, the students can apply their insights to the foreign wedding. This procedure helps students transfer prior knowledge to new situations.

Metacognitive Instruction

Metacognition skills in reading fluency include previewing, predicting, and setting goals for reading. Developing metacognitive skills helps children to acquire fluency by being aware of their own progress (Samuels, Ediger, Willcutt, & Palumbo, 2005). Encourage reflection, pausing, and rereading to reduce situations where students read the text without really understanding what they have decoded. With older ELLs, teachers should capitalize on their level of cognitive maturity. For example, older students should be more capable of developing metacognitive awareness of reading tasks than younger students. Having students summarize books is a great skill to teach students. Discussion of books can also help students relate stories to their own lives. Start these discussions prior to opening the book, during book reading, and when the book is completed.

Measurement

Fluency measurement is an important aspect to consider in regard to NCLB legislation. Snow, Burns, and Griffin (1998) note that the ability to obtain meaning from print depends strongly on reading fluency; thus, it should be regularly assessed in the classroom. There are limited reading-fluency measures. The most frequently used measure to accomplish this goal is a technique called curriculum-based measurement (CBM; Deno, 1985), which is a method of determining a reading rate for each student. Reading rate is used as an indicator of reading fluency. Rate is determined by calculating the number of words read correctly in one minute. CBM provides a relatively quick, formative measure of a student's reading level.

Reading rate, however, may not have as strong a correlation with reading comprehension for ELLs, due to vocabulary problems and differences in grammatical structure of the ELLs' first language. Often a student will read a text silently or aloud with accurate word recognition and moderate speed, only to draw a blank when asked, "What just happened in the story?" Measuring the reading fluency of students with dyslexia can also be accomplished using CBM, and the reading is likely to be characterized by many errors in decoding, resulting in a slower, choppier reading, which will be reflected in reading rate and the ability to demonstrate comprehension. A reading fluency measure that includes a comprehension component might have students read a passage, put that passage away, and then have them retell the story, measuring recall of key ideas. Unlike the Oral Reading Fluency section of the DIBELS (Dynamic Indicators of Basic Early Literacy Skills; Good & Kaminski, 2002), fluency cannot be measured simply by the number of words the student produces in recall. If word count is the only measure, without regard to which words are being recalled, then the validity of the measure is questionable. To be considered a measure of fluency, the recall must include key ideas from the story to be an accurate reflection of the reader's comprehension of the story.

Conclusions

Providing teachers with research-based materials and methods to help special populations of students become successful fluent readers is the purpose of research in fluency instruction. We know that readers in special populations, such as ELLs and students with dyslexia, expend extraordinary effort in their attempt to acquire reading fluency, and that these readers may have different goals and expectations from their reading instruction than other readers. Special focus on related fluency factors should be provided to help each group succeed. Educators may regard fluency as the impossible dream for readers who are struggling just to catch up. With the identification of the particular fluency challenges these groups face, however, and the research to support method effectiveness, it is possible to shape instructional practices to accommodate the reading-fluency needs of ELLs and students with dyslexia.

Questions for Discussion

1. This chapter has described some of the fluency challenges that students with dyslexia experience and proposes some reading

instruction strategies that can help them overcome these challenges. What are some of the techniques described, and what are their advantages and disadvantages for teachers and for students? How do these techniques differ from fluency instruction for all readers? How does fluency instruction relate to comprehension and/or decoding for this population of readers?

2. We know that many students with dyslexia have become successful despite persistent reading problems. How do we know if students with dyslexia have attained fluency? If fluency is attained, are these students no longer dyslexic? What are some indicators of the fluent reader, and how can we measure fluency achievement?

3. Research shows that most gain in reading fluency is made when students read materials that are within their Zone of Proximal Development (Vygotsky, 1934/1978)—not too hard nor too easy. How much increase in reading fluency for ELLs could be made if books were labeled with consistent reading levels for easy identification and access?

4. ELLs have a myriad of constraints to overcome in order to become fluent in reading English. What are these constraints, and what are the means to address each of these?

REFERENCES

Collier, V. (1987). Age and rate of acquisition of second language for academic purposes. *TESOL Quarterly, 21*, 617–641.

Craik, F., & Lockhart, R. (1972). Levels of processing: A framework for memory research. *Journal of Verbal Learning and Verbal Behavior, 11*, 671–684.

Deno, S.L. (1985). Curriculum-based measurement: The emerging alternative. *Exceptional Children, 52*, 219–232.

Dowhower, S.L. (1987). Effects of repeated reading on second-grade transitional readers' fluency and comprehension. *Reading Research Quarterly, 22*, 389–406.

Drucker, M.J. (2003). What reading teachers should know about ESL learners. *The Reading Teacher, 57*, 22–29.

Ehri, L., & McCormick, S. (1998). Phases of word learning: Implications for instruction with delayed and disabled readers. *Reading & Writing Quarterly, 14*(2), 135–163.

Fink, R.P. (1995/1996). Successful dyslexics: A constructivist study of passionate interest reading. *Journal of Adolescent & Adult Literacy, 39*, 268–280.

Fink, R.P. (2002). Successful careers: The secrets of adults with dyslexia. *Career Planning & Adult Development Journal, 18*(1), 118–135.

Fink, R.P. (2006). *Why Jane and John couldn't read—And how they learned: A new look at striving readers.* Newark, DE: International Reading Association.

Good, R.H., & Kaminski, R.A. (Eds.). (2002). *Dynamic Indicators of Basic Early Literacy Skills* (6th ed.). Eugene, OR: Institute for the Development of Educational Achievement.

Graves, M.F., Juel, C., & Graves, B.B. (2004). Reading instruction for English-language learners. In A.M. Ramos & M. Kriener (Eds.), *Teaching reading in the 21st century* (pp. 496–541). Boston: Allyn & Bacon.

Kuhn, M.R., & Stahl, S.A. (2000). *Fluency: A review of developmental and remedial practices* (CIERA report #2-008). Ann Arbor, MI: Center for the Improvement of Early Reading Achievement.

LaBerge, D., & Samuels, S.J. (1974). Toward a theory of automatic information processing in reading. *Cognitive Psychology, 6,* 293–323.

National Institute of Child Health and Human Development (NICHD). (2000). *Report of the National Reading Panel. Teaching children to read: An evidence-based assessment of the scientific research literature on reading and its implications for reading instruction* (NIH Publication No. 00-4769). Washington, DC: U.S. Government Printing Office.

No Child Left Behind Act of 2001, Pub. L. No. 107-110, 115 Stat. 1425 (2002).

O'Shea, L.J., Sindelar, P.T., & O'Shea, D.J. (1985). The effects of repeated readings and attentional cues on reading fluency and comprehension. *Journal of Reading Behavior, 17,* 129–142.

O'Shea, L.J., Sindelar, P.T., & O'Shea, D.J. (1987). The effects of repeated readings and attentional cues on reading fluency and comprehension on learning disabled readers. *Learning Disabilities Research, 2*(2), 103–109.

Palumbo, T.J. (2005). Achieve and measure reading fluency: Expanding the opportunity. In C.C. Block & S.E. Israel (Eds.), *Reading First and beyond: The complete guide for teachers and literacy coaches* (pp. 81–93). Thousand Oaks, CA: Corwin Press.

Samuels, S.J. (1997). The method of repeated readings. *The Reading Teacher, 50,* 376–382.

Samuels, S.J., Ediger, K., Willcutt, J., & Palumbo, T. (2005). Role of automaticity in metacognition and literacy instruction. In S. Israel, K. Bauserman, K. Kinnucan-Welsch, & C.C. Block (Eds.), *Metacognition in literacy learning: Theory, assessment, instruction, and professional development* (pp. 41–59). Mahwah, NJ: Erlbaum.

Samuels, S.J., LaBerge, D., & Bremer, C.D. (1978). Units of word recognition: Evidence for developmental changes. *Journal of Verbal Learning and Verbal Behavior, 17*(6), 715–720.

Schmitt, N., & Carter, R. (2000). The lexical advantages of narrow reading for second language learners. *TESOL Journal, 9*(1), 4–9.

Shaywitz, B.A., Shaywitz, S.E., Blachman, B.A., Pugh, K.R., Fulbright, R.K., Skudlarski, P., et al. (2004). Development of left occipitotemporal systems for skilled reading in children after a phonologically-based intervention. *Biological Psychiatry, 55*(9), 926–933.

Snow, C.E., Burns, M.S., & Griffin, P. (1998). *Preventing reading difficulties in young children.* Washington, DC: National Academy Press.

Snowling, M.J. (2000). *Dyslexia.* Malden, MA: Blackwell.

Spangenberg-Urbschat, K., & Pritchard, R. (1994). *Kids come in all languages: Reading instruction for ESL students.* Newark, DE: International Reading Association.

Stanovich, K. (1986). Matthew effects in reading: Some consequences of individual differences in the acquisition of literacy. *Reading Research Quarterly, 21,* 360–407.

Taylor, B., Frye, B., & Maruyama, G. (1990). Time spent reading and reading growth. *American Educational Research Journal, 27*(2), 351–362.

Vygotsky, L.S. (1978). *Mind in society: The development of higher psychological processes* (M. Cole, V. John-Steiner, S. Scribner, & E. Souberman, Eds. & Trans.). Cambridge, MA: Harvard University Press. (Original work published 1934)

Yeung, A.S. (1999). Cognitive load and learner expertise: Split-attention and redundancy effects in reading comprehension tasks with vocabulary definitions. *Journal of Experimental Education, 67,* 197–217.

Chapter 9

Curriculum-Based Measurement of Oral Reading: An Indicator of Growth in Fluency

Stanley L. Deno and Douglas Marston

Our purpose in this chapter is to describe an approach to measuring reading growth that is also widely used in research as a measure of fluency (Fuchs, Fuchs, Hosp, & Jenkins, 2001; Good, Simmons, & Kame'enui, 2001). That approach is generally known as curriculum-based measurement (CBM; Deno, 1985), and its application results in quantifying the accuracy and speed of passage reading. Shinn (1989, 1998, 2002) has described CBM in two edited books and a book chapter specifically on the topic, and others have contributed to the literature on this topic in a variety of book chapters (Deno, 1991, 1995; Deno, Espin, & Fuchs, 2002; Marston & Magnusson, 1988). The literature on CBM also comprises more than 450 journal articles (more than 150 that are empirical) describing the characteristics, technical adequacy, and use of CBM (Research Institute on Progress Monitoring [RIPM], 2004). Although the initial research and development on CBM was conducted with students in grades 1–6, CBM has been extended upward to secondary students (Espin & Tindal, 1998), downward into early childhood education (McConnell, Priest, Davis, & McEvoy, 2002), early literacy (Good et al., 2001; Marston et al., in press), and to English-language learners (ELLs; Baker & Good, 1995). We will describe CBM, outline its characteristics that have resulted in its being used as a measure of fluency, and summarize the research and development history underlying its procedures. Finally, we will illustrate how CBM data used as an indicator of fluent reading are used to make both individual-level and program-level educational decisions.

At the outset, we would like to address the question of whether CBM is an approach to measuring reading fluency. We understand reading fluency to mean that an individual easily processes text and that the processing of text encompasses both word recognition and comprehension.

What Research Has to Say About Fluency Instruction, edited by S. Jay Samuels and Alan E. Farstrup. © 2006 by the International Reading Association.

Although the measurement procedures at the heart of CBM often are referred to as measures of oral-reading fluency (Fuchs et al., 2001; Good et al., 2001), the program of research resulting in CBM focused on procedures that would produce reliable and valid indicators of student growth in reading proficiency broadly defined (Deno, 1985). The research on CBM has provided a basis for concluding that the number of words read aloud from text in one minute may be the best available measure of reading fluency.

The original purpose of CBM research was to develop a measure of reading growth that could be used across the school years from the beginning of "learning to read" to the point where students are "reading to learn." CBM of oral reading provides a perspective on student reading growth over many years. A simple view of reading development is that it occurs in stages from initial acquisition of word-recognition skills, through fluency in reading text, to comprehension. We do not subscribe to this view and believe it is important not to limit the value of CBM oral reading to determining whether students have achieved "mastered" text reading—a hypothetical stage between initial acquisition of word-reading skill and later comprehension. This idea is what leads many people to the notion that "benchmark" oral-reading rates can, and should, be identified that will guarantee student success in comprehending text. Evidence indicates that CBM oral-reading data reveal student growth in both word recognition and comprehension (Jenkins, Fuchs, van den Broek, Espin, & Deno, 2003), not only reading skill beyond accurate word recognition. Even though CBM oral-reading scores provide a broad indication of reading growth across the years, were we to define fluency as the "number of words read correctly from text in one minute," we would be missing other features of fluent reading, such as prosody (i.e., reading with expression), that are not included in the CBM of oral reading. Ultimately, the readers of this chapter can draw their own conclusions regarding the degree to which the data produced through CBM provide useful facts related to their interests in fluency.

The procedures that have become most widely known as CBM have undergone development for approximately 30 years. The purpose of CBM from its inception has been to provide teachers with the tools to monitor student progress in such a way that they could create more effective instructional programs for their students. CBM is a standardized set of observational procedures for repeatedly measuring growth in core reading, writing, and arithmetic skills. In this chapter we will focus exclusively on the use of those procedures to monitor reading growth.

Research and Development Background

As a result of U.S. federal funding, an empirical research and development program was conducted for six years, 1977–1983, through the University of Minnesota Institute for Research on Learning Disabilities (IRLD). The primary question pursued through that research was whether teachers could use repeated measurement of academic progress like that described initially by Deno and Mirkin (1977) to formatively evaluate their instruction and improve their effectiveness. Ultimately, a field experiment was conducted that established the promise of that approach (Fuchs, Deno, & Mirkin, 1984).

Before that question could be answered, however, a program of empirical research was designed to develop "teacher friendly" procedures for monitoring academic progress in areas of reading, spelling, and written expression (Deno, 1985). That research focused on three key questions: (1) What are the core tasks on which performance should be repeatedly measured? ("what to measure"), (2) How should the measurement activities be structured to produce technically adequate data? ("how to measure"), and (3) How can the data be used to improve educational programs? ("how to use"). The answers to these questions were constrained by three factors: The measures (1) must meet conventional standards of reliability and validity, (2) would have to produce data that teachers could use to make effective instructional decisions, and (3) would have to be logistically feasible within the context of classroom instruction (Deno & Fuchs, 1987). The CBM reading procedures specifying "what to measure," "how to measure," and "how to use" the data have been described in a variety of publications (for example, Deno, Mirkin, & Chiang, 1982; Fuchs, Fuchs, & Maxwell, 1988; Shinn, 1989, 1998). Those publications illustrate that teachers can use CBM basic skills measures to evaluate instruction and improve student outcomes (Fuchs et al., 1984). In the following sections of this chapter, we will describe CBM and illustrate how CBM data are used to make a wide variety of educational decisions.

CBM Progress Measurement: An Example

The results of using the CBM approach to measure reading growth are illustrated in the progress graph of a low-achieving sixth-grade student named Ricky (see Figure 9.1). The teacher obtains the reading scores of Ricky and his peers by presenting them with a text passage and having them read aloud for one minute. The teacher follows along and counts the number of words read correctly and incorrectly by the students during that minute. The teacher then plots Ricky's performance on the graph to clearly depict the number of words read correctly and incorrectly by both Ricky and his peers. For progress-monitoring purpose and to evaluate the effects of Ricky's instruction, his teacher repeats this procedure on a regular basis. The result is a picture of Ricky's growth in CBM oral reading and changes in the rate of his reading growth after his teacher modified his reading program. In what follows, we will use Ricky's progress graph to illustrate how CBM is conducted and to identify its important characteristics.

Figure 9.1. Ricky's CBM reading graph

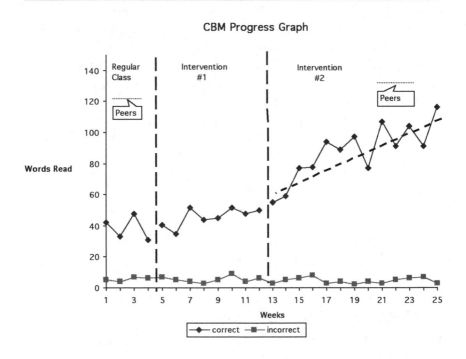

Teacher Use of CBM to Formatively Evaluate Instruction

As stated at the outset, the original and primary purpose of CBM was to provide teachers with simple and direct measurement tools that they could use to do ongoing evaluation of instruction for a student like Ricky. The experiment by Fuchs and colleagues (1984) revealed that when teachers used the approach taken with Ricky, they produced higher levels of reading achievement than the teachers who did not. An important outcome in this experiment was that the students increased in reading comprehensions as well as in their oral reading. In addition to the differences in achievement, differences also existed in the students' knowledge of their reading goals and whether they were achieving those goals. Since that study, additional experiments have been conducted revealing the positive outcomes of teachers using CBM oral-reading data to improve student achievement (Fuchs, Fuchs, & Hamlett, 1989; Stecker & Fuchs 2000). As teachers and administrators have become more familiar with CBM, the oral-reading data have been used for other types of educational decisions, as well.

Procedures and Characteristics of CBM

When measuring reading growth, CBM procedures are said to be *curriculum-based* when the passages from which students read orally are selected directly from the curriculum materials used by the local school—the original approach to CBM. One advantage of drawing the passages directly from the curriculum of the school is that it increases teacher confidence that a close connection exists between the materials they are using for instruction and how they are measuring student progress. A disadvantage of this approach, however, is that it is both time-consuming and difficult to select passages that work well for measurement. For the passages to work well in measurement, they should be as equal in difficulty as possible. This is essential because CBM reading procedures require a student to read a different passage each time performance is measured. Research has demonstrated that stories from the same reading book are often at very different levels of readability (Fuchs, Deno, & Fuchs, 1982), and that readability formulas cannot be used with confidence to estimate equivalence in reading difficulty. In the CBM example illustrated in Figure 9.1, the reading passages read by Ricky were drawn directly from a reading book used in the sixth grade of his school. The reading score of his peers (120 words correct) is their average in reading from the same sixth-grade passages that he read. Many good reasons exist to draw the reading passages directly from the curriculum materials used by the school. At the same time, the same type of measurement procedures used for CBM can be applied to passages that are not drawn from the local school curriculum (Fuchs & Deno, 1994).

CBM procedures are *standardized* in that passages used to assess student reading, the amount of time students read (one minute), and the scoring procedures used are specifically prescribed. Standardization of the procedures is important to increase our confidence in the quality of the data produced. Standardization of the procedures also permits us to aggregate reading scores from different students to get a classwide picture, to examine growth in performance across time, and to compare the performance of different students. Finally, standardization enables us to summarize scores by grade level, by school, and by district to create local norms (Marston & Magnusson, 1988). In Figure 9.1, the fact that the same materials and procedures are used to measure the performance of both Ricky and his classmates allows us to directly compare his performance to theirs in reading from their sixth-grade reader. In making this direct comparison, we see that Ricky read only about one third as many words as his peers when measurement began.

Passage-reading performance is sampled through *direct observation* of the number of words read aloud correctly and incorrectly in one minute of oral reading. Ricky's teacher sat with him while he read those passages, listened to his reading, and recorded his performance. Extensive experience with these procedures confirms that adult readers can easily follow along as a child reads and can accurately record both correctly and incorrectly read words. Research also has been conducted on using a modified cloze procedure (the maze) as a measure of reading growth, but we will not describe that approach here (Fuchs, Fuchs, Hamlett, & Ferguson, 1992).

One of the most distinctive and important features of CBM is that passage oral-reading performance is *repeatedly sampled*. The repeated observations of performance require that students read from passages that are at the same level of difficulty, but each passage that the student reads is different from the last reading sample. Thus, on the first occasion, Ricky read aloud for one minute from a new passage drawn from his sixth-grade text that he had not previously read. On the next occasion, he read again from a different passage from that same text but from a previously unread passage. The purpose of this procedure is to enable us to judge whether the skills that Ricky is learning are generalizing to unfamiliar text. Only when we see such generalized reading growth can we be confident that our instruction is achieving its desired outcomes.

Repeated sampling of reading performance on passages of equal difficulty is the key feature that enables *measurement of growth*. Because the difficulty of the passages is held constant, increases in Ricky's scores mean that his reading proficiency is growing. Both current level of performance and growth are shown on Ricky's graph. *Current level* is obtained from the general level (either the average or the median) of several scores. Growth, on the other hand, can only be seen in the *slope*, or trend, of the scores seen from repeated measurement across time. Growth is most clearly seen and more easily used for decision making when the data are graphically displayed. The *graphic display* of CBM data (see Figure 9.1) becomes central in making key instructional decisions. As we can see in the graph, Ricky's rate of growth is faster under the Second Intervention than after the First Intervention. Using the CBM approach to measuring reading growth has led to efforts to establish typical growth rates in oral reading at different grade levels (Deno, Fuchs, Marston, & Shin, 2001).

What might be less obvious in Figure 9.1 is that multiple references are available for interpreting Ricky's performance. CBM reading scores are individually referenced, peer referenced, and criterion or goal referenced. To say that his scores are *individually referenced* means that we can compare his scores at any point in time with his past scores to see where he is now reading more words correctly in one minute. That makes it possible for us to contrast Ricky's performance at different times to make a judgment about the degree to which he is growing faster as a reader now than he was previously. CBM reading scores also are *peer referenced*, which means that Ricky's reading performance can be compared to that of his classmates. For some purposes, we might be interested only in contrasting Ricky's performance to the students in his classroom. At other times, however, we may be interested in a broader peer sample reflecting all students at the same grade, in the same school, or across schools within a district. The CBM reading measurements also are *goal referenced* because individual progress is plotted on a graph in relation to a *goal line* established for that student. It has become increasingly common for these goals to be determined by establishing grade-level performance standards and making individual adjustments in relation to those standards. Finally, when the measures are obtained using text selected from the curriculum, student growth is *curriculum referenced*, as well. The special value of curriculum referencing is that it allows judgments about the degree to which students in compensatory programs using alternate curricula are progressing satisfactorily in the school's curriculum.

The validity of growth measures rests entirely on the importance of the academic task used in measurement. For example, the increase in scores on Ricky's graph is meaningful only if an increase in reading aloud from text is an important indicator of improvement in generalized reading proficiency. The standard passage-reading task used in CBM has been confirmed through scientific research over many years as a valid indicator of reading proficiency (Fuchs et al., 2001). The high degree of confidence in passage-reading scores as a measure of reading achievement has become evident through its use in research studies to evaluate the effectiveness of different approaches to teaching reading (RIPM, 2004). (Additional CBM research has resulted in identifying the maze task for measuring reading growth. Unlike reading aloud, the maze task can be used for group administration and can be recorded and scored by a computer [Fuchs et al., 1989].)

While considerable evidence exists that CBM oral-reading data can be used effectively to make a wide array of educational decisions (Shinn, 1998), it is important to emphasize that the *validity of the information produced through CBM is entirely dependent on the types of educational decisions to be made* (Good & Jefferson, 1998). For example, CBM data on reading aloud from text provides a good basis for judging growth in general reading proficiency during the elementary and early middle school years, but it probably does less well in helping us judge which of two high-achieving high school students will better comprehend social studies or science texts. At that level of academic achievement, other factors, such as background knowledge, play a more important role in classroom success (Espin & Tindal, 1998). CBM passage-reading data can be used to help us to identify secondary students that might have difficulty in learning from a content area text. A reading disabled student's background knowledge will be a factor in comprehending text, but a reading disabled student's difficulty in rapidly processing the text will almost certainly depress comprehension of text content, as well.

Problems With Traditional Standardized Tests

CBM has emerged as an important and useful alternative to traditional standardized tests for measuring growth in reading because of several limitations associated with those tests.

Lack of Frequent Measurement

Although standardized achievement tests provide norm-referenced data about a student's reading, they are not good measures of pupil progress. One reason for this is they can only be administered once per year, and as Nazzaro (1976) notes, "Only by sampling over time can one gain a fairly accurate picture of a child's potential" (p. 41). If we assess a student's reading performance in September and wish to evaluate his or her progress in October, the "one shot" assessment available through using a commercially available norm-referenced achievement test will not work.

Insensitivity to Growth

In making a distinction between the "psychometric" (norm-referenced) and "edumetric" tests, Carver (1974) points out that

> many standardized tests are used to measure gain or growth without being developed or evaluated from an edumetric standpoint. The danger of this approach is that the psychometrically developed tests may not be sensitive to gain when in fact there is gain. (p. 518)

Scores That Do Not Reflect Growth

For a test to be widely useful, the scores from that test need to be easily understood by the many people who wish to use them. The norm-referenced scores from standardized achievement tests are not helpful for showing growth because they describe a student's relative standing with respect to a standardization sample rather than individual growth across time. A student that scores at the 40th percentile in the third grade and again at the 40th percentile the following year does not appear to have progressed. However, in having kept pace with the normative group, the child did of course make gains. But how much? Technical problems also exist for grade- and age-equivalent scores (Salvia & Ysseldyke, 2001).

School District Use of CBM Oral-Reading Scores: Evidence From 20 Years

In the early 1980s, the Minneapolis Public Schools began using CBM oral-reading data to improve its instructional programs for students in special education. Since the original implementation, district personnel have both extended and examined the use of CBM oral-reading data to make a wide variety of educational decisions across general and compensatory programs. Those extensions and examinations of CBM oral reading will be summarized in the section of this chapter that follows. The descriptions provide illustrations of typical student performance on CBM reading measures across grade levels and within different educational subgroups. In addition, evidence for the use of CBM reading measures to make different educational decisions is provided. The section concludes with a description of the district's efforts to use CBM reading data to address two increasingly difficult issues faced by the schools: (1) monitoring progress toward success on high-stakes tests and (2) assessing the performance of ELLs.

Initial Use of CBM Oral-Reading Measures

In 1984 the Minneapolis school system began its CBM implementation by developing district norms (Marston & Magnusson, 1985). The means and standard deviations for oral-reading fluency in the fall, winter, and spring from the original published work are shown below in Table 9.1. By reviewing this table, teachers have been able to establish the norma-

Table 9.1. CBM oral-reading scores of students in grades 1–6

Grade	Fall		Winter		Spring	
	Mean	SD	Mean	SD	Mean	SD
1	14.7	31.6	36.7	39.9	68.5	40.8
2	53.0	44.8	83.0	47.8	98.4	46.8
3	81.3	39.7	100.6	41.9	119.9	39.5
4	91.5	39.0	108.3	39.0	114.9	38.4
5	103.3	40.0	116.6	39.1	124.1	39.7
6	129.8	38.8	138.0	38.1	143.4	39.8

From Marston, D., & Magnusson, D. (1985). Implementing curriculum-based measurement in special and regular education settings. *Exceptional Children, 52*(3), 266–276. Copyright 1985 by the Council for Exceptional Children. Reprinted with permission.

tive CBM oral-reading score for students across several grade levels. These data, which were based on a random sample of 8,460 students in grades 1 to 6, reflect the number of words read correctly on grade-level passages (i.e., first graders read passages with readability levels of grade 1, and fifth graders read passages at the grade 5 level).

As shown in Table 9.1, oral-reading fluency levels increase significantly with grade level. In the fall of first grade, when most students are just learning to read, first graders read about 14 words correct on their first-grade passages. However, sixth graders read approximately 130 words correct when administered sixth-grade passages. Teachers in the district use this information to determine whether students are at levels normal for their grade level or discrepant from peers. Also evident in Table 9.1 is fairly consistent growth within each grade level from fall to spring, where the greatest gains are demonstrated at the earlier grade levels. Again, these data help the teachers who are trying to ascertain whether students are making significant gains during the school year.

The implementation of new assessment procedures in the classroom creates questions regarding logistics, ease of use, and validity. In studying the district implementation of CBM oral-reading procedures, Marston and Magnusson (1985) addressed the issues of feasibility and cost effectiveness, teacher and administrator attitudes, validity of measurement system, sensitivity to pupil growth, and judging program-placement efficacy. Survey data from the teachers indicated that assessment time necessary for listening to the students read was minimal and that implementation was realistic on a schoolwide basis. Seventy-two percent of these respondents also found "the data useful for tracking student progress in reading" (p. 268). Marston and Magnusson examined the CBM oral-reading scores of general education students, students needing Title I reading services, and students with disabilities. As the data in Figure 9.2 clearly illustrate, the average performance of these groups consistently differ in predictable directions within grade levels. For example, in second grade the average general education student is reading almost 93 words correct, whereas Title I students are reading 37 words correct and special education students only 23 words correct. Marston and Magnusson (1988) and Tindal and Marston (1996) obtained similar findings. Additional inspection of Figure 9.2 reveals that third-grade special education students have CBM reading scores lower than typical first-grade general education students. Although the scores of these groups are not directly comparable because they are reading different

Figure 9.2. Comparison of general education, Title I, and special education students' CBM oral-reading scores

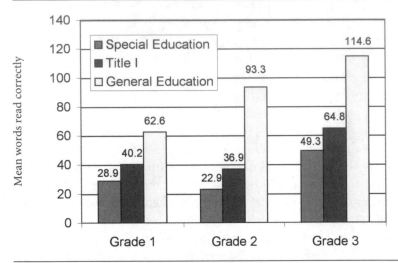

Adapted from Marston, D., & Magnusson, D. (1985). Implementing curriculum-based measurement in special and regular education settings. *Exceptional Children, 52*(3), 266–276. Copyright 1985 by the Council for Exceptional Children. Reprinted with permission.

passages, this finding would appear to correspond with the perception that special education students are typically two or more years behind their general education peers. Such a finding also provides support for the validity of the CBM oral-reading measures. The 1985 Marston and Magnusson article is particularly useful because it describes how Minneapolis Public Schools began to use CBM reading data for screening, compensatory program eligibility, program planning, progress monitoring, and program evaluation.

Problem-Solving Model

For more than 10 years, the Minneapolis Public Schools has used a response-to-intervention (RTI) model for identifying struggling readers and implementing an instructional modification (Marston, Muyskens, Lau, & Canter, 2003). In part, this model rests on early research that reading disability could be sensitively detected by using CBM of oral reading (Deno, Marston, Shinn, & Tindal, 1983). The system's problem-solving model provides teachers with a four-step approach to examine student response to intervention by (1) defining student academic difficulties, (2) generating hypotheses and interventions for addressing the student's needs, (3) frequently collecting reading data for the purpose of evaluating the effectiveness of the student's response to the intervention, and (4) recycling through these steps as necessary. These four steps are repeated within the three stages of problem solving: Stage 1 or Classroom Intervention, Stage 2 or Problem Solving Team, and Stage 3 or Special Education Evaluation. CBM of oral fluency plays a key role in implementing the model and measuring the student's response to instruction. School staffs use the CBM growth charts shown in Figure 9.3 in much the same way height and weight charts are used to identify students in need of intervention.

Once students enter the problem-solving model process, their progress is monitored across the school year. The classroom example in Figure 9.4 shows how teachers can evaluate the progress of their students across fall, winter, and spring with the CBM reading data. In this second-grade class, where the students have been rank ordered based on the number of words read correctly in the fall, there are some students reading only 10–20 words correct who show little growth during the year. The class, however, also has several students who initially read about 40

Figure 9.3. Normative growth chart showing 20th, 50th, and 80th percentile CBM oral-reading scores for second-grade students

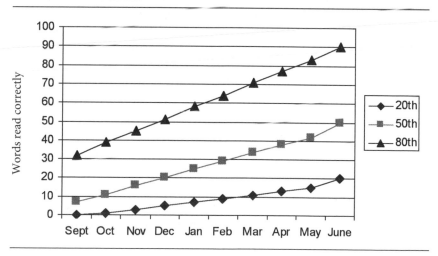

Figure 9.4. Within-year growth in CBM oral-reading scores for a class of second-grade students*

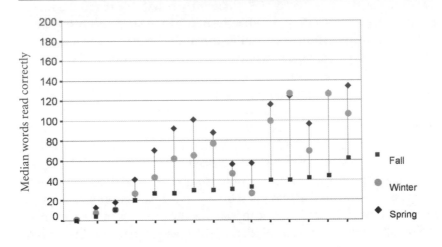

Student's Last Name

* Each vertical line represents the CBM oral-reading score of a student in a second-grade classroom. Students have been ranked based on their words read correctly in the fall.

words correct in the fall and gain more than 60 words during the course of the academic year. This chart provides an efficient way for the teacher to review an entire class with respect to level and growth of reading performance and indicates that students showing small gains need more intensive instructional support.

Teachers often ask what growth rates can be expected at the different stages of the problem-solving model. As part of our program evaluation efforts, the district has aggregated CBM oral-reading scores across the various stages of the model and presented these growth rates from grades 1 to 6 (Marston et al., 2003). Growth rates for first-grade students in each stage of the problem-solving model are displayed in Figure 9.5. Not surprisingly, general education students succeeding in the mainstream curriculum have the highest CBM reading scores in the fall and make the greatest gains by spring. First graders needing more assistance begin with lower CBM reading scores and make less progress.

Figure 9.5. CBM oral-reading growth of first-grade students in general education, Stage 1, Stage 2, and Stage 3 of the problem-solving model

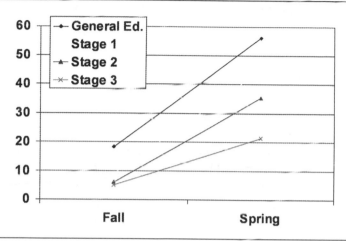

From Marston, D., Muyskens, P., Lau, M., & Canter, A. (2003). Problem-solving model for decision-making with high-incidence disabilities: The Minneapolis experience. *Learning Disabilities Research & Practice, 18*(3), 187–200. Copyright 2003 by Blackwell Publishing. Reprinted with permission.

Program Evaluation

As a result of increased confidence in the data, CBM oral-reading scores have been used in the district to assist in evaluating a variety of program alternatives. Those evaluations have included the use of noncategorical delivery of special education services (Marston, 1987), special education effectiveness (Marston, 1988), collaborative service delivery (Self, Benning, Marston, & Magnusson, 1991), types of special education service (Marston, 1996), and as a tool to review the effectiveness of specific reading instruction strategies (Marston, Deno, Kim, Diment, & Rogers, 1995).

CBM of Reading and High-Stakes Tests

Earlier we noted that CBM oral-reading scores were highly correlated with standardized achievement tests of reading (Marston, 1989). More recently, we have continued to find this pattern for oral reading and the district's reading achievement test, the Northwest Achievement Levels

Test with a median correlation of .76 for grades 2–7. However, with the advent of graduation tests for high school students and the assessment of adequate yearly progress for schools through No Child Left Behind (NCLB, 2002), the need has increased to monitor student progress toward "passing" these new high-stakes tests. Since 1996 Minnesota has had a Basic Standards Test (MBST) in reading that determines whether a student graduates from high school. For that reason, the district has examined the utility of CBM of oral reading to predict progress on high-stakes tests. The initial research found that CBM of oral reading could be used to predict whether a seventh-grade student was on track to pass the MBST (Fuchs, Deno, & Marston, 1997). The analysis revealed that the number of words read aloud correctly in one minute predicted passing the test with 82% accuracy. The level of oral-reading score for seventh graders that predicted success on the eighth-grade MBST was approximately 150 words correct in one minute. Muyskens and Marston (2003) subsequently confirmed this finding by computing a correlation of .70 between CBM reading scores and the MBST for eighth-grade students.

In addition to the tests used to establish graduation standards for secondary students, the district also has implemented state accountability measures for the No Child Left Behind initiative. These tests, known as the Minnesota Comprehension Assessment (MCA), to date have been administered at grades 3, 5, 7, and 10. The MCAs provide scores used for determining whether schools are making adequate yearly progress (AYP).

To assist teachers with doing early screening and prediction of success on the MCAs, the district examined the concurrent and predictive validity of CBM oral-reading scores for predicting the MCA performance of 5,828 third and fifth graders (Marston, Muyskens, Betts, & Heistad, 2004). The students were culturally and linguistically diverse: 73.4% students of color, 67% in poverty, 26.6% ELLs, and 10.9% in special education. The correlation between the CBM oral-reading scores at the time of MCA test administration was .75. To extend the analysis, the CBM reading scores of the third- and fifth-grade cohorts were obtained for the previous three years. The average CBM reading score for students scoring above and below the proficiency standard of 1420 on the MCA reading test for each of those three years was then computed for each cohort. As can be seen in Figure 9.6, the differences between students scoring above and below 1420 at third grade are considerable. By the end of third grade, students who are proficient on the MCA averaged almost 130 words correct whereas third graders who are not proficient averaged almost 80 words correct. Such

Figure 9.6. Average CBM oral-reading scores in first, second, and third grade for a cohort of third-grade students scoring above and below the 1420 benchmark on the statewide third-grade MCA reading test

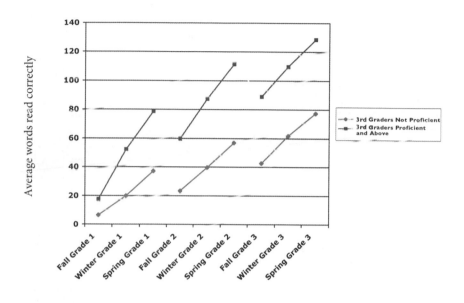

Adapted from Marston, D., Muyskens, P., Betts, J., & Heistad, D. (2004). *Tracking the progress of diverse learners toward success on tests of accountability: A three-year study.* Manuscript submitted for publication.

data increases teacher confidence in the CBM reading data and gives them multiple opportunities during the school year to screen and predict their students' likely success on the state tests.

The differences in the CBM oral-reading scores for successful fifth graders are just as dramatic. In Figure 9.7, students meeting the state standard at the end of fifth grade read about 145 words correctly in one minute from fifth-grade text, whereas those not meeting the standard for proficiency average slightly less than 100 correctly read words from the same text. The availability of such evidence now provides teachers with empirical guides for using CBM reading data to set goals and monitor student progress toward high-stakes outcomes.

Figure 9.7. Average CBM oral-reading scores in third, fourth, and fifth grade for a cohort of fifth-grade students scoring above and below the 1420 benchmark on the statewide fifth-grade MCA reading tests

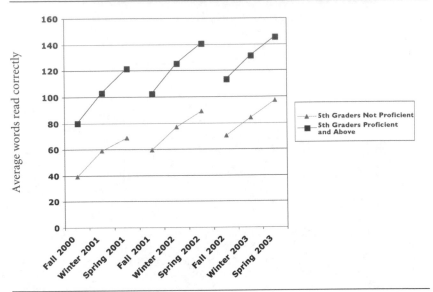

Adapted from Marston, D., Muyskens, P., Betts, J., & Heistad, D. (2004). *Tracking the progress of diverse learners toward success on tests of accountability: A three-year study.* Manuscript submitted for publication.

English-Language Learners

With the large influx of ELLs, teachers in the district needed evidence regarding the appropriateness of CBM reading procedures for assessing ELLs. To answer this question, district personnel (Muyskens & Marston, 2003) examined the relationship between CBM oral-reading scores and MBST results for eighth-grade ELLs in the district and obtained a moderately high correlation (.68). An analysis was also conducted to compare the correlations of CBM oral-reading scores with scores on the Northwest Achievement Levels Test (NALT), the district's standardized achievement test, for the fifth-grade students from the district's three largest language groups—English, Spanish, and Hmong. Substantial correlations were obtained for all language groups with the highest (.76) for English-speaking students and somewhat lower correlations for the Spanish- and Hmong-speaking students (.62 and .67, respectively).

Having established that a relationship existed between the CBM oral-reading scores and both state and district tests, the CBM oral-reading data were then used to compare the level of performance and their growth patterns when in fourth and fifth grade. The CBM oral-reading scores were compared for students who were assessed in the fall, winter, and spring of both fourth grade and fifth grade. The sample consisted of 777 English-speaking students, 112 Spanish-speaking students, and 135 Hmong-speaking students. Both the Hmong- and the Spanish-speaking groups were similar in that virtually all of these students were reported to be receiving free and reduced lunch (95% of Spanish-speaking students and 98% of Hmong-speaking students) and ELL services (96% of Spanish-speaking students and 95% of Hmong-speaking students). In contrast, only 55% of the English-speaking group received free and reduced lunch; however, of the Spanish-speaking group 21.4% reported that they had lived in the United States for less than five years; whereas, none of the Hmong group reported that they had lived in the United States for less than 5 years. The CBM oral-reading scores for the groups are presented in Figure 9.8.

Figure 9.8. Mean CBM oral-reading scores for three language cohorts assessed in fourth and fifth grade

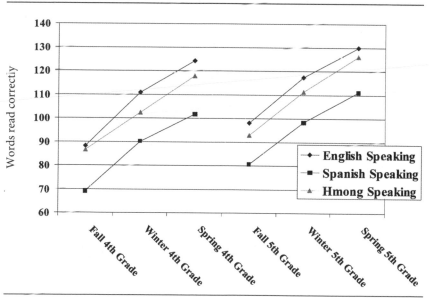

As can be seen, the mean CBM reading scores for the language groups differed consistently for both years. The rank ordering of group performance is consistent with their experience in English: Native-English speakers have the highest scores; the Hmong students who have been in the United States for at least five years do next best; and the Spanish-speaking students, where many have been exposed to English for less than five years, score the lowest in CBM oral reading. These findings for the CBM oral-reading data are consistent with group performance on the district's standardized reading achievement test. The median percentile rank on NALT reading test during the fifth grade for each group was 46 for native-English students, 31 for Hmong students, and 20 for Spanish students.

Of additional interest in Figure 9.8 is the growth pattern of the CBM oral-reading scores for the different language groups. The average gain in words read aloud correctly in one minute for each of the three groups ranged between 30 and 36 words, with the English-speaking group slightly more than both the Spanish-speaking and Hmong-speaking students, whose gains were comparable. Based on the evidence from these analyses, it would appear the CBM oral-reading scores can be a useful tool for helping teachers to screen ELLs, to monitor their progress in learning to read, and to predict success on high-stakes tests.

Extensions of CBM of Reading

The success in developing curriculum-based measures of reading has extended to written expression and arithmetic, and it has precipitated efforts to develop measures for different populations and different content areas. Since the initial developmental efforts focused on students in elementary school, the application of those measures to secondary-level students was unknown. Work by a number of different researchers has addressed both the application of basic curriculum-based measures and the development of alternative measures (Espin & Tindal, 1998) to *secondary school programs*. At the other end of the age spectrum, the Early Childhood Research Institute on Developing Individual Growth and Development Indicators at the University of Minnesota extended the basic CBM procedures to measuring growth in *early childhood* with some success (McConnell et al., 2002).

As CBM procedures have become more widely disseminated in public education, the potential for their development as commercial products has increased. In the 1980s, the Basic Skills Monitoring Program (Pro-Ed, 2005) included the use of the maze-reading procedure to conduct CBM-type growth evaluation with computers. At about the same time, the Test of Reading Fluency (TORF; Children's Educational Services, 1987) appeared, consisting of a generic set of grade-level oral-reading passages for screening and companion progress monitoring. The Standard Reading Passages of the TORF have since become part of a more elaborate Web-based system for progress monitoring called Edcheckup (2005). The Grade 1 Standard Reading Passages from the TORF were subsequently used in the initial research to develop the Dynamic Indicators of Basic Early Literacy Skills (DIBELS; Kaminski & Good, 1996) now commercially available. Another online progress-monitoring system called AimsWeb (Edformation, 2005), like Edcheckup, uses the basic CBM reading measures that were developed in the original CBM research. A Web-based system called Yearly Progress Pro (CTB/McGraw Hill, 2005) is also available that utilizes the same basic measurement concepts embedded in CBM. The development and sale of these commercial products is significant because they indicate both the degree of acceptability and the perceived potential of the CBM reading-measurement approach on which those products are based. We only hope as this move to commercialize CBM of oral reading occurs that both the reliability and validity of those procedures is preserved in the commercial products.

Conclusions

Research on the development and uses of CBM to measure reading growth now spans nearly 30 years. Evidence exists that CBM of oral reading provides reliable data on reading growth that are valid for a wide range of educational decisions. Often, CBM oral-reading measures are used to operationalize the construct of reading fluency (Fuchs et al., 2001). More often, CBM data are used to assess whether students are growing satisfactorily as readers, whether they are at risk for reading failure, and whether their instruction should be modified. Use of CBM oral-reading data is becoming more widespread as the NCLB law mandates the use of high-stakes tests and schools seek to meet its stringent requirements. As the NCLB requirement to assure that students in all subgroups succeed, research continues on the potential use of CBM with diverse learners at all ages. Although most of the technical characteristics of CBM oral reading are well known, many questions about these procedures remain to be answered. Whether or not CBM of oral reading is a sufficient index of reading fluency is not a question that will be answered through that research, however.

Questions for Discussion

1. When CBM is used as an indication of reading fluency, it narrows the focus to two dimensions of performance in reading text passages. What are those two dimensions, and why have they become so widely used to measure reading fluency?

2. While CBM seems clearly to be a direct measure of fluent word recognition, it does not seem to incorporate a focus on measuring comprehension. If reading fluency requires both word recognition and comprehension, why would CBM be used as a measure of reading fluency?

3. A different text passage is used every time a student's performance is sampled using CBM. Why is this done, and how might it aid in determining whether a student's reading fluency has improved?

4. It is September, and district and state reading tests are not administered for several months. However, you want to know immediately about each student's level of reading performance. Based on this chapter, describe how you could evaluate each student in reading and determine which students may need some extra reading instruction.

5. You are interested in how well students in your classroom are improving in reading. Based on this chapter, describe how you might check their reading progress during the school year.

REFERENCES

Baker, S.K., & Good, R.H. (1995). Curriculum-based measurement of English reading with bilingual Hispanic students: A validation study with second-grade students. *School Psychology Review, 24*, 561–578.

Carver, R.P. (1974). Two dimensions of tests: Psychometric and edumetric. *American Psychologist, 29*, 512–518.

Children's Educational Services. (1987). *Test of Reading Fluency (TORF)*. Eden Prairie, MN: Author.

CTB/McGraw-Hill. (2005). Yearly Progress Pro [Computer software]. Chicago: Author.

Deno, S.L. (1985). Curriculum-based measurement: The emerging alternative. *Exceptional Children, 52*(3), 219–232.

Deno, S.L. (1991). Curriculum-based measurement: The emerging alternative. In J. Kramer (Ed.), *Curriculum-based assessment: Examining old problems, evaluating new solutions*. Hillsdale, NJ: Erlbaum.

Deno, S.L. (1995). The school psychologist as problem solver. In J. Grimes & A. Thomas (Eds.), *Best practices in school psychology III* (pp. 471–484). Bethesda, MD: National Association of School Psychologists.

Deno, S.L., Espin, C., & Fuchs, L. (2002). Evaluation strategies for preventing and remediating basic skill deficits. In G. Stoner, M. Shinn, & H. Walker (Eds.), *Interventions for achievement and behavior problems* (pp. 213–242). Bethesda, MD: National Association of School Psychologists.

Deno, S.L., & Fuchs, L.S. (1987). Developing curriculum-based measurement systems for data-based special education problem solving. *Focus on Exceptional Children, 19*(8), 1–16.

Deno, S.L., Fuchs, L.S., Marston, D., & Shin, J. (2001). Using curriculum-based measurement to establish growth standards for students with learning disabilities. *School Psychology Review, 30*(4), 507–524.

Deno, S.L., Marston, D., Shinn, M.R., & Tindal, G. (1983). Oral reading fluency: A simple datum for scaling reading disability. *Topics in Learning and Learning Disabilities, 2*(4), 53–59.

Deno, S.L., & Mirkin, P.K. (1977). *Data-based program modification: A manual.* Arlington, VA: Council for Exceptional Children.

Deno, S.L., Mirkin, P.K., & Chiang, B. (1982). Identifying valid measures of reading. *Exceptional Children, 49*(1), 36–45

Edcheckup. (2005). *Edcheckup.* Edina, MN: Author.

Edformation. (2005). *AimsWeb.* Eden Prairie, MN: Author.

Espin, C.A., & Tindal, G. (1998). Curriculum-based measurement for secondary students. In M.R. Shinn (Ed.), *Advanced applications of curriculum-based measurement* (pp. 214–253). New York: Guilford.

Fuchs, L.S., & Deno, S.L. (1994). Must instructionally useful performance assessment be based in the curriculum? *Exceptional Children, 61*, 15–24.

Fuchs, L.S., Deno, S.L., & Fuchs, D. (1982). Reliability and validity of curriculum-based informal reading inventories. *Reading Research Quarterly, 18*, 16–26.

Fuchs, L.S., Deno, S.L., & Marston, D. (1997, February 7). *Alternative measures of student progress and state standards testing.* Paper presented at the Pacific Coast Research Conference, San Diego, CA.

Fuchs, L.S., Deno, S.L., & Mirkin, P. (1984). Effects of frequent curriculum-based measurement and evaluation on pedagogy, student achievement, and student awareness of learning. *American Educational Research Journal, 21*, 449–460.

Fuchs, L.S., Fuchs, D., & Hamlett, C.L. (1989). Effects of instrumental use of curriculum-based measurement to enhance instructional programs. *Remedial & Special Education, 10*(2), 43–52.

Fuchs, L.S., Fuchs, D., Hamlett, C.L., & Ferguson, C. (1992). Effects of expert system consultation within curriculum-based measurement using a reading maze task. *Exceptional Children, 58*(5), 436–450.

Fuchs, L.S., Fuchs, D., Hosp, M., & Jenkins, J.R. (2001). Oral reading fluency as an indicator of reading competence: A theoretical, empirical, and historical analysis. *Scientific Studies of Reading, 5*, 239–256.

Fuchs, L.S., Fuchs, D., & Maxwell, L. (1988). The validity of informal reading comprehension measures. *Remedial and Special Education, 9*, 20–28.

Good, R.H., & Jefferson, G. (1998). Contemporary perspectives on curriculum-based measurement validity. In M.R. Shinn (Ed.), *Advanced applications of curriculum-based measurement* (pp. 61–88). New York: Guilford.

Good, R.H., Simmons, D.C., & Kame'enui, E.J. (2001). The importance and decision-making utility of a continuum of fluency-based indicators of foundational reading skills for third-grade high stakes outcomes. *Scientific Studies of Reading, 5*, 257–288.

Jenkins, J., Fuchs, L.S., van den Broek, P., Espin, C., & Deno, S.L. (2003). Sources of individual differences in reading comprehension and reading fluency. *Journal of Educational Psychology, 95*, 719–729.

Kaminski, R.A., & Good, R.H. (1996). Toward a technology for assessing basic early literacy skills. *School Psychology Review, 25*, 215–227.

Marston, D. (1987). Does categorical teacher certification benefit the mildly handicapped child? *Exceptional Children, 63*(5), 423–431.

Marston, D. (1988). The effectiveness of special education: A time series analysis of reading performance in regular and special education. *Journal of Special Education, 21*(4), 13–26.

Marston, D. (1989). A curriculum-based approach to assessing academic performance: What it is and why do it. In M.R. Shinn (Ed.), *Curriculum-based measurement: Assessing special children* (pp. 19–78). New York: Guilford.

Marston, D. (1996). A comparison of inclusion only, pull-out only, and combined service models for students with mild disabilities. *Journal of Special Education, 30*(2), 121–132.

Marston, D., Deno, S.L., Kim, D., Diment, K., & Rogers, D. (1995). Comparison of reading intervention approaches for students with mild disabilities. *Exceptional Children, 62*(1), 20–37.

Marston, D., & Magnusson, D. (1985). Implementing curriculum-based measurement in special and regular education settings. *Exceptional Children, 52*(3), 266–276.

Marston, D., & Magnusson, D. (1988). Curriculum-based measurement: District level implementation. In J. Graden, J. Zins, & M. Curtis (Eds.), *Alternative educational delivery systems: Enhancing instructional options for all students* (pp. 137–172). Bethesda, MD: National Association of School Psychologists.

Marston, D., Muyskens, P., Betts, J., & Heistad, D. (2004). *Tracking the progress of diverse learners toward success on tests of accountability: A three-year study.* Manuscript submitted for publication.

Marston, D., Muyskens, P., Lau, M., & Canter, A. (2003). Problem-solving model for decision-making with high-incidence disabilities: The Minneapolis experience. *Learning Disabilities Research & Practice, 18*(3), 187–200.

Marston, D., Pickart, M., Reschly, A.R., Heistad, D., Muyskens, P., & Tindal, G. (in press). Early literacy measures for improving student reading achievement: Translating research into practice. *Exceptionality.*

McConnell, S., Priest, J., Davis, S., & McEvoy, M. (2002). Best practices in measuring growth and development for preschool children. In A. Thomas & J. Grimes (Eds.), *Best practices in school psychology IV* (pp. 1231–1246). Bethesda, MD: National Association of School Psychologists.

Muyskens, P., & Marston, D. (2003). *The relationship between curriculum-based measurement and outcomes on high-stakes tests with secondary students.* Manuscript submitted for publication.

Nazzaro, J. (1976). Comprehensive assessment for educational planning. In J. Weintraub, A. Abeson, J. Ballard, & M. LaVor (Eds.), *Public policy and the education of exceptional children* (p. 41). Arlington, VA: Council for Exceptional Children.

No Child Left Behind Act of 2001, Pub. L. No. 107-110, 115 Stat. 1425 (2002).

Pro-Ed. (2005). *Monitoring basic skills progress.* Austin, TX: Author.

Research Institute on Progress Monitoring (RIPM). (2004). *Literature review: Curriculum-based measurement progress monitoring.* Unpublished manuscript.

Salvia, J., & Ysseldyke, J. (2001). *Assessment.* Boston: Houghton Mifflin.

Self, H., Benning, A., Marston, D., & Magnusson, D. (1991). Cooperative Teaching Project: A model for students at risk. *Exceptional Children, 58*(1), 26–34.

Shinn, M.R. (Ed.). (1989). *Curriculum-based measurement: Assessing special children.* New York: Guilford.

Shinn, M.R. (Ed.). (1998). *Advanced applications of curriculum-based measurement.* New York: Guilford.

Shinn, M.R. (2002). Best practices in using curriculum-based measurement in a problem-solving model. In A. Thomas & J. Grimes (Eds.), *Best practices in school psychology IV* (pp. 671–697). Bethesda, MD: National Association of School Psychologists.

Stecker, P.M., & Fuchs, L.S. (2000). Effecting superior achievement using curriculum-based measurement: The importance of individual progress monitoring. *Learning Disabilities Research and Practice, 15,* 128–135.

Tindal, G., & Marston, D. (1996). Technical adequacy of alternative reading measures as performance assessments. *Exceptionality, 6*(4), 201–230.

Chapter 10

Becoming Fluent: Repeated Reading With Scaffolded Texts

Elfrieda H. Hiebert

The interaction between reader and text is at the center of definitions of reading comprehension (RAND Reading Study Group, 2002). The common perspective is that when teachers are there to scaffold and guide the interaction, features of texts, such as engagingness, content, and length, are as important in determining text difficulty as the ability of children to read the words (Fountas & Pinnell, 1999; Hoffman & Schallert, 2004). Although teachers have a central role in guiding the interactions of beginning and struggling readers with texts, the development of independent reading also requires that children read many texts with minimal teacher support. An underlying premise of this chapter is that the word-level features of texts that beginning and struggling readers are given to read will support the fluency that contributes to meaningful comprehension of text. Just as teachers scaffold reading events, the characteristics of texts serve to scaffold the reading act for beginning and struggling readers.

A second premise of this chapter is that the selections in reading textbooks offered by major U.S. publishers for primary-grade instruction have not been chosen with fluency development in mind. As demonstrated by several researchers (Foorman, Francis, Davidson, Harm, & Griffin, 2004; Hiebert, 2005a; Hoffman, Sailors, & Patterson, 2002), the word-level features of instructional texts for the primary grades—during which period the foundations of fluency are laid—have changed substantially over the past 15 to 20 years. The nature of these changes can be seen in the first two excerpts in Table 10.1.

These two excerpts, published by the same company about 15 years apart, appear in the middle of the second-grade basal reading program. Excerpt 1, part of the 1982 program (Clymer & Venezky, 1982), comes from a text in which approximately one out of every 100 words is both multisyllabic and rare (i.e., *not* among the 1,000 most frequent words

---

What Research Has to Say About Fluency Instruction, edited by S. Jay Samuels and Alan E. Farstrup. © 2006 by the International Reading Association.

Table 10.1. Excerpts from different types of texts (second-grade level)

Excerpt number	Text type	Excerpt
1	Controlled reading text	She reached into her hat, and pulled out ... a chicken! "That's great!" said May. "A chicken is not a rabbit," said Jimmy Smith. "Give me a little time," said Madge. She waved her wand. She reached back into her hat. She said the magic words, and pulled out...a fox! (Clymer & Venezky, 1982)
2	Literature text (used in study)	Alphonse was delighted to see all the swimmers. "It's a submarine from another planet!" bellowed the coach. "Call the police! Call the Navy!" "No! It's a tadpole!" cried Louis. "He's my pet!" The coach was upset and confused. "You have until tomorrow," he cried, "to get that creature out of the pool!" (Kellogg, 1977, in Pearson et al., 1998)
3	Scaffolded text (used in study)	George Washington Carver was a scientist who knew about plants. He learned that soil wears out when farmers grow the same crop every year. When soil wears out, crops are poor. George Washington Carver showed farmers how to grow one crop in one year. Then they would grow a different crop in the next year. (Hiebert, 2003)
4	Science textbook text	Flowers and fruits Seeds form inside the flowers of many adult plants. Pollen, a powdery material, is made by one part of the flower. Pollen is needed to make seeds form. There are tiny eggs inside some flowers. When pollen lands on the eggs, seeds may start to form. (Badders et al., 2000)
5	HI/LV text	Frog was in his garden. Toad came walking by. "What a fine garden you have, Frog," he said. "Yes," said Frog. "It's very nice, but it was hard work." "I wish I had a garden," said Toad. "Here are some flower seeds." (Lobel, 1979)
6	Literature anthology text, example 1	"My, my!" sighed Mrs. Frye. "Cool!" said Ira Baker. "Brr!" chattered Mr. Boyle. "Wheee!" squealed the babies. "OOOO!" said the gathering crowd, thrilled to be chilled to the bone. No wonder no one noticed a little breeze rippling the haze and turning the leaves inside out. (Poydar, 1996, in Afflerbach et al., 2000)
7	Literature anthology text, example 2	When the lights go on in the town, the worker's day is done. "Goodnight, my dear white bench," he says. "You must be very tired. I'll see you tomorrow." He turns on the lights of his little motor cart and drives home. The park is covered with darkness. (Takeshita, 1988, in Afflerbach et al., 2000)

in written English; Carroll, Davies, & Richman, 1971); these are words such as *chicken, rabbit,* and *magician.* Excerpt 2, from the 1998 program, comes from a textbook that consisted of trade book selections, such as *The Mysterious Tadpole* (Kellogg, 1977). In that selection, approximately 7 out of every 100 words are both multisyllabic and rare; these are words such as *submarine, bellowed,* and *creature.* Not only are there more rare multisyllabic words in the more recently published program, but the familiarity of these words for second graders also differs. Although *chicken* and *rabbit* may not occur among the 1,000 most frequent words in written English, second graders are likely to be familiar with the concepts. Words such as *bellowed* and *creature* will require more explanation.

These observations regarding text features are made to illustrate that different types of texts have important but unique roles in instructional programs. Although trade books develop literary knowledge, texts with high percentages of highly frequent and common decodable words support the development of automatic, meaningful reading for beginning and struggling readers. This chapter is concerned with texts that support the latter goal—the attainment of fluency among beginning and struggling readers. My intent is to portray the background and evidence for the role of a particular type of text in fluency development among beginning and struggling readers by (a) presenting a model of text difficulty that recognizes the role of word-level features, (b) summarizing research and theory on the kinds of texts that promote fluency, (c) presenting the results of a study in which the texts for fluency practice were selections from a literature-based basal series or "scaffolded" texts that emphasized the 1,000 most frequent words, and (d) proposing implications of the foregoing for classrooms.

A Definition of Fluency

In fluent reading, word recognition is sufficiently automatic and accurate so that a reader's attention is focused on the meaning of the text (LaBerge & Samuels, 1974; Samuels, 2002). Fluent reading does not preclude hesitating or pausing to decode unknown words. However, it is unlikely that readers will have a high-quality interpretation of a text when many words need to be decoded. The breaking point at which the number of known words is insufficient for constructing a useful interpretation of a text is determined by reader proficiency and background knowledge. For example, reading educators who read this chapter facilely but who are not researchers in neuroscience may find it difficult to give anything but a superficial interpretation to an article on the molecular organization of the olfactory septal organ (Tian & Ma, 2004) in the *Journal of Neuroscience*.

Fluent readers know the majority of the words automatically and attend to less frequent words in texts; thus, the aim of fluency practice would seem to be to increase the automatic response of beginning and struggling readers to the words that account for the majority of the words in texts. Fortunately for the instruction of fluency, a very small group of unique words accounts for the majority of the total words in written language (Adams, 1990). In addition, a small group of vowel patterns appears consistently in many common words that appear in texts for beginning readers (Wylie & Durrell, 1970).

As yet, analyses that pinpoint the size and the content of the vocabularies of young readers who attain fluency as first graders remain to be conducted. Research indicates that differences in the automaticity of beginning readers with the majority of the words in typical first-grade texts are already substantial by mid-first grade (Good, Wallin, Simmons, Kame'enui, & Kaminski, 2002; Lesgold, Resnick, & Hammond, 1985). Research also provides insight into how readers develop this automaticity. Less skilled readers process all words, even words that appear frequently, letter by letter, unlike skilled readers, who process the same words holistically (Samuels, LaBerge, & Bremer, 1978). When confronted with an unfamiliar word, skilled readers may engage initially in letter-by-letter processing but move to a holistic strategy with increased exposure to the word (Samuels, Miller, & Eisenberg, 1979). Familiar words are responded to quickly; familiarity comes from repeated experiences. In a subsequent section of this chapter, I discuss the texts that provide the repeated experiences with the vocabulary that accounts for the majority of the words in written language. Research shows that reading of texts with high percentages of unique words that are both rare and multisyllabic is unlikely to support increases in automaticity with the words that appear frequently in texts.

Oral-reading fluency is a fairly robust proxy for silent-reading comprehension (Fuchs, Fuchs, Hamlett, Walz, & Germann, 1993; Pinnell et al., 1995). However, because reading is typically a silent act, automaticity and accuracy in silent reading, not oral reading, is the ultimate goal. Readers—even beginning and struggling readers—have greater latitude in strategies during silent reading than oral reading. When reading aloud for an adult, beginning and struggling readers may stumble repeatedly over a word such as the name of a character in a narrative (e.g., Alphonse) that they may skip over in silent reading. Although oral reading provides the means for capturing fluency, it should not be viewed as the be-all and end-all of fluency practice. Ultimately, what matters is the student's ability to transfer fluency from oral to silent reading.

Successful fluency interventions need to provide opportunities for students to transfer their skills to silent reading. Giving students a purpose for reading a text and a definite time period in which to accomplish it provides scaffolding for silent reading (Manning & Manning, 1984; Samuels, 2005). This scaffolded silent reading is quite different than the independent silent reading for which the National Reading Panel (NRP) found little experimental evidence for positively influencing fluency (National Institute of Child Health and Human Development [NICHD], 2000). While research has yet to experimentally address the efficacy of scaffolded silent-reading events, the ability of students to transfer fluency from oral-reading events to silent-reading events determines their performance on national and state assessments.

The Text Elements by Task (TExT) Model and Fluency Development

After establishing the degree to which textbooks for beginning and struggling readers had changed (from controlled to literature-based texts in the late 1980s and then from literature-based to decodable texts in the mid-1990s; Hiebert, 1999), Hiebert and colleagues began to develop a model for the effects of text on word recognition and fluency among beginning and struggling readers (e.g., Hiebert, 2005a; Hiebert & Fisher, 2005; Hiebert, Martin, & Menon, 2005). This model, called the Text Elements by Task (TExT) model, focuses on the task that a text poses for beginning and struggling readers. Although many other factors (see Gray & Leary, 1935) influence reading proficiency, beginning and struggling readers must be able to identify words to read a text independently. In the TExT model, two features of text are seen to influence the success of beginning and struggling readers in identifying words in text: the linguistic content (e.g., the letter–sound patterns within words in the text and the frequency of words within written English) and the variety in this linguistic content (e.g., the cognitive load required to process the linguistic content).

The Components of the TExT Model

Linguistic knowledge refers to the size and features of a word corpus a reader needs to know in order to read a text independently. It has long been recognized that a relatively small number of words accounts for a substantial percentage of the total words in text (Thorndike, 1921). Based on a sample of 17.25 million words in texts used from kindergarten through college, Zeno, Ivens, Millard, and Duvvuri (1995) reported that 25 words account for 33% of the total words in the corpus. When the number of unique words gets to around 5,575, approximately 90% of the total words in texts from third through ninth grade (Carroll et al., 1971) and about 80% of the total words in texts from kindergarten through college (Zeno et al., 1995) are accounted for. The remaining words in texts come from an enormous corpus of 150,000 or more words. Even when the corpus is reduced substantially by clustering words with shared root words (Nagy & Anderson, 1984), it is impractical to teach all of these words. However, students can be expected to use knowledge of word parts and syntax together with general background knowledge to establish the meanings of rarely occurring unique words and have sufficient cognitive resources to comprehend texts, if they are automatic with the words that account for 80%–90% of their texts (Samuels, 1979, 2002).

Automaticity with the majority of words also assumes that students have the ability to generalize common and consistent letter–sound patterns within less frequent words. For example, even though the word *mat* is not within the 5,575 most frequent words, the presence of numerous words within the 5,575 that share the *at* rime (*bat, fat, hat, pat, rat, sat, that*) leads to the expectation that *mat* would be recognized more readily than another word with similar frequency but with a more complex structure, such as *punctuation*. Consequently, the analyses of corpora according to the TExT model consider both the frequency and the linguistic structure of words.

Cognitive load refers to the number of words in a text that are not recognized automatically by readers and thus require conscious processing. Although these unknown words vary among individual readers, some general characteristics of texts can be identified that are likely to influence many beginning and struggling readers. In a review of word learning from text, Swanborn and de Glopper (1999) found that the number of rare words in text was a critical feature. They reported that the probability of learning a word is about .30 when the density of unknown words in a text is 1:150 words. This probability drops to .14 when the ratio is 1:75. In current second-grade literature textbook anthologies where the ratio of rare multisyllabic single-appearing words is 7:100 (Hiebert, 2005a), the cognitive load is high. Struggling readers are unlikely to become automatic readers of texts when they are stopping to decode and retrieve the meaning of numerous rare words such as *submarine* and *bellowed* (see Excerpt 2 in Table 10.1). Even after several repeated readings of a text, these numerous rare words may continue to serve as obstacles to beginning and struggling readers. With students who have at least basic reading proficiency, a range of 6–12 repetitions is required for meaningful recognition of words (Jenkins, Stein, & Wysocki, 1984; McKeown, Beck, Omanson, & Pople, 1985).

A Review of Existing Research on Fluency and the TExT Model

The National Reading Panel recently concluded that fluency can be attained through repeated and guided reading (NICHD, 2000). This conclusion was based on a review of a sample of studies selected to meet certain methodological criteria. Although the NRP listed the nature and difficulty of the various texts that were used in treatments in their sample of studies, they did not differentiate their findings on fluency by either text difficulty or type. Following the NRP's report, Hiebert and Fisher (2005) reviewed the original reports of the 51 studies identified by the NRP (16 studies that the NRP used in a meta-analysis and 35 additional studies in its extended database) to establish the characteristics of texts used in repeated and guided reading interventions. Four types of texts were identified: (1) pre-1990 basal texts, (2) children's literature, (3) skill builders, and (4) high-interest/low-vocabulary texts (HI/LV). When texts with controlled vocabulary were clustered (i.e., pre-1990 basal, skill builder, and HI/LV texts), they accounted for 73% of the studies overall and 74% of the studies used in the meta-analysis. The four studies (26%) in the meta-analysis that used texts from children's literature were further examined to establish their contribution to the overall effect size of .48 (across measures of fluency, vocabulary, and comprehension) reported by the NRP. Only one of these four studies reported a fluency outcome; in that study, the treatment and comparison groups did not differ significantly on fluency. Thus the effect size for fluency reported by the NRP came from the studies that used text types with some level of controlled vocabulary. It follows that the panel's fluency finding, in the absence of additional data, cannot be generalized beyond texts with some level of controlled vocabulary.

Hiebert and Fisher (2005) also analyzed the unique words in proto-typical texts for each of the four text types (i.e., children's literature, pre-1990 basal textbooks, skill builders, and HI/LV). Not surprisingly, the children's literature text type differed from the other three text types in number and kinds of unique words. On average, 92% of the words in the three controlled text types were included in the 3,000 most frequent words, 83% in the literature text type. Multisyllabic words that appeared as single-time words accounted for 3.8% of the words in the controlled text types; in samples of children's literature, 10%.

Further review of the fluency studies reviewed by the NRP (NICHD, 2000) revealed that text characteristics were typically not manipulated. Most often, instructional conditions (e.g., repeated reading with or without teacher guidance) were manipulated, but participants in all conditions read the same text. In one of the few studies of repeated reading where text had been manipulated, Rashotte and Torgesen (1985) found that repeated reading resulted in improved fluency only when students read stories that shared a high percentage of words. When the percentage of shared words was low, repeated reading did not result in increased fluency levels. Because this finding could reflect shared content and not shared words, Faulkner and Levy (1994) examined students' reading rate and accuracy after reading texts with similar content that did not share critical vocabulary (e.g., the word *automobile* appears in one text, and the word *car* in the other) and texts with shared vocabulary that did not share content (e.g., *birdie* in a game of golf or a young child's description of a bird). Good and poor readers had the most transfer when words and content were shared. Poor readers, unlike good readers, also improved in reading rate and accuracy when texts had high levels of word overlap but did not share content.

Other than these two studies (Faulkner & Levy, 1994; Rashotte & Torgesen, 1985), the texts in fluency treatments have not been manipulated systematically. Furthermore, in both of these studies, experimenters (rather than teachers) conducted the training sessions, and training sessions were limited in scope. The limited research and the limitations of the research on effects of text features on fluency led Hiebert (2005b) to conduct a study of teachers providing the fluency instruction to their classes using different kinds of texts.

Two groups of second-grade classes participated in Fluency-Oriented Reading Instruction (FORI; Stahl, Heubach, & Cramond, 1997). The literature group read texts from the district's literature-based reading program. The scaffolded-text group read from a set of science and social studies texts that were written to have few, if any, rare multisyllabic single-appearing words. A passive control group read from the district's literature-based program. Both intervention groups made greater fluency gains than the control group; in addition, the scaffolded-text group made greater fluency gains than the literature group.

Although it was not by design, it came to light that a substantial difference in time allocation to reading occurred between the literature- and scaffolded-text groups. A federal school reading improvement grant was implemented in the school where literature texts were used for repeated reading. This grant required that second-grade teachers devote three hours daily to reading and language arts. Teachers in the school using scaffolded texts complied with the district guideline of 75 minutes per day for reading and language arts. As a result, the superior performance of the scaffolded-text treatment was accomplished in about 60% of the time spent on reading by the literature group. That is, shorter periods of time with less difficult texts resulted in higher performances when compared to longer periods of time with difficult texts.

More than 30 years ago, Barr (1974) reported that effective teachers compensate for difficult texts by spending more time on them. Despite extensive research on the importance of engaged learning time (see Fisher & Berliner, 1985), this factor has not been systematically addressed in the research on fluency. Unlike the research on phonemic awareness, about which the NRP (NICHD, 2000) was able to make definitive conclusions about the point of diminishing returns in the investment of time, the corpus of fluency studies did not support analogous conclusions, nor did it suggest guidelines for optimal lengths of fluency training.

In educational practice, a common interpretation of research findings on time allocation is to assume that if a little is good, more will be better (Fisher & Berliner, 1985). As students approach automaticity, however, longer and more fluency sessions may have little effect (Logan, Taylor, & Etherton, 1999). Further, as Underwood and Pearson (2004) have suggested, excessive fluency practice could serve to compromise students' engagement and comprehension. Federal mandates requiring substantial investments of instructional time in reading instruction (No

Child Left Behind Act of 2001 [NCLB], 2002) create questions that merit further investigation about the amount of time spent on reading instruction during a school day and, in particular, the amount of reading instruction that should be spent on fluency.

A Study of Text Effects on Second-Grade Readers' Fluency Development

This project was a follow-up to the study of scaffolded texts (Hiebert, 2005b) described earlier. This second study examined fluency gains when the length of the intervention with scaffolded texts was half of the duration used in the first study. The two studies were conducted with different grade 2 cohorts at the same schools. Data from the two studies were compared to assess effects of treatment length on fluency.

The study was similar in design to the first investigation (Hiebert, 2005b) where students read repeatedly using different types of text for a portion of the daily reading period. One group read from literature with a high number of rare words, while the other group read from a set of "scaffolded" texts—texts with a small percentage of rare words. The rare words that occurred in the scaffolded texts always appeared more than once in a given text. In both studies, students reading the scaffolded texts also read literature, but repeated-reading activities occurred only with the scaffolded texts. Unlike the first study, in which repeated reading with scaffolded texts occurred over a 20-week period, the second intervention with the scaffolded texts occurred for 10 weeks.

Although the relationship between comprehension and fluency is strong (Fuchs et al., 1993; Pinnell et al., 1995), concerns have been voiced within the reading education community that fluency practice may result in faster reading but have no appreciable gains—and may even have negative effects—on comprehension (Underwood & Pearson, 2004). The hypothesis underlying the study under discussion is that fluency interventions, when conducted with accessible but engaging texts, will sustain students' comprehension. When literature is used for fluency treatments (as in the comparison group in the present research), significant effects have been found for comprehension, although not for fluency (Hiebert & Fisher, 2005). In this study, the prediction was that students whose repeated reading occurred with the scaffolded texts would have comprehension performances equivalent to students whose repeated reading occurred with literature texts. Although prosody data were gathered, no hypotheses were made regarding effects of text type on expressiveness in oral reading or prosody.

Intervention Participants, Procedures, and Materials

The literature text (literature) group consisted of 54 students from four second-grade classes in one school; the group whose repeated-reading experiences occurred with scaffolded texts consisted of 45 students from three classes in a second school. A passive-control treatment that comprised a set of classrooms in a third school was eliminated when state mandates made it necessary for this school to implement a reading intervention or risk state and federal sanctions. In lieu of a passive-control group, students' changes in fluency in the two intervention groups were compared to data from the previous study (Hiebert, 2005b), as well as to national norms (Hasbrouck & Tindal, in press).

The intervention occurred over a 10-week period during the second half of the school year. The teachers of students in both groups had been trained in the implementation of FORI with literature texts at the beginning of the school year. The FORI procedure with a text begins with teacher modeling of fluent reading in a guided reading lesson. The reading is followed by comprehension activities and a review of key vocabulary from the story. During one day of the cycle with a text, children reread the text with a partner. Another day of the cycle is devoted to extension activities for typically developing students and repeated reading of the text for struggling students. During the 10 weeks of the study, the texts in the basal literature anthology were the content for a teacher-guided lesson for both groups. During the partner reading and the extension portion of the FORI cycle, the students in the scaffolded-text group read and reread scaffolded texts, rather than the literature.

The 10 literature texts that were read over the 10-week intervention came from the district's adopted basal reading program (Pearson et al., 1998). The scaffolded texts came from a set of science and social studies texts (Hiebert, 2003). Topics came from national content standards and represented major disciplines in each content area (i.e., life, earth, and physical sciences in science and civics, geography/economics, and history in social studies). A topic of a content area was made up of five texts, each from 90 to 110 words in length. For example, Excerpt 3 in Table 10.1 comes from a set of five texts on the topic of "Brave Americans."

A HyperCard application (Hiebert & Martin, 2003) was used to establish the number of unique or different words within a text, high-frequency ratings of unique words, and the decodability patterns of unique words. Data for the two types of text are presented in Table 10.2.

Table 10.2 shows that the scaffolded texts had fewer unique words than the literature texts: 13 new unique words per 100 words in scaffolded texts and 18 new unique words per 100 words in literature texts. The 1,000 most frequent words accounted for a higher percentage of scaffolded texts than literature texts: 75% for the former and 50% for the latter. The greatest difference between the two types of text was in the number of rare multisyllabic single-appearing words: 19% of the literature corpus and 1% of the scaffolded-text corpus.

This follow-up study used similar assessment procedures as those in the previous study (Hiebert, 2005b). Graduate students in reading education who had been trained in administration of clinical assessments, including the Gray Oral Reading Test (GORT; Wiederholt & Bryant, 2001), individually assessed all students at the beginning and end of the intervention. Students were asked to read a passage aloud and then to give an oral summary of the passage. Administration procedures of the GORT (i.e., counting substitutions, insertions, and omissions as errors and discontinuing the task when students made 10 consecutive oral-reading errors) were used for the recording of miscues. Test administrators also gave students a rating for phrasing and expressiveness, or prosody, during the oral reading, using the four-point scale developed

Table 10.2. Features of literature, scaffolded, and science texts

Text type	Total number of words per text	Number of new, unique words per 100	Percentage of high-frequency words	Percentage of multisyllabic words (singletons)
Literature texts (Pearson et al., 1998)	727	18	51	27 (19)
Scaffolded texts (Hiebert, 2003)	486	13	75	9 (1)
Science texts (Badders et al., 2000)	708	11	61	20 (8)

for the special study of the 1994 National Assessment of Educational Progress (NAEP; Pinnell et al., 1995). Test administrators recorded students' oral summaries, which were subsequently evaluated according to the scale used for open-ended comprehension items on the NAEP (Donahue, Finnegan, Lutkus, Allen, & Campbell, 2001). This score was used as the index of comprehension.

Findings and Conclusions for the Follow-Up Study

Students' fluency scores were computed as the number of words read correctly per minute (WCPM). The fluency scores of students in the scaffolded- and literature-text groups were examined in several ways: (1) mean differences between groups, (2) weekly average gains in the 10-week intervention compared to gains in the previous 20-week intervention (Hiebert, 2005b), and (3) changes in attainment of benchmark levels of fluency. In addition, mean differences on comprehension and prosody scores were examined.

Means for WCPM (and standard deviations) were as follows: literature text pretest 37.5 ($SD = 34.6$) and posttest 62.9 ($SD = 38.9$), and scaffolded text pretest 53.1 ($SD = 30.4$) and posttest 84.2 ($SD = 32.3$). Fluency scores were analyzed using analysis of covariance with pretest scores as covariate. The adjusted means for the two groups—69.7 WCPM (literature) and 76.0 WCPM (scaffolded)—were significantly different at the .09 level. Both groups made substantial gains over the 10-week intervention. However, the gains for students using the scaffolded text were somewhat greater than those of the literature-text group.

On the comprehension measure, scaffolded-text students' mean posttest scores (2.3) were slightly higher than those of students in the literature group (2.0) but not significantly different. As predicted, students in the scaffolded-text group performed well on the comprehension measure. On the prosody measure, the adjusted means for the two groups (literature = 2.8; scaffolded = 2.9) were not significantly different.

The next set of analyses examined the average gain per week made by students in the two treatments. Data on the average weekly growth of reading speed for students in both the first (Hiebert, 2005b) and second studies appear in Table 10.3.

Fuchs et al. (1993) have suggested that a weekly increase of at least 0.5 WCPM above typical growth is needed if struggling readers are to attain satisfactory fluency levels. According to available norms (Hasbrouck & Tindal, in press), the typical weekly growth of second graders is 1.2

Table 10.3. **Mean gains in words read correctly per minute (WCPM) over intervention periods**

Text type	Weekly gain over 10 weeks	Weekly gain over 20 weeks (Hiebert, 2005b)
Scaffolded texts	3.1	1.7
Literature texts	2.5	1.5
Typical instruction	1.2	1.2

words per week, a rate that students in both intervention groups exceeded. The average gain of 2.5 words per week for the literature-text students exceeded the typical growth rate by more than a word per week. The scaffolded-text students' gain of 3.1 words per week was 2.6 times that of the typical expected growth.

The data in Table 10.3 also show that students in the 20-week intervention did not attain the weekly growth rate of students in the 10-week intervention. The inability of students to sustain the higher growth rate over a 20-week period may be explained by the phenomenon described earlier in which students who are approaching automaticity do not appear to benefit from longer and more fluency sessions (Logan et al., 1999).

The final set of analyses examined students' attainment of fluency standards. Because Reading First legislation requires that students be evaluated by the same standards, the number of students who attain particular levels is an increasingly important issue. The standards against which students' performances were examined were those reported by Hasbrouck and Tindal (in press) for the 25th, 50th, and 75th percentiles in winter and spring of second grade. Percentages of students at these three percentiles are shown in Table 10.4 for students in the literature- and scaffolded-text groups (second study only).

In both groups, approximately 15% more students reached the 25th percentile or higher at the end of the 10-week period. However, in the middle segments of the distribution, the scaffolded-text group did considerably better than the literature group. The scaffolded-text treatment increased the percentage of students reaching at least the 50th percentile by 15, while the literature group increased by only 1 percent.

When all of the analyses of fluency are considered (mean differences, average weekly growth, and attainment of standards), students who read scaffolded texts for fluency practice had an advantage over peers who

Table 10.4. Attainment of standards: Cumulative percentages at three percentile levels by text type and time period

Percentile levels	Literature winter (2002)	Literature spring (2002)	Scaffolded winter (2002)	Scaffolded spring (2002)
75	2	7	7	9
50	21	22	25	40
25	36	50	61	76

used literature texts. The present study confirmed the NRP's (NICHD, 2000) conclusions that repeated, guided reading of text supported second graders in attaining higher than expected levels of fluency. When texts had a degree of control for number of rare multisyllabic words, students had higher fluency gains than those who read from texts that were not controlled for rare multisyllabic words. Even a 10-week intervention with scaffolded texts was sufficient to change children's standing when evaluated by the benchmarks in a national sample (Hasbrouck & Tindal, in press). In both intervention groups, an additional 14–15% of students reached the 25th percentile of a national norming sample. The scaffolded-text intervention, however, was effective in moving a sizable group of students—15% of the sample—from the 25th to 50th percentile groups. Given the stability of children's reading relative to their peers in typical instructional settings (Juel, 1988), this latter finding may be especially important.

Equally critical, the comprehension scores of students in both groups also improved. Students using scaffolded texts, where high-frequency words accounted for more of the unique words than in the literature texts, had higher, but not significantly higher, gains in comprehension. The present findings suggest that fluency and comprehension can be supported in the same instructional events.

Implications for Educational Practice

The NRP (NICHD, 2000) concluded that fluency must be part of instructional programs if a significant portion of American students is to achieve proficient or even basic reading standards. Their emphasis was on the instructional activities that support increased fluency: repeated and guided reading. The review of literature and results of the study reported in the previous section point to the importance of two additional elements: features of texts used for fluency instruction and the allocation of time. The greatest gains in the archival studies on repeated and guided reading used in the NRP's meta-analysis came from texts emphasizing highly frequent words and words with common and consistent letter–sound patterns. Texts for fluency development should maximize these words and minimize rare words, especially those with complex multisyllabic structures, so that students have a higher probability of becoming automatic with high-frequency words and words that have common, consistent letter–sound patterns.

Although the study requires substantial replication and extension, it showed that the best results for fluency were obtained when scaffolded texts were used over short practice periods rather than when literature with uncontrolled vocabulary was used over extended practice periods. In the interventions using scaffolded texts with high percentages of high-frequency words, students continued to have guided reading lessons with literature texts from their basal program. However, for at least a portion of the reading and language arts period, students in the scaffolded-text group were involved with texts that had a high percentage of words that account for the majority of words in written English and words with common, consistent letter–sound relationships. Even though scaffolded texts were used for a small portion of the school day and for a relatively small portion of the school year, this opportunity made a difference beyond the repeated and guided reading practices described by the NRP (NICHD, 2000). Fluency practice is not the sole aim of an elementary school curriculum; it is one of several aims. Fluency practice that is too long may be counterproductive.

A question that educators frequently ask is whether texts that consist almost entirely of highly frequent and phonetically regular words also can be engaging and merit rereading for different purposes. In a previous era, controlled texts were common in schools. Such texts (see Excerpt 1 in Table 10.1) fell out of fashion because the stilted language that came from an overabundance of highly frequent words was seen to have negative effects on comprehension (Beck, McKeown, Omanson, & Pople, 1984). Even though the studies that considered controlled vocabulary and comprehension were few, their findings were generalized to developmental levels and aspects of reading that were not part of the investigations. Neither did these generalizations consider the role of genre. Whereas authors of children's literature do not use a word repeatedly to describe the trait or action of a character in a narrative text—the genre used in the studies on negative effects of controlled vocabulary on comprehension—writers of informational text do repeat words as they describe a concept (Hiebert, 2005c).

Because repetition of core vocabulary is a feature of informational text, several research projects (Moje et al., 2004; Pearson, Cervetti, Hiebert, Bravo, & Arya, 2005), including the line of work reported on in this chapter (see also Hiebert, 2005a) have selected informational texts for the instruction of fluency and vocabulary comprehension. Pearson et al. (2005) have reported that science texts that were written with high percentages of high-frequency and phonetically regular words (approximately 97% of the unique words) can have a positive effect on vocabulary learning, in addition to fluency development. A considerable number of HI/LV texts, such as the Frog and Toad series, from which Excerpt 5 in Table 10.1 comes, also show that engaging narrative texts can be written where vocabulary is controlled.

As standards related to fluency—which are included in Reading First mandates (NCLB, 2002)—become more widespread, publishers of mainstream textbook programs may begin addressing the scaffolded texts that are now confined to a handful of projects. Until scaffolded texts are part of mainstream reading programs, educators who recognize that particular types of texts are needed for fluency development will need to select carefully from available options. The kinds of texts that are needed for integrating focused fluency practice during reading instruction can come from several sources, some of which are already in classrooms. However, before identifying sources of texts, a general guideline about the features of texts may be in order. The long-standing guideline regarding instructional-level text applies. That is, there should be fewer than a handful of infrequent multisyllabic words per 100 words of running text. This guideline does not have to be applied rigidly. Some multisyllabic words that appear rarely in texts represent familiar concepts (e.g., words such as *chickens* and *rabbits*). However, texts containing a substantial number of multisyllabic words that are beyond children's experiences (e.g., *severed* or *imprint*) are unlikely candidates for fluency practice.

Literature texts within a basal program will vary in the numbers and types of rare words. Consider two texts that are excerpted in Table 10.1 from a second-grade basal program (Afflerbach et al., 2000). In Excerpt 6, the literature selection from *Cool Ali* (Poydar, 1996), numerous words are likely to be unfamiliar to second graders, including words such as

chattered, thrilled, chilled, squealed, rippling, breeze, and *haze,* and ono-
matopoeic words such as *wheee, brr,* and *oooo.* Excerpt 7, from *The Park
Bench* (Takeshita, 1988), illustrates a text that is more likely to be appropriate for developing fluency. The phrase with a rare word—*motor
cart*—refers to a concrete object pictured in the text's illustrations. This
text is likely to be a good context for experiencing fluent reading. Even
though the teacher's edition of this program suggests that the two texts
be treated similarly, their differing demands for word recognition and
vocabulary serve different functions in a reading program.

Many literature-based programs include at least one or two HI/LV
texts in their anthology components. In the basal programs that were
adopted recently in California and Texas, three of the six second-grade
programs included selections from Arnold Lobel's Frog and Toad series. Even though the teacher's editions give the same comprehensive lesson plans for every text, HI/LV texts such as Frog and Toad vary in
conceptual demands from *Cool Ali* (Poydar, 1996) or *The Mysterious
Tadpole* (Kellogg, 1977). HI/LV texts were initiated after Dr. Seuss (1960)
proved with *Green Eggs and Ham* that an inventive text could be written with the Dolch (1948) 220 most frequent words. Excerpt 5 in Table
10.1 from *Frog and Toad Together* (Lobel, 1979) shows that HI/LV texts
emphasize high-frequency and phonetically regular words.

Another source of texts for fluency practice that already exists in
classrooms is science texts. A sample of text from a widely used science
textbook was analyzed for the presence of high-frequency words and
rare multisyllabic single-appearing words (see Table 10.1). Although
the percentage of multisyllabic words is higher than in scaffolded texts,
the percentage of rare multisyllabic single-appearing words is lower than
in literature texts. Excerpt 4 in Table 10.1 from a science textbook also
shows one of the hallmarks of good informational text: Rare words that
represent critical concepts are repeated often and in close proximity.
Such features provide the repetition that students require to learn and
remember new vocabulary (McKeown et al., 1985).

In instructional settings where students require additional support to
become fluent readers, teachers may need to go a little further afield than
existing programs. In some locations, teachers may find that the store-
rooms of county and district offices have old textbook programs. As the
re-analysis of the NRP fluency studies showed (Hiebert & Fisher, 2005),
textbooks prior to the late 1980s and early 1990s exaggerate high-frequency
words. Although these texts have often been viewed as less engaging (Bruce,

1984), their use for short periods of time may support struggling readers to perform smoothly and fluidly. In addition, texts called "skill builders" were written for, and used in, some of the studies in the archival literature. Several of these programs are still published, as well as newer programs with informational content (see Excerpt 3 in Table 10.1).

A guideline in selecting from the available materials should be that texts have few rare words that represent unfamiliar concepts in texts used for fluency instruction and practice. Fluency practice should not dominate the curriculum, but when it is the focus, the texts should give students an opportunity to read fluidly without having to grapple with the pronunciation and meaning of many rare multisyllabic, single-appearing words. The research that has been reviewed and presented in this chapter indicates that, when texts with such characteristics also present information, students' comprehension can be supported along with fluency.

Conclusions

Numerous questions remain about the development of fluency during children's elementary school years. This chapter has focused on two topics that the NRP report (NICHD, 2000) does not address: the role of text and allocation of time for fluency practice. If fluency is to approach levels expected in current policy initiatives, levels that the NRP indicates are possible, then text features cannot be ignored. Different kinds of text serve different functions in a reading program. Texts that support fluency are not intended to displace literature. However, just as literature is critical in achieving goals of strategic thinking and expanded vocabularies, so too is text with few rare multisyllabic, single-appearing words useful in increasing students' fluency with the core words that account for significant percentages of the total words in text.

Questions for Discussion

1. Assume that you're part of a committee in a school district reviewing texts for use in a comprehensive reading program. Based on the information in this chapter, what functions within the program might the following texts serve?

   (a) texts where the ratio of multisyllabic, rare words is approximately 7 for every 100 words of text; and

   (b) texts where the ratio of multisyllabic, rare words is approximately 2 for every 100 words of text.

2. Among the students with whom you work, identify

(a) those who could benefit from experiences with the scaffolded texts that are described in this chapter, and

(b) those who are reading at sufficient fluency and comprehension levels where such texts are not necessary.

3. Select a sample of texts that are commonly used in the educational agency in which you work. Identify the texts that meet the definition of "scaffolded texts" that is described in this chapter.

REFERENCES

Adams, M.J. (1990). *Beginning to read: Thinking and learning about print.* Cambridge, MA: MIT Press.

Afflerbach, P., Beers, J., Blachowicz, C., Boyd, C.D., Diffily, D., Gaunty-Porter, D., et al. (2000). *Scott Foresman Reading.* Glenview, IL: Scott Foresman.

Badders, W., Bethel, L.J., Fu, V., Peck, D., Sumners, C., & Valentino, C. (2000). *Houghton Mifflin Science DiscoveryWorks* (California ed.). Boston: Houghton Mifflin.

Barr, R. (1974). The effect of instruction on pupil reading strategies. *Reading Research Quarterly, 10,* 555–582.

Beck, I.L., McKeown, M., Omanson, R., & Pople, M. (1984). Improving the comprehensibility of stories: The effects of revisions that improve coherence. *Reading Research Quarterly, 19,* 263–277.

Bruce, B.C. (1984). A new point of view on children's stories. In R.C. Anderson, J. Osborn, & R.J. Tierney (Eds.), *Learning to read in American schools: Basal readers and content texts* (pp. 153–174). Hillsdale, NJ: Erlbaum.

Carroll, J.B., Davies, P., & Richman, B. (1971). *The American Heritage word frequency book.* Boston: Houghton Mifflin.

Dolch, E.W. (1948). *Problems in reading.* Champaign, IL: Garrard Press.

Donahue, P.L., Finnegan, R.J., Lutkus, A.D., Allen, N.L., & Campbell, J.R. (2001). *The nation's report card for reading: Fourth grade.* Washington, DC: National Center for Education Statistics.

Faulkner, H.J., & Levy, B.A. (1994). Fluent and nonfluent forms of transfer in reading: Words and their message. *Psychonomic Bulletin and Review, 6,* 111–116.

Fisher, C.W., & Berliner, D.C. (Eds.). (1985). *Perspectives on instructional time.* New York: Longman.

Foorman, B.R., Francis, D.J., Davidson, K.C., Harm, M.W., & Griffin, J. (2004). Variability in text features in six grade 1 basal reading programs. *Scientific Studies of Reading, 8,* 167–197.

Fountas, I.C., & Pinnell, G.S. (1999). *Matching books to readers: Using leveled books in guided reading, K–3.* New York: Heinemann.

Fuchs, L.S., Fuchs, D., Hamlett, C.L., Walz, L., & Germann, G. (1993). Formative evaluation of academic progress: How much growth can we expect? *School Psychology Review, 22,* 27–48.

Good, R.H., Wallin, J.U., Simmons, D.C., Kame'enui, E.J., & Kaminski, R.A. (2002). *System-wide percentile ranks for DIBELS Benchmark Assessment* (Technical Report No. 9). Eugene: University of Oregon.

Gray, W.S., & Leary, B.W. (1935). *What makes a book readable.* Chicago: University of Chicago Press.

Hasbrouck, J.E., & Tindal, G. (in press). Oral reading fluency norms: A valuable tool for reading teachers. *The Reading Teacher.*

Hiebert, E.H. (1999). Text matters in learning to read. *The Reading Teacher, 52,* 552–568.

Hiebert, E.H. (2003). *QuickReads.* Parsipanny, NJ: Pearson Learning Group.

Hiebert, E.H. (2005a). State reform policies and the reading task for first graders. *The Elementary School Journal, 105,* 245–266.

Hiebert, E.H. (2005b). The effects of text difficulty on second graders' fluency development. *Reading Psychology, 26,* 1–27.

Hiebert E.H. (2005c, May). *Five reasons for making science content/texts central to language arts/reading.* Keynote address at Preconvention Institute, Bringing Science Into the Literacy Curriculum...and Literacy Into Science, at the annual convention of the International Reading Association, San Antonio, TX.

Hiebert, E.H., & Fisher, C.W. (2005). A review of the National Reading Panel's studies on fluency: On the role of text. *The Elementary School Journal, 105,* 443–460.

Hiebert, E.H., & Martin, L.A. (2003). *TExT (Text Elements by Task) software* (4th ed.). Santa Cruz, CA: TextProject.

Hiebert, E.H., Martin, L.A., & Menon, S. (2005). Are there alternatives in reading textbooks? An examination of three beginning reading programs. *Reading & Writing Quarterly, 21*(1), 7–32.

Hoffman, J.V., Sailors, M., & Patterson, E.U. (2002). Decodable texts for beginning reading instruction: The year 2000 basals. *Journal of Literacy Research, 34,* 269–298.

Hoffman, J.V., & Schallert, D.L. (2004). *The texts in elementary classrooms.* Mahwah, NJ: Erlbaum.

Jenkins, J., Stein, M., & Wysocki, K. (1984). Learning vocabulary through reading. *American Educational Research Journal, 21*(4), 767–787.

Juel, C. (1988). Learning to read and write: A longitudinal study of fifty-four children from first through fourth grades. *Journal of Educational Psychology, 80,* 437–447.

LaBerge, D., & Samuels, S.J. (1974). Toward a theory of automatic information processing in reading. *Cognitive Psychology, 6,* 293–323.

Lesgold, A., Resnick, L.B., & Hammond, K. (1985). Learning to read: A longitudinal study of word skill development in two curricula. In G.E. Mackinnon & T.G. Waller (Eds.), *Reading research: Advances in theory and practice* (Vol. 4, pp. 107–138). New York: Academic.

Logan, G.D., Taylor, S.E., & Etherton, J.L. (1999). Attention and automaticity: Toward a theoretical integration. *Psychological Research, 62,* 165–181.

Manning, G.L., & Manning, M. (1984). What models of recreational reading make a difference. *Reading World, 23,* 375–380.

McKeown, M.G., Beck, I.L., Omanson, R.C., & Pople, M.T. (1985). Some effects of the nature and frequency of vocabulary instruction on the knowledge and use of words. *Reading Research Quarterly, 20,* 522–535.

Moje, E.B., Sutherland, L.M., Krajcik, J., Blumenfeld, P., Peek-Brown, D., & Marx, R.W. (2004, November). *Reading and writing like scientists: Toward developing scientific literacy in project-based science.* Paper presented at the 82nd annual convention of the National Council of Teachers of English, Indianapolis, IN.

Nagy, W.E., & Anderson, R.C. (1984). How many words are there in printed school English? *Reading Research Quarterly, 19,* 304–330.

National Institute of Child Health and Human Development (NICHD). (2000). *Report of the National Reading Panel. Teaching children to read: An evidence-based assessment of the scientific research literature on reading and its implications for reading instruction* (NIH Publication No. 00-4769). Washington, DC: U.S. Government Printing Office.

No Child Left Behind Act of 2001, Pub. L. No. 107-110, 115 Stat. 1425 (2002). Retrieved January 13, 2006, from http://www.ed.gov/nclb

Pearson, P.D., Block, K.C., deLain, M.T., Dewitz, P.A., Englebretson, R., Florio-Ruane, S., et al. (1998). *Literature works.* Chicago: Pearson Education.

Pearson, P.D., Cervetti, G.N., Hiebert, E.H., Bravo, M., & Arya, D. (2005, April). *Reading and writing in the service of acquiring scientific knowledge and dispositions: In search of synergies.* Paper presented at the Research Institute of the International Reading Association, San Antonio, TX.

Pinnell, G.S., Pikulski, J.J., Wixson, K.K., Campbell, J.R., Gough, P.B., & Beatty, A.S. (1995). *Listening to children read aloud: Data from NAEP's integrated reading performance record (IRPR) at grade 4.* Washington, DC: Office of Educational Research and Improvement, U.S. Department of Education; Princeton, NJ: Educational Testing Service.

RAND Reading Study Group. (2002). *Reading for understanding: Toward a research and development program in reading comprehension.* Washington, DC: RAND Corporation.

Rashotte, C., & Torgesen, J.K. (1985). Repeated reading and reading fluency in learning disabled children. *Reading Research Quarterly, 20,* 180–188.

Samuels, S.J. (1979). The method of repeated readings. *The Reading Teacher, 32,* 403–408.

Samuels, S.J. (2002). Reading fluency: Its development and assessment. In A.E. Farstrup & S.J. Samuels (Eds.), *What research has to say about reading instruction* (3rd ed., pp. 166–183). Newark, DE: International Reading Association.

Samuels, S.J. (2005, May). *A response to the National Reading Panel: Experimental evidence that reading more raises achievement under certain conditions.* Paper presented at the annual convention of the International Reading Association, San Antonio, TX.

Samuels, S.J., LaBerge, D., & Bremer, C.D. (1978). Units of word recognition: Evidence for developmental changes. *Journal of Verbal Learning and Verbal Behavior, 17,* 715–720.

Samuels, S.J., Miller, N., & Eisenberg, P. (1979). Practice effects on the unit of word recognition. *Journal of Educational Psychology, 71,* 514–520.

Stahl, S.A., Heubach, K., & Cramond, B. (1997). *Fluency-oriented reading instruction* (Research Report No. 79). Athens, GA: National Reading Research Center.

Swanborn, M.S.L., & de Glopper, K. (1999). Incidental word learning while reading: A meta-analysis. *Review of Educational Research, 69,* 261–285.

Thorndike, E.L. (1921). *The teacher's word book.* New York: Columbia University Press.

Tian, H., & Ma, M. (2004). Molecular organization of the olfactory septal organ. *Journal of Neuroscience, 24*, 8383–8390.

Underwood, T., & Pearson, P.D. (2004). Teaching struggling adolescent readers to comprehend what they read. In T.L. Jetton & J.A. Dole (Eds.), *Adolescent literacy research and practice* (pp. 135–161). New York: Guilford.

Wiederholt, J.L., & Bryant, B.R. (2001). *Gray Oral Reading Test* (4th ed). Austin, TX: Pro-Ed.

Wylie, R.E., & Durrell, D.D. (1970). Teaching vowels through phonograms. *Elementary English, 47*, 787–791.

Zeno, S.M., Ivens, S.H., Millard, R.T., & Duvvuri, R. (1995). *The educator's word frequency guide.* New York: Touchstone Applied Science.

CHILDREN'S LITERATURE CITED

Clymer, T., & Venezky, R.L. (1982). *Glad to meet you.* Boston: Ginn & Company.

Kellogg, S. (1977). *The mysterious tadpole.* New York: Dial Books for Young Readers.

Lobel, A. (1979). *Frog and toad together.* New York: HarperTrophy.

Poydar, N. (1996). *Cool Ali.* New York: McElderry.

Takeshita, F. (1988). *The park bench.* New York: Kane/Miller.

Seuss, Dr. (1960). *Green eggs and ham.* New York: Random House.

Author Index

GASKINS, J.C., 53
GASKINS, R.W., 53
GAUNTY-PORTER, D., 205, 220
GERMANN, G., 207, 213, 216
GIBSON, E.J., 11
GILBERT, T., 119
GILLISPIE, M., 54, 150
GOLDEN, J., 148
GOOD, R.H., 40–41, 94, 175, 179–180,
    186, 199, 207
GOSWAMI, U., 50
GOUGH, P.B., 14, 34, 60, 71–72, 207, 213,
    216
GRAVES, B.B., 164
GRAVES, M.F., 82, 164
GRAY, W.S., 208
GREENE, F.P., 89
GRIFFIN, J., 204
GRIFFIN, P., 84–85, 88, 174
GRIFFITH, L.W., 119
GUTHRIE, J.T., 98–99, 101–102

H
HAINES, L.P., 52
HAMILTON, A.M., 95, 134–135
HAMLETT, C.L., 183–184, 186, 207, 213, 216
HAMMOND, K., 207
HARM, M.W., 204
HARRIS, T.L., 72
HART, B., 83
HARTER, N., 24
HARTY, K.R., 100
HASBROUCK, J.E., 18, 214, 216–218
HASSLER, L., 130
HEBB, D.O., 25
HECHT, S., 130
HECKELMAN, R.G., 13, 89, 117
HEISTAD, D., 179, 194–196
HERRON, J., 147
HEUBACH, K.M., 17, 56, 72–73, 212
HIEBERT, E.H., 64, 77, 87, 96, 153, 204–205,
    208, 210–211, 213–216, 220–221
HILDEN, K., 43, 95
HIRSCH, E.D., 83
HITE, S., 55, 115, 119
HODGES, R.E., 72
HOFFMAN, J.V., 6–7, 9–11, 16–17, 96,
    115, 204
HOFFMAN, T.V., 16, 18
HOGABOAM, T.W., 54
HOGAN, J., 124

HOGAN, T.P., 60
HOIEN, T., 150
HOLDAWAY, D., 16
HOLLINGSWORTH, P.M., 11, 13, 16–17,
    102, 117
HOMAN, S., 55, 115, 119
HOOVER, W.A., 71
HORN, C., 54
HOSKISSON, K., 13, 118–119
HOSP, M., 10, 61, 130, 179–180, 186, 199
HOWLETT, N., 11
HUDSON, R.F., 133, 153
HUEY, E.B., 7, 25
HUMENICK, N.M., 101
HUNT, E., 141
HYATT, A.V., 5–9

I
IHNOT, C., 18
IMLACH, R.H., 94
INVERNIZZI, M., 78–79
IVENS, S.H., 209

J
JACOBS, V.A., 76
JAMES, W., 6
JASPERS, J., 119
JEFFERSON, G., 41, 186
JENKINS, J.R., 10, 57, 130, 136, 138, 143,
    179–180, 186, 199, 210
JERNIGAN, M., 119
JOHNSON, D.D., 81
JOHNSTON, F., 78–79
JOHNSTON, P.H., 101
JUEL, C., 164, 218

K
KAHNEMAN, D., 35
KAIL, R.V., 54, 137, 150
KAME'ENUI, E.J., 35, 179–180, 207
KAMINSKI, R.A., 40, 94, 175, 199, 207
KASTLER, L., 96
KELLOGG, S., 205–206, 221
KENNEDY, A., 148
KIM, D., 193
KING, S., 119
KLESIUS, P., 55, 115, 119
KOSKINEN, P.S., 17, 118
KOUZEKANANI, K., 119
KRAJCIK, J., 220
KROHM, B., 118–119

Subject Index

Note: Page numbers followed by *f* and *t* indicate figures and tables, respectively.

A

ABILITY: and effect of time spent reading, 33

ACCURACY: and fluency, 133; versus speed, and fluency, 139–140

ADEQUATE YEARLY PROGRESS (AYP), 194

ADVANCED FLUENCY, 76; development of, 86–88

AIMSWEB, 199

ALPHABET, 1

ALPHABETIC PRINCIPLE, 77, 84

ARROW TECHNIQUE, 116–117

ASSESSMENT: of fluency, 89–90; of prosody, 136; research on, 181. *See also* measurement of fluency

ASSISTANCE: adult, for struggling readers, 55–56

ASSISTED READING, 13–14, 116–118; for ELLs and students with dyslexia, 167

ATTENTION: ability and, 34; and constructing meaning, 71; in reading process, 35

AURAL-READ-RESPOND-ORAL-WRITTEN (ARROW) TECHNIQUE, 116–117

AUTOMATICITY THEORY, 11–13, 34–39, 160

AYP. *See* adequate yearly progress

B

BACKGROUND KNOWLEDGE: in ELLs and students with dyslexia, 173–174; and fluency, 87–88

BALANCED INSTRUCTION: for struggling readers, 63–64

BASIC FLUENCY, 76, 86

BASIC SKILLS MONITORING PROGRAM, 198–199

BEGINNING READERS: and reading process, 36–37, 37*f*; severely struggling, phonics instruction and, 54

BEHAVIORISM, 26

BENCHMARK SCHOOL, 48, 52, 64–65; and sight words, 58–60

BOOKS IN BAGS, 59

BRAIN DEVELOPMENT: and fluency, 50–51; phonics and, 51–52

BROCA'S AREA, 50

C

CATTELL, JAMES McKEEN, 24

CBM. *See* curriculum-based measurement

CHORAL READING, 30*t*, 167; for struggling readers, 55

COGNITIVE LOAD, 209–210

COGNITIVE PSYCHOLOGY: and fluency, 26–27

COMPREHENSION: elements of, 47; in ELLs and students with dyslexia, 173–174; fluency and, 14–15, 72–73, 207; oral-reading speed and, 41–42; prosody and, 134–136; in reading process, 34–35, 71; strategies, for struggling readers, 62–63

COMPUTER-AIDED INSTRUCTION: for repeated reading, 28, 29*t*

CONCEPTS OF PRINT: lack of, 163

CONFIDENCE: and fluency, 108–110

CONSOLIDATED ALPHABETIC STAGE, 75–76

CONSTRUCTIVELY RESPONSIVE READING: elements of, 47

CONTEXT: and fluency, 138

CONTROLLED TEXTS: problems with, 219–220

CULTURE: and dysfluency, 163

CURRICULUM-BASED MEASUREMENT (CBM), 174–175, 179–203; example of, 181–186, 182*f*; extensions of, 198–199; oral-reading scores, school district use of, 188–198, 188*f*; procedures and characteristics of, 183–186; research and development background of, 181

D

DECODING: dyslexia and, 162; efficiency of, and fluency, 141; in reading process, 34, 71; skills needed for fluency, 77–81; speed of, and fluency,

233

READING EXPERIENCES: high-success, and fluency, 98

READING FLUENCY. *See* fluency

READING INSTRUCTION: developmental approach and, 77–83; diversity in, 49, 64; and dysfluency, 96–97; for ELLs and students with dyslexia, methods for, 165–169; evaluation of, CBM and, 183, 193; scaffolded texts and, 218–222

READING MATERIALS: for ELLs and students with dyslexia, 169–173

READING PROCESS: in beginning readers, 36–37, 37*f*; components of, 34–35; in fluent readers, 38–39, 38*f*

READING READINESS: lack of, 163

READING TO STUDENTS: for ELLs and students with dyslexia, 168–169

READING VOLUME: and fluency, 98–100

READING WHILE LISTENING (RWL), 13–14, 16, 116–117

RECITATION, 6

RECREATIONAL READING, 167–168

REMEDIATION: with older struggling readers, difficulty in, 132, 145–148, 146*f*

REPEATED READINGS (RR), 13, 15–16; for ELLs and students with dyslexia, 166–167; and fluency, 115–116; forms of, 29*t*–30*t*; research on, 27–31; with scaffolded texts, 204–226; for struggling readers, 89

REPEATED SAMPLING: in CBM, 184–185

RESEARCH ON FLUENCY, 1–3; and CBM, 181; future directions for, 18–19; history of, 24–27; and TExT model, 210–213; trends in, 24–32

RESILIENCE: and fluency, 108–110

RESPONSE TO INTERVENTION (RTI) MODEL, 190–192, 191*f*–193*f*

RETELL FLUENCY (RF), 40, 43

RIMES, 79

ROUND-ROBIN READING, 10–11

RR. *See* repeated readings

RTI. *See* response to intervention model

RWL. *See* reading while listening

S

SAMPLING: repeated, in CBM, 184–185

SBE. *See* shared-book experience

SCAFFOLDED TEXTS: and educational practice, 218–222; features of, 215*t*; repeated reading with, 204–226

SCAFFOLDING: and fluency, 110

SCIENCE TEXTS: features of, 215*t*, 220–221

SECOND GRADE: and fluency development, 85–86; fluency development in, text effects and, 213–222

SELF-EFFICACY: and fluency, 108–110

SHARED-BOOK EXPERIENCE (SBE), 16

SHARED READING, 167

SIGHT WORDS: children with reading disabilities and, 147–148; as compensation, 60–62; limits of, 60; processing speed for, and fluency, 137; proportion of, and fluency, 136–137; reading efficiency of, and fluency, 140–141; for struggling readers, 56–62

SILENT READING: rise of, 7–10; scaffolded, 208

SKILL BUILDERS: features of, 222

SPECIAL EDUCATION STUDENTS: CBM scores of, 189, 190*f*

SPEED: versus accuracy, and fluency, 139–140

SPELLING PATTERNS, 79

STAGE THEORIES: of reading development, 73–76

STANDARDIZATION: of CBM, 184

STANDARDIZED TESTING: and fluency, 15; problems with, 187; and silent reading, 10. *See also* high-stakes tests

STORY METHOD, 6

STRATEGIC FLUENCY, 111–112; definition of, 107

STRATEGIES: for decoding, 80–81; for struggling readers, 62–63

STRESS PATTERNS: and prosody, 134

STRUGGLING READERS: balanced instruction for, 63–64; comprehension strategies for, 62–63; developing fluency in, 88–89; diversity among, 48–49, 64; fluency in, 47–69, 130–158, 131*t*; instruction and, 96; interventions for, effectiveness of, 132, 145–148, 146*f*; observation of, 100–101; oral reading with adult feedback for, 55–56; phonics instruction for, 50–54; with severe difficulties, 54; sight words for, 56–62

SUPPORT: and fluency, 110